HARPER'S THISTLE EDITION

OF

THE WAVERLEY NOVELS

COMPLETE IN FORTY-EIGHT VOLUMES

VOLUME XLIV

LUCERNE.

THE WAVERLEY NOVELS

ANNE OF GEIERSTEIN

BY

SIR WALTER SCOTT, Bart.

Vol. II.

HARPER & BROTHERS PUBLISHERS
NEW YORK AND LONDON
1902

Sco86aq
v.2

List of Illustrations.

SUBJECT.	PAGE
Lucerne. *Frontispiece*	4
Peasant, Canton of Schwytz	9
Falls of the Rhine	16
Arnsberg Castle, a seat of the Vehme Gericht	40
Interior of Strasburg Cathedral	59
Castle of Hohen Syburg, a seat of the Vehme Gericht	83
Street in Strasburg	104
Strasburg Cathedral	122
Arthur Philipson kneeling to Queen Margaret	128
Monumental Pillar, near Wooler, Northumberland, to the memory of Sir Ralph Percy, a Partisan of Queen Margaret	165
Interview with Charles the Bold	171
Parliament of Charles the Bold, from an old Illumination	190
A Tournament. After an original drawing by King René, preserved in the Royal Library, Paris	230
King René. From the original portrait, supposed to have been painted by himself	240

LIST OF ILLUSTRATIONS.

SUBJECT.	PAGE
Ruins at Aix, Provence	257
Town of Aix, Provence	276
Queen Margaret. From an ancient picture in the late collection at Strawberry Hill	297
Death of Queen Margaret	319
Costume of Princess in the Court of King René	336
Peasants, Canton of Zurich	348
Roman Fountain near Aix, Provence	349
Effigy of King René	352
Discovery of the body of Charles the Bold	382
Monumental Effigy of Charles the Bold	384

ANNE OF GEIERSTEIN;

OR, THE MAIDEN OF THE MIST.

CHAPTER THE NINETEENTH.

First Carrier.—What, ostler !—a plague on thee, hast never an eye in thy head ? Canst thou not hear ? An 'twere not as good a deed as drink to break the pate of thee, I am a very villain—Come, and be hanged—Hast thou no faith in thee ?

Gadshill.—I pray thee, lend me thy lantern, to see my gelding in the stable.

Second Carrier.—Nay, soft, I pray you—I know a trick worth two of that.

Gadshill.—I prithee lend me thine.

Third Carrier.—Ay, when ? Canst tell ?— Lend thee my lantern, quotha ? Marry, I'll see thee hanged first.—HENRY IV.

SWISS PEASANT.

THE social spirit peculiar to the French nation had already introduced into the inns of that country the gay and cheerful character of welcome, upon which Erasmus, at a later period, dwells with strong emphasis, as a contrast to the saturnine and sullen reception which strangers were apt to meet with at a German caravansera. Philipson was, therefore, in expectation of being received by the busy, civil, and talkative host—by the hostess and her daughter, all softness, coquetry, and glee—the smiling and supple waiter—the officious and dimpled chambermaid. The better inns in France boast also separate rooms, where strangers could change or put in order their dress, where they might sleep without company in their bedroom, and where they could deposit their baggage in privacy and safety. But all these luxuries were as yet unknown in Germany; and in Alsace, where the scene now lies, as well as in the other dependencies of the Empire, they regarded as effeminacy every thing beyond such provisions as were absolutely necessary for the supply of the wants of travellers; and even these were coarse and indifferent, and, excepting in the article of wine, sparingly ministered.

The Englishman, finding that no one appeared at the gate, began to make his presence known by calling aloud, and finally by alighting, and smiting with all his might on the doors of the hostelrie for a long time, without attracting the least attention. At length the head of a grizzled servitor was thrust out at a small window, who, in a voice which sounded like that of one displeased at the interruption, rather than hopeful of advantage from the arrival of a guest, demanded what he wanted.

"Is this an inn?" replied Philipson.

"Yes," bluntly replied the domestic, and was about to withdraw from the window, when the traveller added,—

"And if it be, can I have lodgings?"

"You may come in," was the short and dry answer.

"Send some one to take the horses," replied Philipson.

"No one is at leisure," replied this most repulsive of waiters; "you must litter down your horses yourself, in the way that likes you best."

"Where is the stable?" said the merchant, whose prudence and temper were scarce proof against this Dutch phlegm.

The fellow, who seemed as sparing of his words, as if, like the Princess in the fairy tale, he had dropped ducats with each of them, only pointed to a door in an outer building, more resembling that of a cellar than of a stable, and, as if weary of the conference, drew in his head, and shut the window sharply against the guest, as he would against an importunate beggar.

Cursing the spirit of independence which left a traveller to his own resources and exertions, Philipson, making a virtue of necessity, led the two nags towards the door pointed out as that of the stable, and was rejoiced at heart to see light glimmering through its chinks. He entered with his charge into a place very like the dungeon vault of an ancient castle, rudely fitted up with some racks and mangers. It was of considerable extent in point of length, and at the lower end two or three persons were engaged in tying up their horses, dressing them, and dispensing them their provender.

This last article was delivered by the ostler, a very old lame man, who neither put his hand to wisp or curry-comb, but sat weighing forth hay by the pound, and counting out corn, as it seemed, by the grain, so anxiously did he bend over his task, by the aid of a blinking light enclosed within a horn lantern. He did not even turn his head at the noise which the Englishman made on entering the place with two additional horses, far less did he seem disposed to give himself the least trouble, or the stranger the smallest assistance.

In respect of cleanliness, the stable of Augeas bore no small resemblance to that of this Alsatian dorff; and it would have been an exploit worthy of Hercules to have restored it to such a state of cleanliness, as would have made it barely decent in the eyes, and tolerable to the nostrils, of the punctilious Englishman. But this was a matter which disgusted Philipson himself much more than those of his party which were principally concerned. They, *videlicet* the two horses, seeming perfectly to understand that the rule of the place was, "first come first served," hastened to occupy the empty stalls which happened to be nearest to them. In this one of them at least was disappointed, being received by a groom with a blow across the face with a switch.

"Take that," said the fellow, "for forcing thyself into the place taken up for the horses of the Baron of Randelsheim."

Never in the course of his life had the English merchant more pain to retain possession of his temper than at that moment. Reflecting, however, on the discredit of quarrelling with such a man in such a cause, he contented himself with placing the animal, thus repulsed from the stall he had chosen, into one next to that of his companion, to which no one seemed to lay claim.

The merchant then proceeded, notwithstanding the fatigue of the day, to pay all that attention to the mute companions of his journey, which they deserve from every traveller who has any share of prudence, to say nothing of humanity. The unusual degree of trouble which Philipson took to arrange his horses, although his dress, and much more his demeanour, seemed to place him above this species of servile labour, appeared to make an impression even upon the iron insensibility of the old ostler himself. He shewed some alacrity in furnishing the traveller, who knew the business of a groom so well, with corn, straw, and hay, though in small quantity, and at exorbitant rates, which were instantly to be paid; nay, he even went as far as the door of the stable, that he might point across the court to the well, from which Philipson was obliged to fetch water with his own hands. The duties of the stable being finished, the merchant concluded that he had gained such an interest with the grim master of the horse, as to learn of him whether he might leave his bales safely in the stable.

"You may leave them if you will," said the ostler; "but touching their safety, you will do much more wisely if you take them with you, and give no temptation to any one by suffering them to pass from under your own eyes."

So saying, the man of oats closed his oracular jaws, nor could he be prevailed upon to unlock them again by any inquiry which his customer could devise.

In the course of this cold and comfortless reception, Philipson recollected the necessity of supporting the character of a prudent and wary trader, which he had forgotten once before in the course of the day; and, imitating what he saw the others do, who had been, like himself, engaged in taking charge of their horses, he took up his baggage, and removed himself and his property to the inn. Here he was suffered to enter, rather than admitted, into the general or public *stubé*, or room of entertainment, which, like the ark of the patriarch, received all raks without distinction, whether clean or unclean.

The *stubé*, or stove, of a German inn, derived its name from the great hypocaust, which is always strongly heated to secure the warmth of the apartment in which it is placed. There travellers of every age and description assembled — there their upper garments were indiscriminately hung up around the stove to dry or to air—and the guests themselves were seen employed in various acts of ablution or personal arrangement, which are generally, in modern times, referred to the privacy of the dressing-room.

The more refined feelings of the Englishman were disgusted with this scene, and he was reluctant to mingle in it. For this reason he inquired for the private retreat of the landlord himself, trusting that, by some of the arguments powerful among his tribe, he might obtain separate quarters from the crowd, and a morsel of food, to be eaten in private. A grey-haired Ganymede, to whom he put the question where the landlord was, indicated a recess behind the huge stove, where, veiling his glory in a very dark and extremely hot corner, it pleased the great man to obscure himself from vulgar gaze. There was something remarkable about this person. Short, stout, bandy-legged, and consequential, he was in these respects like many brethren of the profession in all countries. But the countenance of the man, and still more his manners, differed more from the merry host of France or England, than even the experienced Philipson was prepared to expect. He knew German customs too well to expect the suppliant and serviceable qualities of the master of a French inn, or even the more blunt and frank manners of an English landlord. But such German innkeepers as he had yet seen, though indeed arbitrary and peremptory in their country fashions, yet, being humoured in these, they, like tyrants in their hours of relaxation, dealt kindly with the guests over whom their sway extended, and mitigated, by jest and jollity, the harshness of their absolute power. But this man's brow was like a tragic volume, in which you were as unlikely to find anything of jest or amusement, as in a hermit's breviary. His answers were short, sudden, and repulsive, and the air and manner with which they were delivered was as surly as their tenor; which will appear from the following dialogue betwixt him and his guest:—

"Good host," said Philipson, in the mildest tone he could assume, "I am fatigued, and far from well—may I request to have a separate apartment, a cup of wine, and a morsel of food, in my private chamber?"

FALLS OF THE RHINE AT SCHAFFHAUSEN.

"You may," answered the landlord; but with a look strangely at variance with the apparent acquiescence which his words naturally implied.

"Let me have such accommodation, then, with your earliest convenience."

"Soft!" replied the innkeeper. "I have said that you may request these things, but not that I would grant them. If you would insist on being served differently from others, it must be at another inn than mine."

"Well, then," said the traveller, "I will shift without supper for a night—nay, more, I will be content to pay for a supper which I do not eat, if you will cause me to be accommodated with a private apartment?"

"Seignor traveller," said the innkeeper, "every one here must be accommodated as well as you, since all pay alike. Whoso comes to this house of entertainment, must eat as others eat, drink as others drink, sit at table with the rest of my guests, and go to bed when the company have done drinking."

"All this," said Philipson, humbling himself where anger would have been ridiculous, "is highly reasonable; and I do not oppose myself to your laws or customs. But," added he, taking his purse from his girdle, "sickness craves some privilege; and when the patient is willing to pay for it, methinks the rigour of your laws may admit of some mitigation?"

"I keep an inn, Seignor, and not an hospital. If you remain here, you shall be served with the same attention as others,—if you are not willing to do as others do, leave my house and seek another inn."

On receiving this decisive rebuff, Philipson gave up the contest, and retired from the *sanctum sanctorum* of his ungracious host, to await the arrival of supper, penned up like a bullock in a pound amongst the crowded inhabitants of the *stubê*. Some of these, exhausted by fatigue, snored away the interval between their own arrival and that of the expected repast; others conversed together on the news of the country; and others, again, played at dice, or such games as might serve to consume the time. The company were of various ranks, from those who were apparently wealthy and well-appointed, to some whose garments and manners indicated that they were but just beyond the grasp of poverty.

A begging friar, a man apparently of a gay and pleasant temper, approached Philipson, and engaged him in conversation. The Englishman was well enough acquainted with the world to be aware, that whatever of his character and purpose it was desirable to conceal, would be best hidden under a sociable and open demeanour. He, therefore, received the friar's approaches graciously, and conversed with him upon the state of Lorraine, and the interest which the Duke of Burgundy's attempt to seize that fief into his own hands was likely to create both in France and Germany. On these subjects, satisfied with hearing his fellow-traveller's sentiments, Philipson expressed no opinion of his own, but, after receiving such intelligence as the friar chose to communicate, preferred rather to talk upon the geography of the country, the facilities afforded to commerce, and the rules which obstructed or favoured trade.

While he was thus engaged in the conversation which seemed most to belong to his profession, the landlord suddenly entered the room, and, mounting on the head of an old barrel, glanced his eye slowly and steadily round the crowded apartment, and when he had completed his survey, pronounced, in a decisive tone, the double command,—"Shut the gates— Spread the table."

"The Baron Saint Antonio be praised!" said the friar, "our landlord has given up hope of any more guests to-night, until which blessed time, we might have starved for want of food before he had relieved us. Ay, here comes the cloth, the old gates of the courtyard are now bolted fast enough, and when Ian Mengs has once said, 'Shut the gates,' the stranger may knock on the outside as he will, but we may rest assured that it shall not be opened to him."

"Meinherr Mengs maintains strict discipline in his house," said the Englishman.

"As absolute as the Duke of Burgundy," answered the friar. "After ten o'clock, no admittance—the 'seek another inn,' which is before that a conditional hint, becomes, after the clock has struck, and the watchmen have begun their rounds, an absolute order of exclusion. He that is without remains without, and he that is within must, in like manner, continue there until the gates open at break of day. Till then the house is almost like a beleaguered citadel, John Mengs its seneschal——"

"And we its captives, good father," said Philipson. "Well, content am I; a wise traveller must submit to the control of the leaders of the people, when he travels; and I hope a goodly fat potentate, like John Mengs, will be as clement as his station and dignity admit of."

While they were talking in this manner, the aged waiter, with many a weary sigh, and many a groan, had drawn out certain boards, by which a table, that stood in the midst of the *stubé*, had the capacity of being extended, so as to contain the company present, and covered it with a cloth, which was neither distinguished by extreme cleanliness nor fineness of texture. On this table, when it had been accommodated to receive the necessary number of guests, a wooden trencher and spoon, together with a glass drinking cup, were placed before each, he being expected to serve himself with his own knife for the other purposes of the table. As for forks, they were unknown until a much later period, all the Europeans of that day making the same use of the fingers to select their morsels and transport them to the mouth, which the Asiatics now practice.

The board was no sooner arranged, than the hungry guests hastened to occupy their seats around it; for which purpose the sleepers were awakened, the dicers resigned their game, and the idlers and politicians broke off their sage debates, in order to secure their station at the supper-table, and be ready to perform their part in the interesting solemnity which seemed about to take place. But there is much between the cup and the lip, and not less sometimes between the covering of a table and the placing food upon it. The guests sat in order, each with his knife drawn, already menacing the victuals which were still subject to the operations of the cook. They had waited, with various degrees of patience, for full half an hour, when at length the old attendant before mentioned entered with a pitcher of thin Moselle wine, so light and so sharp-tasted, that Philipson put down his cup with every tooth in his head set on edge by the slender portion which he had swallowed. The landlord, John Mengs, who had assumed a seat somewhat elevated at the head of the table, did not omit to observe this mark of insubordination, and to animadvert upon it.

"The wine likes you not, I think, my master?" said he to the English merchant.

"For wine, no," answered Philipson; "but could I see any thing requiring such sauce, I have seldom seen better vinegar."

This jest, though uttered in the most calm and composed manner, seemed to drive the innkeeper to fury.

"Who are you," he exclaimed, "for a foreign pedlar, that ventures to quarrel with my wine, which has been approved of by so many princes, dukes, reigning dukes, graves, rhinegraves, counts, barons, and knights of the Empire, whose shoes you are altogether unworthy even to clean? Was it not of this wine that the Count Palatine of Nimmersatt drank six quarts before he ever rose from the blessed chair in which I now sit?"

"I doubt it not, mine host," said Philipson; "nor

should I think of scandalizing the sobriety of your honourable guest, even if he had drunken twice the quantity."

"Silence, thou malicious railer!" said the host; "and let instant apology be made to me, and the wine which you have calumniated, or I will instantly command the supper to be postponed till midnight."

Here there was a general alarm among the guests, all abjuring any part in the censures of Philipson, and most of them proposing that John Mengs should avenge himself on the actual culprit, by turning him instantly out of doors, rather than involve so many innocent and famished persons in the consequences of his guilt. The wine they pronounced excellent; some two or three even drank their glass out, to make their words good; and they all offered, if not with lives and fortunes, at least with hands and feet, to support the ban of the house against the contumacious Englishman. While petition and remonstrance were assailing John Mengs on every side, the friar, like a wise counsellor, and a trusty friend, endeavoured to end the feud, by advising Philipson to submit to the host's sovereignty.

"Humble thyself, my son," he said; "bend the stubbornness of thy heart before the great lord of the spigot and butt. I speak for the sake of others as well as my own; for Heaven alone knows how much longer they or I can endure this extenuating fast!"

"Worthy guests," said Philipson, "I am grieved to have offended our respected host, and am so far from objecting to the wine, that I will pay for a double flagon of it, to be served all round to this honourable company—so, only, they do not ask me to share of it."

These last words were spoken aside; but the Englishman could not fail to perceive, from the wry mouths of some of the party who were possessed of a nicer palate, that they were as much afraid as himself of a repetition of the acid potation.

The friar next addressed the company with a proposal, that the foreign merchant, instead of being amerced in a measure of the liquor which he had scandalized, should be mulcted in an equal quantity of the more generous wines which were usually produced after the repast had been concluded. In this, mine host, as well as the guests, found their advantage; and, as Philipson made no objection, the proposal was unanimously adopted, and John Mengs gave, from his seat of dignity, the signal for supper to be served.

The long-expected meal appeared, and there was twice as much time employed in consuming as there had been in expecting it. The articles of which the supper consisted, as well as the mode of serving them up, were as much calculated to try the patience of the company as the delay which had preceded its appearance. Messes of broth and vegetables followed in succession, with platters of meat sodden and roasted, of which each in its turn took a formal course around the ample table, and was specially subjected to every one in rotation. Black puddings, hung beef, dried fish, also made the circuit, with various condiments, called Botargo, Caviare, and similar names, composed of the roes of fish mixed with spices, and the like preparations, calculated to awaken thirst and encourage deep drinking. Flagons of wine accompanied these stimulating dainties. The liquor was so superior in flavour and strength to the ordinary wine which had awakened so much controversy, that it might be objected to on the opposite account, being so heady, fiery, and strong, that, in spite of the rebuffs which his criticism had already procured, Philipson ventured to ask for some cold water to allay it.

"You are too difficult to please, sir guest," replied the landlord, again bending upon the Englishman a stern and offended brow; "if you find the wine too strong in my house, the secret to allay its strength is to drink the less. It is indifferent to us whether you drink or not, so you pay the reckoning of those good fellows who do." And he laughed a gruff laugh.

Philipson was about to reply, but the friar, retaining his character of mediator, plucked him by the cloak, and entreated him to forbear. "You do not understand the ways of the place," said he; "it is not here as in the hostelries of England and France, where each guest calls for what he desires for his own use, and where he pays for what he has required, and for no more. Here we proceed on a broad principle of equality and fraternity. No one asks for any thing in particular; but such provisions as the host thinks sufficient are set down before all indiscriminately; and as with the feast, so is it with the reckoning. All pay their proportions alike, without reference to the quantity of wine which one may have swallowed more than another; and thus the sick and infirm, nay, the female and the child, pay the same as the hungry peasant and strolling *lanzknecht.*"

"It seems an unequal custom," said Philipson; "but travellers are not to judge. So that when a reckoning is called, every one, I am to understand, pays alike?"

"Such is the rule," said the friar,—"excepting, perhaps, some poor brother of our own order, whom Our Lady and Saint Francis send into such a scene as this, that good Christians may bestow their alms upon him, and so make a step on their road to Heaven."

The first words of this speech were spoken in the open and independent tone in which the friar had begun the conversation; the last sentence died away into the professional whine of mendicity proper to the convent, and at once apprised Philipson at what price he was to pay for the friar's counsel and mediation. Having thus explained the custom of the country, good Father Gratian turned to illustrate it by his example, and, having no objection to the new service of wine on account of its strength, he seemed well disposed to signalize himself amongst some stout topers, who, by drinking deeply, appeared determined to have full pennyworths for their share of the reckoning. The good wine gradually did its office, and even the host relaxed his sullen and grim features, and smiled to see the kindling flame of hilarity catch from one to another, and at length embrace almost all the numerous guests at the table d'hôte, except a few who were too temperate to partake deeply of the wine, or too fastidious to enter into the discussions to which it gave rise. On these the host cast, from time to time, a sullen and displeased eye.

Philipson, who was reserved and silent, both in consequence of his abstinence from the wine-pot, and his unwillingness to mix in conversation with strangers, was looked upon by the landlord as a defaulter in both particulars; and as he aroused his own sluggish nature with the fiery wine, Mengs began to throw out obscure hints about kill-joy, mar-company, spoil-sport, and such like epithets, which were plainly directed against the Englishman. Philipson replied, with the utmost equanimity, that he was perfectly sensible that his spirits did not at this moment render him an agreeable member of a merry company, and that, with the leave of those present, he would withdraw to his sleeping apartment, and wish them all a good evening, and continuance to their mirth.

But this very reasonable proposal, as it might have elsewhere seemed, contained in it treason against the laws of German compotation.

"Who are you," said John Mengs, "who presume to leave the table before the reckoning is called and settled? Sapperment der teufel! we are not men upon whom such an offence is to be put with impunity! You may exhibit your polite pranks in Rams-Alley if you will, or in Eastcheap, or in Smithfield; but it shall not be in John Mengs's Golden Fleece; nor will I suffer one guest to go to bed to blink out of the reckoning, and so cheat me and all the rest of my company."

Philipson looked round, to gather the sentiments of the company, but saw no encouragement to appeal to their judgment. Indeed, many of them had little judgment left to appeal to, and those who paid any attention to the matter at all, were some quiet old soakers, who were already beginning to think of the reckoning, and were disposed to agree with the host in considering the English merchant as a flincher, who was determined to evade payment of what might be drunk after he left the room; so that John Mengs received the applause of the whole company, when he concluded his triumphant denunciation against Philipson.

"Yes, sir, you may withdraw if you please; but, poz element! it shall not be for this time to seek for another inn, but to the court-yard shall you go, and no further, there to make your bed upon the stable litter; and good enough for the man that will needs be the first to break up good company."

"It is well said, my jovial host," said a rich trader from Ratisbon; "and here are some six of us—more or less—who will stand by you to maintain the good old customs of Germany; and the—umph—laudable and—and praiseworthy rules of the Golden Fleece."

"Nay, be not angry, sir," said Philipson; "yourself and your three companions, whom the good wine has multiplied into six, shall have your own way of ordering the matter; and since you will not permit me to go to bed, I trust that you will take no offence if I fall asleep in my chair."

"How say you? what think you, mine host?" said the citizen from Ratisbon; "may the gentleman, being drunk, as you see he is, since he cannot tell that three and one make six—I say, may he, being drunk, sleep in the elbow-chair?"

This question introduced a contradiction on the part of the host, who contended that three and one made four, not six; and this again produced a retort from the Ratisbon trader. Other clamours rose at the same time, and were at length with difficulty silenced by the stanzas of a chorus song of mirth and good fellowship, which the friar, now become somewhat oblivious of the rule of Saint Francis, thundered forth with better good-will than he ever sung a canticle of King David. Under cover of this tumult, Philipson drew himself a little aside, and though he felt it impossible to sleep, as he had proposed, was yet enabled to escape the reproachful glances with which John Mengs distinguished all those who did not call for wine loudly, and drink it lustily. His thoughts roamed far from the *stubé* of the Golden Fleece, and upon matter very different from that which was discussed around him, when his attention was suddenly recalled by a loud and continued knocking on the door of the hostelry.

"What have we here?" said John Mengs, his nose reddening with very indignation; "who the foul fiend presses on the Golden Fleece at such an hour, as if he thundered at the door of a bordel? To the turret window some one—Geoffrey, knave ostler, or thou, old Timothy, tell the rash man there is no admittance into the Golden Fleece save at timeous hours."

The men went as they were directed, and might be

heard in the *stubé* vying with each other in the positive denial which they gave to the ill-fated guest, who was pressing for admission. They returned, however, to inform their master, that they were unable to overcome the obstinacy of the stranger, who refused positively to depart until he had an interview with Mengs himself.

Wroth was the master of the Golden Fleece at this ill-omened pertinacity, and his indignation extended, like a fiery exhalation, from his nose, all over the adjacent regions of his cheeks and brow. He started from his chair, grasped in his hand a stout stick, which seemed his ordinary sceptre or leading staff of command, and muttering something concerning cudgels for the shoulders of fools, and pitchers of fair or foul water for the drenching of their ears, he marched off to the window which looked into the court, and left his guests nodding, winking, and whispering to each other, in full expectation of hearing the active demonstrations of his wrath. It happened otherwise, however ; for, after the exchange of a few indistinct words, they were astonished when they heard the noise of the unbolting and unbarring of the gates of the inn, and presently after the footsteps of men upon the stairs; and the landlord entering, with an appearance of clumsy courtesy, prayed those assembled to make room for an honoured guest, who came, though late, to add to their numbers. A tall dark form followed, muffled in a travelling cloak: on laying aside which, Philipson at once recognised his late fellow-traveller, the Black Priest of Saint Paul's.

There was in the circumstance itself nothing at all surprising, since it was natural that a landlord, however coarse and insolent to ordinary guests, might yet shew deference to an ecclesiastic, whether from his rank in the church, or from his reputation for sanctity. But what did appear surprising to Philipson, was the effect produced by the entrance of this unexpected guest. He seated himself, without hesitation, at the highest place of the board, from which John Mengs had dethroned the aforesaid trader from Ratisbon, notwithstanding his zeal for ancient German customs, his steady adherence and loyalty to the Golden Fleece, and his propensity to brimming goblets. The priest took instant and unscrupulous possession of his seat of honour, after some negligent reply to the host's unwonted courtesy; when it seemed that the effect of his long black vestments, in place of the slashed and flounced coat of his predecessor, as well as of the cold grey eye with which he slowly reviewed the company, in some degree resembled that of the fabulous Gorgon, and if it did not literally convert those who looked upon it into stone, there was yet something petrifying in the steady unmoved glance with which he seemed to survey them, looking as if desirous of reading their very inmost souls, and passing from one to another, as if each upon whom he looked in succession was unworthy of longer consideration.

Philipson felt, in his turn, that momentary examination, in which, however, there mingled nothing that seemed to convey recognition. All the courage and composure of the Englishman could not prevent an unpleasant feeling while under this mysterious man's eye, so that he felt a relief when it passed from him and rested upon another of the company, who seemed in turn to acknowledge the chilling effects of that freezing glance. The noise of intoxicated mirth and drunken disputation, the clamorous argument, and the still more boisterous laugh, which had been suspended on the priest's entering the eating apartment, now, after one or two vain attempts to resume them, died away, as if the feast had been changed to a funeral, and the jovial guests had been at once converted into the lugubrious mutes who attend on such solemnities. One little rosy-faced man, who afterwards proved to be a tailor from Augsburg, ambitious, perhaps, of shewing a degree of courage not usually supposed consistent with his effeminate trade, made a bold effort; and yet it was with a timid and restrained voice, that he called on the jovial friar to renew his song. But whether it was that he did not dare to venture on an uncanonical pastime in presence of a brother in orders, or whether he had some other reason for declining the invitation, the merry churchman hung his head, and shook it with such an expressive air of melancholy, that the tailor drew back as if he had been detected in cabbaging from a cardinal's robes, or cribbing the lace of some cope or altar gown. In short, the revel was hushed into deep silence, and so attentive were the company to what should arrive next, that the bells of the village church, striking the first hour after midnight, made the guests start as if they heard them rung backwards, to announce an assault or conflagration. The

Black Priest, who had taken some slight and hasty repast, which the host had made no kind of objection to supplying him with, seemed to think the bells, which announced the service of lauds, being the first after midnight, a proper signal for breaking up the party.

"We have eaten," he said, "that we may support life; let us pray that we may be fit to meet death; which waits upon life as surely as night upon day, or the shadow upon the sunbeam, though we know not when or from whence it is to come upon us."

The company, as if mechanically, bent their uncovered heads, while the priest said, with his deep and solemn voice, a Latin prayer, expressing thanks to God for protection throughout the day, and entreating for its continuance during the witching hours which were to pass ere the day again commenced. The hearers bowed their heads in token of acquiescence in the holy petition; and, when they raised them, the Black Priest of Saint Paul's had followed the host out of the apartment, probably to that which was destined for his repose. His absence was no sooner perceived, than signs, and nods, and even whispers, were exchanged between the guests; but no one spoke above his breath, or in such connected manner, as that Philipson could understand anything distinctly from them. He himself ventured to ask the friar, who sat near him, observing at the same time the under-tone which seemed to be fashionable for the moment, whether the worthy ecclesiastic who had left them, was not the Priest of Saint Paul's, on the frontier town of La Ferette.

"And if you know it is he," said the friar, with a countenance and a tone, from which all signs of intoxication were suddenly banished, "why do you ask of me?"

"Because," said the merchant, "I would willingly learn the spell which so suddenly converted so many merry tipplers into men of sober manners, and a jovial company into a convent of Carthusian friars?"

"Friend," said the friar, "thy discourse savoureth mightily of asking after what thou knowest right well. But I am no such silly duck as to be taken by a decoy. If thou knowest the Black Priest, thou canst not be ignorant of the terrors which attend his presence, and that it were safer to pass a broad jest in the holy House of Loretto than where he shews himself."

So saying, as if desirous of avoiding further discourse, he withdrew to a distance from Philipson.

At the same moment the landlord again appeared, and, with more of the usual manners of a publican than he had hitherto exhibited, commanded his waiter, Geoffrey, to hand round to the company a sleeping-drink, or pillow-cup of distilled water, mingled with spices, which was indeed as good as Philipson himself had ever tasted. John Mengs, in the meanwhile, with somewhat of more deference, expressed to his guests a hope that his entertainment had given satisfaction; but this was in so careless a manner, and he seemed so conscious of deserving the affirmative which was expressed on all hands, that it became obvious there was very little humility in proposing the question. The old man, Timothy, was in the meantime mustering the guests, and marking with chalk on the bottom of a trencher the reckoning, the particulars of which were indicated by certain conventional hieroglyphics, while he shewed on another the division of the sum total among the company, and proceeded to collect an equal share of it from each. When the fatal trencher, in which each man paid down his money, approached the jolly friar, his countenance seemed to be somewhat changed. He cast a piteous look towards Philipson, as the person from whom he had the most hope of relief; and our merchant, though displeased with the manner in which he had held back from his confidence, yet not unwilling in a strange country to incur a little expense, in the hope of making a useful acquaintance, discharged the mendicant's score as well as his own. The poor friar paid his thanks in many a blessing in good German and bad Latin, but the host cut them short; for, approaching Philipson with a candle in his hand, he offered his own services to shew him where he might sleep, and even had the condescension to carry his mail, or portmanteau, with his own landlordly hands.

"You take too much trouble, mine host," said the merchant, somewhat surprised at the change in the manner of John Mengs, who had hitherto contradicted him at every word.

"I cannot take too much pains for a guest," was the reply, "whom my venerable friend, the Priest of Saint Paul's, hath especially recommended to my charge."

He then opened the door of a small bedroom, prepared for the occupation of a guest, and said to Philipson,—" Here you may rest till to-morrow at what hour you will, and for as many days more as you incline. The key will secure your wares against theft or pillage of any kind. I do not this for every one; for, if my guests were every one to have a bed to himself, the next thing they would demand might be a separate table; and then there would be an end of the good old German customs, and we should be as foppish and frivolous as our neighbours."

He placed the portmanteau on the floor, and seemed about to leave the apartment, when, turning about, he began a sort of apology for the rudeness of his former behaviour.

" I trust there is no misunderstanding between us, my worthy guest. You might as well expect to see one of our bears come aloft and do tricks like a jackanapes, as one of us stubborn old Germans play the feats of a French or an Italian host. Yet I pray you to note, that if our behaviour is rude our charges are honest, and our articles what they profess to be. We do not expect to make Moselle pass for Rhenish, by dint of a bow and a grin, nor will we sauce your mess with poison, like the wily Italian, and call you all the time Illustrissimo and Magnifico."

He seemed in these words to have exhausted his rhetoric, for, when they were spoken, he turned abruptly and left the apartment.

Philipson was thus deprived of another opportunity to inquire who or what this ecclesiastic could be, that had exercised such influence on all who approached him. He felt, indeed, no desire to prolong a conference with John Mengs, though he had laid aside in such a considerable degree his rude and repulsive manners; yet he longed to know who this man could be, who had power with a word to turn aside the daggers of Alsatian banditti, habituated as they were, like most borderers, to robbery and pillage, and to change into civility the proverbial rudeness of a German innkeeper. Such were the reflections of Philipson, as he doffed his clothes to take his much-needed repose, after a day of fatigue, danger, and difficulty, on the pallet afforded by the hospitality of the Golden Fleece, in the Rhein-Thal.

CHAPTER THE TWENTIETH.

Macbeth.—How now, ye secret, black, and midnight hags
What is't ye do?
Witches.—A deed without a name.
MACBETH.

WE have said in the conclusion of the last chapter, that, after a day of unwonted fatigue and extraordinary excitation, the merchant, Philipson, naturally expected to forget so many agitating passages in that deep and profound repose, which is at once the consequence and the cure of extreme exhaustion. But he was no sooner laid on his lowly pallet, than he felt that the bodily machine, over-laboured by so much exercise, was little disposed to the charms of sleep. The mind had been too much excited, the body was far too feverish, to suffer him to partake of needful rest. His anxiety about the safety of his son, his conjectures concerning the issue of his mission to the Duke of Burgundy, and a thousand other thoughts which recalled past events, or speculated on those which were to come, rushed upon his mind like the waves of a perturbed sea, and prevented all tendency to repose. He had been in bed about an hour, and sleep had not yet approached his couch, when he felt that the pallet on which he lay was sinking below him, and that he was in the act of descending along with it he knew not whither. The sound of ropes and pullies was also indistinctly heard, though every caution had been taken to make them run smooth; and the traveller, by feeling around him, became sensible that he and the bed on which he lay had been spread upon a large trap-door, which was capable of being let down into the vaults, or apartments beneath.

Philipson felt fear in circumstances so well qualified to produce it; for how could he hope a safe termination to an adventure which had begun so strangely? But his apprehensions were those of a brave, ready-witted man, who, even in the extremity of danger, which appeared to surround him, preserved his presence of mind. His descent seemed to be cautiously managed, and he held himself in readiness to start to his feet and defend himself, as soon as he should be once more upon firm ground. Although somewhat advanced in years, he was a man of great personal vigour and activity, and unless taken at advantage, which no doubt was at present much to be apprehended, he was likely to make a formidable defence. His plan of resistance, however, had been anticipated. He no sooner reached the bottom of the vault, down to which he was lowered, than two men, who had been waiting there till the operation was completed, laid hands on him from either side, and forcibly preventing him from starting up as he intended, cast a rope over his arms, and made him a prisoner as effectually as when he was in the dungeons of La Ferette. He was obliged, therefore, to rumain passive and unresisting, and await the termination of this formidable adventure.

Secured as he was, he could only turn his head from one side to the other; and it was with joy that he at length saw lights twinkle, but they appeared at a great distance from him.

From the irregular manner in which these scattered lights advanced, sometimes keeping a straight line, sometimes mixing and crossing each other, it might be inferred that the subterranean vault in which they appeared was of very considerable extent. Their number also increased; and as they collected more together, Philipson could perceive that the lights proceeded from many torches, borne by men muffled in black cloaks, like mourners at a funeral, or the Black Friars of Saint Francis's Order, wearing their cowls drawn over their heads so as to conceal their features. They appeared anxiously engaged in measuring off a portion of the apartment; and, while occupied in that employment, they sung, in the ancient German language, rhymes more rude than Philipson could well understand, but which may be imitated thus:—

> Measurers of good and evil,
> Bring the square, the line, the level,—
> Rear the altar, dig the trench,
> Blood both stone and ditch shall drench.
> Cubits six, from end to end,
> Must the fatal bench extend,—
> Cubits six, from side to side,
> Judge and culprit must divide.
> On the east the Court assembles,
> On the west the Accused trembles—
> Answer, brethren, all and one,
> Is the ritual rightly done?

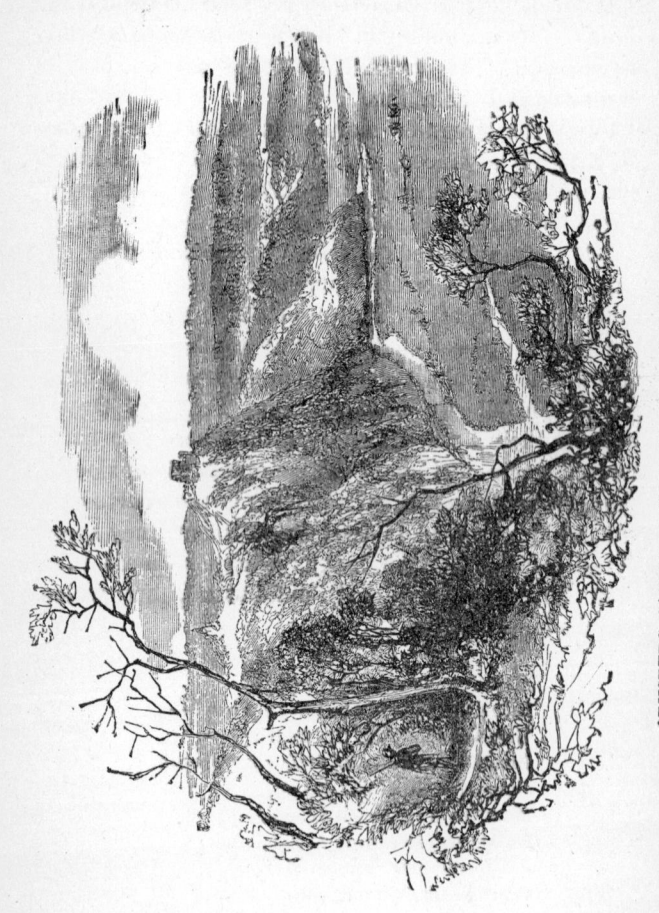

ARNSBERG CASTLE, A SEAT OF THE VEHME GERICHT.

A deep chorus seemed to reply to the question. Many voices joined in it, as well of persons already in the subterranean vault, as of others who as yet remained without in various galleries and passages which communicated with it, and whom Philipson now presumed to be very numerous. The answer chanted ran as follows:—

> On life and soul, on blood and bone,
> One for all, and all for one,
> We warrant this is rightly done.

The original strain was then renewed in the same manner as before—

> How wears the night?—Doth morning shine
> In early radiance on the Rhine?
> What music floats upon his tide?
> Do birds the tardy morning chide?
> Brethren, look out from hill and height,
> And answer true, how wears the night?

The answer was returned, though less loud than at first, and it seemed that those by whom the reply was given were at a much greater distance than before; yet the words were distinctly heard.

> The night is old; on Rhine's broad breast
> Glance drowsy stars which long to rest.
> No beams are twinkling in the east.
> There is a voice upon the flood,
> The stern still call of blood for blood;
> 'Tis time we listen the behest.

The chorus replied with many additional voices—

> Up, then, up! When day's at rest,
> 'Tis time that such as we are watchers;

> Rise to judgment, brethren, rise!
> Vengeance knows not sleepy eyes,
>   He and night are matchers.

The nature of the verses soon led Philipson to comprehend that he was in presence of the Initiated, or the Wise Men; names which were applied to the celebrated Judges of the Secret Tribunal, which continued at that period to subsist in Swabia, Franconia, and other districts of the east of Germany, which was called, perhaps from the frightful and frequent occurrence of executions by command of those invisible judges, the Red Land. Philipson had often heard that the seat of a free Count, or chief of the Secret Tribunal, was secretly instituted even on the left bank of the Rhine, and that it maintained itself in Alsace, with the usual tenacity of those secret societies, though Duke Charles of Burgundy had expressed a desire to discover and discourage its influence so far as was possible, without exposing himself to danger from the thousands of poniards which that mysterious tribunal could put in activity against his own life;—an awful means of defence, which for a long time rendered it extremely hazardous for the sovereigns of Germany, and even the Emperors themselves, to put down by authority those singular associations.

So soon as this explanation flashed on the mind of Philipson, it gave some clew to the character and condition of the Black Priest of Saint Paul's. Supposing him to be a president, or chief official of the secret association, there was little wonder that he should confide so much in the inviolability of his terrible office, as to propose vindicating the execution of De Hagenbach; that his presence should surprise Bartholomew, whom he had power to have judged and executed upon the spot; and that his mere appearance at supper on the preceding evening should have appalled the guests; for though every thing about the institution, its proceedings and its officers, was preserved in as much obscurity as is now practised in free-masonry, yet the secret was not so absolutely well kept as to prevent certain individuals from being guessed or hinted at as men initiated and intrusted with high authority by the Vehme-gericht, or tribunal of the bounds. When such suspicion attached to an individual, his secret power, and supposed acquaintance with all guilt, however secret, which was committed within the society in which he was conversant, made him at once the dread and hatred of every one who looked on him; and he enjoyed a high degree of personal respect, on the same terms on which it would have been yielded to a powerful enchanter, or a dreaded genie. In conversing with such a person, it was especially necessary to abstain from all questions alluding, however remotely, to the office which he bore in the Secret Tribunal; and, indeed, to testify the least curiosity upon a subject so solemn and mysterious, was sure to occasion some misfortune to the inquisitive person.

All these things rushed at once upon the mind of the Englishman, who felt that he had fallen into the hands of an unsparing tribunal, whose proceedings were so much dreaded by those who resided within the circle of their power, that the friendless stranger must stand a poor chance of receiving justice at their hands, whatever might be his consciousness of innocence. While Philipson made this melancholy reflection, he resolved, at the same time, not to forsake his own cause, but defend himself as he best might; conscious as he was that these terrible and irresponsible judges were nevertheless governed by certain rules of right and wrong, which formed a check on the rigours of their extraordinary code.

He lay, therefore, devising the best means of obviating the present danger, while the persons whom he beheld glimmered before him, less like distinct and individual forms, than like the phantoms of a fever, or the phantasmagoria with which a disease of the optic nerves has been known to people a sick man's chamber. At length they assembled in the centre of the apartment where they had first appeared, and seemed to arrange themselves into form and order. A great number of black torches were successively lighted, and the scene became distinctly visible. In the centre of the hall, Philipson could now perceive one of the altars which are sometimes to be found in ancient subterranean chapels. But we must pause, in order briefly to describe, not the appearance only, but the nature and constitution, of this terrible court.

Behind the altar, which seemed to be the central point, on which all eyes were bent, there were placed in parallel lines two benches covered with black cloth. Each was occupied by a number of persons, who seemed assembled as judges; but those who held the foremost bench were fewer, and appeared of a rank superior to those who crowded the seat most remote from the altar. The first seemed to be all men of some consequence, priests high in their order, knights or noblemen; and notwithstanding an appearance of equality which seemed to pervade this singular institution, much more weight was laid upon their opinion, or testimonies. They were called Free Knights, Counts, or whatever title they might bear, while the inferior class of the judges were only termed Free and worthy Burghers. For it must be observed, that the Vehmique Institution,* which was the name that it commonly bore, although its power consisted in a wide system of espionage, and the tyrannical application of force which acted upon it, was yet (so rude were the ideas of enforcing public law) accounted to confer a privilege on the country in which it was received, and only freemen were allowed to experience its influence. Serfs and peasants could neither have a place among the Free Judges, their assessors, or assistants; for there was in this assembly even some idea of trying the culprit by his peers.

Besides the dignitaries who occupied the benches, there were others who stood around, and seemed to guard the various entrances to the hall of judgment, or, standing behind the seats on which their supe-

* The word Wehme, pronounced Vehme, is of uncertain derivation, but was always used to intimate this inquisitorial and secret Court. The members were termed Wissenden, or Initiated, answering to the modern phrase of Illuminati. Mr. Palgrave seems inclined to derive the word *Vehme* from *Ehme*, i. e., *Law*, and he is probably right.

riors were ranged, looked prepared to execute their commands. These were members of the order, though not of the highest ranks. Schöppen is the name generally assigned to them, signifying officials, or sergeants of the Vehmique Court, whose doom they stood sworn to enforce, through good report and bad report, against their own nearest and most beloved, as well as in cases of ordinary malefactors.

The Schöppen, or Scabini, as they were termed in Latin, had another horrible duty to perform, that, namely, of denouncing to the tribunal whatever came under their observation, that might be construed as an offence falling under its cognizance; or, in their language, a crime against the Vehme. This duty extended to the judges as well as the assistants, and was to be discharged without respect of persons; so that, to know, and wilfully conceal, the guilt of a mother or brother, inferred, on the part of the unfaithful official, the same penalty as if he himself had committed the crime which his silence screened from punishment. Such an institution could only prevail at a time when ordinary means of justice were excluded by the hand of power, and when, in order to bring the guilty to punishment, it required all the influence and authority of such a confederacy. In no other country than one exposed to every species of feudal tyranny, and deprived of every ordinary mode of obtaining justice or redress, could such a system have taken root and flourished.

We must now return to the brave Englishman, who, though feeling all the danger he encountered from so tremendous a tribunal, maintained nevertheless a dignified and unaltered composure.

The meeting being assembled, a coil of ropes, and a naked sword, the well-known signals and emblems of Vehmique authority, were deposited on the altar; where the sword, from its being usually straight, with a cross handle, was considered as representing the blessed emblem of Christian Redemption, and the cord as indicating the right of criminal jurisdiction, and capital punishment. Then the president of the meeting, who occupied the centre seat on the foremost bench, arose, and laying his hand on the symbols, pronounced aloud the formula expressive of the duty of the tribunal, which all the inferior judges and assistants repeated after him, in deep and hollow murmurs.

"I swear by the Holy Trinity, to aid and co-operate, without relaxation, in the things belonging to the Holy Vehme, to defend its doctrines and institutions against father and mother, brother and sister, wife and children; against fire, water, earth, and air; against all that the sun enlightens; against all that the dew moistens; against all created things of heaven and earth, or the waters under the earth; and I swear to give information to this holy judicature, of all that I know to be true, or hear repeated by credible testimony, which, by the rules of the Holy Vehme, is deserving of animadversion or punishment; and that I will not cloak, cover, or conceal, such my knowledge, neither for love, friendship, or family affection, nor for gold, silver, or precious stones; neither will I associate with such as are under the sentence of this

Sacred Tribunal, by hinting to a culprit his danger, or advising him to escape, or aiding and supplying him with counsel, or means to that effect; neither will I relieve such culprit with fire, clothes, food, or shelter, though my father should require from me a cup of water in the heat of summer-noon, or my brother should request to sit by my fire in the bitterest cold night of winter: And further, I vow and promise to honour this holy association, and do its behests, speedily, faithfully, and firmly, in preference to those of any other tribunal whatsoever—so help me God, and his holy Evangelists."

When this oath of office had been taken, the President addressing the assembly, as men who judge in secret and punish in secret, like the Deity, desired them to say, why this "child of the cord"* lay before them bound and helpless? An individual rose from the more remote bench, and in a voice which, though altered and agitated, Philipson conceived that he recognised, declared himself the accuser, as bound by his oath, of the child of the cord, or prisoner, who lay before them.

"Bring forward the prisoner," said the President, "duly secured, as is the order of our secret law; but not with such severity as may interrupt his attention to the proceedings of the tribunal, or limit his power of hearing and replying."

Six of the assistants immediately dragged forward the pallet and platform of boards on which Philipson lay, and advanced it towards the foot of the altar.

* The term *Strick-kind*, or child of the cord, was applied to the person accused before these awful assemblies.

This done, each unsheathed his dagger, while two of them unloosed the cords by which the merchant's hands were secured, and admonished him in a whisper, that the slightest attempt to resist or escape, would be the signal to stab him dead.

"Arise!" said the President; "listen to the charge to be preferred against you, and believe you shall in us find judges equally just and inflexible."

Philipson carefully avoiding any gesture which might indicate a desire to escape, raised his body on the lower part of the couch, and remained seated, clothed as he was in his under-vest and *calecons*, or drawers, so as exactly to face the muffled President of the terrible court. Even in these agitating circumstances, the mind of the undaunted Englishman remained unshaken, and his eyelid did not quiver, nor his heart beat quicker, though he seemed, according to the expression of Scripture, to be a pilgrim in the Valley of the Shadow of Death, beset by numerous snares, and encompassed by total darkness, where light was most necessary for safety.

The President demanded his name, country, and occupation?

"John Philipson," was the reply; "by birth an Englishman, by profession a merchant."

"Have you ever borne any other name, and profession?" demanded the Judge.

"I have been a soldier, and, like most others, had then a name by which I was known in war."

"What was that name?"

"I laid it aside when I resigned my sword, and I do not desire again to be known by it. Moreover, I never bore it where your institutions have weight and authority," answered the Englishman.

" Know you before whom you stand ? " continued the Judge.

" I may at least guess," replied the merchant.

" Tell your guess, then," continued the interrogator. " Say who we are, and wherefore you are be-before us ? "

" I believe that I am before the Unknown, or Secret Tribunal, which is called Vehme-gericht."

" Then are you aware," answered the Judge, " that you would be safer if you were suspended by the hair over the Abyss of Schaffhausen, or if you lay below an axe, which a thread of silk alone kept back from the fall. What have you done to deserve such a fate ? "

" Let those reply by whom I am subjected to it," answered Philipson, with the same composure as before.

" Speak, accuser," said the President, " to the four quarters of Heaven !—To the ears of the free judges of this tribunal, and the faithful executors of their doom !—And to the face of the child of the cord, who denies or conceals his guilt, make good the substance of thine accusation !"

" Most dreaded," answered the accuser, addressing the President, " this man hath entered the Sacred Territory, which is called the Red Land,—a stranger under a disguised name and profession. When he was yet on the Eastern side of the Alps, at Turin, in Lombardy, and elsewhere, he at various times spoke of the Holy Tribunal in terms of hatred and contempt, and declared that were he Duke of Burgundy, he would not permit it to extend itself from Westphalia, or Swabia, into his dominions. Also, I charge him, that, nourishing this malevolent intention against the Holy Tribunal, he who now appears before the bench as child of the cord, has intimated his intention to wait upon the court of the Duke of Burgundy, and use his influence with him, which he boasts will prove effectual, to stir him up to prohibit the meetings of the Holy Vehme in his dominions, and to inflict on their officers, and the executors of their mandates, the punishment due to robbers and assassins."

"This is a heavy charge, brother!" said the President of the assembly, when the accuser ceased speaking—"How do you purpose to make it good?"

"According to the tenor of those secret statutes, the perusal of which is prohibited to all but the initiated," answered the accuser.

"It is well," said the President; "but I ask thee once more, What are those means of proof?— You speak to holy and to initiated ears."

"I will prove my charge," said the accuser, " by the confession of the party himself, and by my own oath upon the holy emblems of the Secret Judgment —that is, the steel and the cord."

"It is a legitimate offer of proof," said a member of the aristocratic bench of the assembly; "and it much concerns the safety of the system to which we are bound by such deep oaths, a system handed down to us from the most Christian and holy Roman Emperor, Charlemagne, for the conversion of the heathen Saracens, and punishing such of them as revolted again to their Pagan practices, that such criminals should be looked to. This Duke Charles of Burgundy hath already crowded his army with foreigners, whom he can easily employ against this Sacred Court, more especially with English, a fierce insular people, wedded to their own usages, and hating those of every other nation. It is not unknown to us, that the Duke hath already encouraged opposition to the officials of the Tribunal in more than one part of his German dominions; and that in consequence, instead of submitting to their doom with reverent resignation, children of the cord have been found bold enough to resist the executioners of the Vehme, striking, wounding, and even slaying those who have received commission to put them to death. This contumacy must be put an end to; and if the accused shall be proved to be one of those by whom such doctrines are harboured and inculcated, I say let the steel and cord do their work on him."

A general murmur seemed to approve what the speaker had said; for all were conscious that the power of the Tribunal depended much more on the opinion of its being deeply and firmly rooted in the general system, than upon any regard or esteem for an institution, of which all felt the severity. It followed, that those of the members who enjoyed consequence by means of their station in the ranks of the Vehme, saw the necessity of supporting its terrors by occasional examples of severe punishment; and none could be more readily sacrificed, than an unknown and wandering foreigner. All this rushed upon Philipson's mind, but did not prevent his making a steady reply to the accusation.

"Gentlemen," he said, "good citizens, burgesses, or by whatever other name you please to be addressed, know, that in my former days I have stood in as great peril as now, and have never turned my heel to save my life. Cords and daggers are not calculated to strike terror into those who have seen sword and lances. My answer to the accusation is, that I am an Englishman, one of a nation accustomed to yield and to receive open-handed and equal justice dealt forth in the broad light of day. I am, however, a traveller, who knows that he has no right to oppose the rules and laws of other nations, because they do not resemble those of his own. But this caution can only be called for in lands, where the system about which we converse is in full force and operation. If we speak of the institutions of Germany, being at the time in France or Spain, we may, without offence to the country in which they are current, dispute concerning them, as students debate upon a logical thesis in a university. The accuser objects to me, that at Turin, or elsewhere in the north of Italy, I spoke with censure of the institution under which I am now judged. I will not deny that I remember something of the kind; but it was in consequence of the question being in a manner forced upon me by two guests, with whom I chanced to find myself at table. I was much and earnestly solicited for an opinion ere I gave one."

"And was that opinion," said the presiding Judge,

"favourable or otherwise to the Holy and Secret Vehme-gericht? Let truth rule your tongue—remember, life is short, judgment is eternal!"

"I would not save my life at the expense of a falsehood. My opinion was unfavourable; and I expressed myself thus:—No laws or judicial proceedings can be just or commendable, which exist and operate by means of a secret combination. I said, that justice could only live and exist in the open air, and that when she ceased to be public, she degenerated into revenge and hatred. I said, that a system, of which your own jurists have said, *non frater a fratre, non hospes a hospite, tutus*, was too much adverse to the laws of nature, to be connected with or regulated by those of religion."

These words were scarcely uttered, when there burst a murmur from the Judges highly unfavourable to the prisoner,—"He blasphemes the Holy Vehme —Let his mouth be closed for ever!"

"Hear me," said the Englishman, "as you will one day wish to be yourselves heard! I say such were my sentiments, and so I expressed them—I say also, I had a right to express these opinions, whether sound or erroneous, in a neutral country, where this Tribunal neither did, nor could, claim any jurisdiction. My sentiments are still the same. I would avow them if that sword were at my bosom, or that cord around my throat. But I deny that I have ever spoken against the institutions of your Vehme, in a country where it had its course as a national mode of justice. Far more strongly, if possible, do I denounce the absurdity of the falsehood, which represents me, a wandering foreigner, as commissioned to traffic with the Duke of Burgundy about such high matters, or to form a conspiracy for the destruction of a system, to which so many seem warmly attached. I never said such a thing, and I never thought it."

"Accuser," said the presiding Judge, "thou hast heard the accused—What is thy reply?"

"The first part of the charge," said the accuser, "he hath confessed in this high presence, namely, that his foul tongue hath basely slandered our holy mysteries; for which he deserves that it should be torn out of his throat. I myself, on my oath of office, will aver, as use and law is, that the rest of the accusation, namely, that which taxes him as having entered into machinations for the destruction of the Vehmique institutions, are as true as those which he has found himself unable to deny."

"In justice," said the Englishman, "the accusation, if not made good by satisfactory proof, ought to be left to the oath of the party accused, instead of permitting the accuser to establish by his own deposition the defects in his own charge."

"Stranger," replied the presiding Judge, "we permit to thy ignorance a longer and more full defence than consists with our usual forms. Know that the right of sitting among these venerable judges confers on the person of him who enjoys it a sacredness of character, which ordinary men cannot attain to. The oath of one of the initiated must counterbalance the most solemn asseveration of every one that is not acquainted with our holy secrets. In the Vehmique court all must be Vehmique. The averment of the

Emperor, he being uninitiated, would not have so much weight in our counsels as that of one of the meanest of these officials. The affirmation of the accuser can only be rebutted by the oath of a member of the same Tribunal, being of superior rank."

"Then, God be gracious to me, for I have no trust save in Heaven!" said the Englishman, in solemn accents. "Yet I will not fall without an effort. I call upon thee, thyself, dark spirit, who presidest in this most deadly assembly—I call upon thyself, to declare on thy faith and honour, whether thou holdest me guilty of what is thus boldly averred by this false calumniator—I call upon thee by thy sacred character—by the name of——"

"Hold!" replied the presiding Judge. "The name by which we are known in open air must not be pronounced in this subterranean judgment-seat."

He then proceeded to address the prisoner and the assembly,—"I, being called on in evidence, declare that the charge against thee is so far true as it is acknowledged by thyself, namely, that thou hast in other lands than the Red Soil,[*] spoken lightly of this holy institution of justice. But I believe in my soul, and will bear witness on my honour, that the rest of the accusation is incredible and false. And

---

[*] The parts of Germany subjected to the operation of the Secret Tribunal, were called, from the blood which it spilt, or from some other reason, (Mr. Palgrave suggests the ground tincture of the ancient banner of the district,) the Red Soil. Westphalia, as the limits of that country were understood in the middle ages, which are considerably different from the present boundaries, was the principal theatre of the Vehme.

this I swear, holding my hand on the dagger and the cord.—What is your judgment, my brethren, upon the case which you have investigated?"

A member of the first-seated and highest class amongst the judges, muffled like the rest, but the tone of whose voice, and the stoop of whose person, announced him to be more advanced in years than the other two who had before spoken, arose with difficulty, and said with a trembling voice,—

"The child of the cord who is before us, has been convicted of folly and rashness in slandering our holy institution. But he spoke his folly to ears whcih had never heard our sacred laws — He has, therefore, been acquitted by irrefragable testimony, of combining for the impotent purpose of undermining our power, or stirring up princes against our holy association, for which death were too light a punishment — He hath been foolish, then, but not criminal; and as the holy laws of the Vehme bear no penalty save that of death, I propose for judgment that the child of the cord be restored without injury to society, and to the upper world, having been first duly admonished of his errors."

"Child of the cord," said the presiding Judge, "thou hast heard thy sentence of acquittal. But as thou desirest to sleep in an unbloody grave, let me warn thee, that the secrets of this night shall remain with thee, as a secret not to be communicated to father nor mother, to spouse, son, or daughter; neither to be spoken aloud nor whispered; to be told in words or written in characters; to be carved or to be painted, or to be otherwise communicated, either directly, or by parable and emblem. Obey this behest, and thy life is in surety. Let thy heart then rejoice within thee, but let it rejoice with trembling. Never more let thy vanity persuade thee that thou art secure from the servants and Judges of the Holy Vehme. Though a thousand leagues lie between thee and the Red Land, and thou speakest in that where our power is not known; though thou shouldst be sheltered by thy native island, and defended by thy kindred ocean, yet, even there, I warn thee to cross thyself when thou dost so much as think of the Holy and Invisible Tribunal, and to retain thy thoughts within thine own bosom; for the Avenger may be beside thee, and thou mayst die in thy folly. Go hence, be wise, and let the fear of the Holy Vehme never pass from before thine eyes."

At the concluding words, all the lights were at once extinguished with a hissing noise. Philipson felt once more the grasp of the hands of the officials, to which he resigned himself as the safest course. He was gently prostrated on his pallet-bed, and transported back to the place from which he had been advanced to the foot of the altar. The cordage was again applied to the platform, and Philipson was sensible that his couch rose with him for a few moments, until a slight shock apprised him that he was again brought to a level with the floor of the chamber in which he had been lodged on the preceding night, or rather morning. He pondered over the events that had passed, in which he was sensible that he owed Heaven thanks for a great deliverance. Fatigue at length prevailed over anxiety,

ANNE OF GEIERSTEIN. 59

and he fell into a deep and profound sleep, from
which he was only awakened by returning light.
He resolved on an instant departure from so dangerous a spot, and without seeing any one of the household but the old ostler, pursued his journey to
Strasburg, and reached that city without farther
accident.

INTERIOR OF STRASBURG CATHEDRAL.

CHAPTER THE TWENTY-FIRST.

Away with these!—True Wisdom's world will be
Within its own creation, or in thine,
Maternal Nature! for who teems like thee
Thus on the banks of thy majestic Rhine?
There Harold gazes on a work divine,
A blending of all beauties, streams, and dells—
Fruit, foliage, crag, wood, cornfield, mountain, vine,
And chiefless castles breathing stern farewells,
From grey but leafy walls, where ruin greenly dwells.
CHILDE HAROLD'S PILGRIMAGE, *Canto III.*

WHEN Arthur Philipson left his father, to go on board the bark which was to waft him across the Rhine, he took but few precautions for his own subsistence, during a separation of which he calculated the duration to be very brief. Some necessary change of raiment, and a very few pieces of gold, were all which he thought it needful to withdraw from the general stock; the rest of the baggage and money he left with the sumpter-horse, which he concluded his father might need, in order to sustain his character as an English trader. Having embarked with his horse and his slender appointments on board a fishing skiff, she instantly raised her temporary mast, spread a sail across the yard, and, supported by the force of the wind against the downward power of the current, moved across the river obliquely in the direction of Kirch-hoff, which, as we have said, lies somewhat lower on the river than Hans-Chapelle. Their passage was so favourable, that they reached the opposite side in a few minutes, but not until Arthur, whose eye and thoughts were on the left bank, had seen his father depart from the Chapel of the Ferry, accompanied by two horsemen, whom he readily concluded to be the guide Bartholomew, and some chance traveller who had joined him; but the second of whom was in truth the Black Priest of Saint Paul's, as has been already mentioned.

This augmentation of his father's company was, he could not but think, likely to be attended with an increase of his safety, since it was not probable he would suffer a companion to be forced upon him, and one of his own choosing might be a protection, in case his guide should prove treacherous. At any rate, he had to rejoice that he had seen his father depart in safety from the spot where they had reason to apprehend some danger awaited him. He resolved, therefore, to make no stay at Kirch-hoff, but to pursue his way, as fast as possible, towards Strasburg, and rest, when darkness compelled him to stop, in one of the dorffs, or villages, which were situated on the German side of the Rhine. At Strasburg, he trusted, with the sanguine spirit of youth, he might again be able to rejoin his father; and if he could not altogether subdue his anxiety on their separation, he fondly nourished the hope that he might meet him in safety. After some short refreshment and repose afforded to his horse, he lost no time in proceeding on his journey down the eastern bank of the broad river.

He was now upon the most interesting side of the Rhine, walled in and repelled as the river is on that shore by the most romantic cliffs, now mantled with vegetation of the richest hue, tinged with all the variegated colours of autumn; now surmounted by fortresses, over whose gates were displayed the pennons of their proud owners; or studded with hamlets, where the richness of the soil supplied to the poor labourer the food, of which the oppressive hand of his superior threatened altogether to deprive him. Every stream which here contributes its waters to the Rhine, winds through its own tributary dell, and each valley possesses a varying and separate character, some rich with pastures, cornfields, and vineyards, some frowning with crags and precipices, and other romantic beauties.

The principles of taste were not then explained or analysed as they have been since, in countries where leisure has been found for this investigation. But the feelings arising from so rich a landscape as is displayed by the valley of the Rhine, must have been the same in every bosom, from the period when our Englishman took his solitary journey through it, in doubt and danger, till that in which it heard the indignant Childe Harold bid a proud farewell to his native country, in the vain search of a land in which his heart might throb less fiercely.

Arthur enjoyed the scene, although the fading daylight began to remind him, that, alone as he was, and travelling with a very valuable charge, it would be matter of prudence to look out for some place of rest during the night. Just as he had formed the resolution of inquiring at the next habitation he passed, which way he should follow for this purpose, the road he pursued descended into a beautiful amphitheatre filled with large trees, which protected from the heats of summer the delicate and tender herbage of the pasture. A large brook flowed through it, and joined the Rhine. At a short mile up the brook, its waters made a crescent round a steep craggy eminence, crowned with flanking walls, and Gothic towers and turrets, enclosing a feudal castle of the first order. A part of the savanna that has been mentioned, had been irregularly cultivated for wheat, which had grown a plentiful crop. It was gathered in, but the patches of deep yellow stubble contrasted with the green of the undisturbed pasture land, and with the seared and dark-red foliage of the broad oaks which stretched their arms athwart the level space. There a lad, in a rustic dress, was employed in the task of netting a brood of partridges, with the assistance of a trained spaniel; while a young woman, who had the air rather of a domestic in some family of rank, than that of an ordinary villager, sat on the stump of a decayed tree, to watch the progress of the amusement. The spaniel, whose duty it was to drive the partridges under the net, was perceptibly disturbed at the approach of the traveller; his attention was divided, and he was obviously in danger of marring the sport, by barking and putting up the covey, when the maiden quitted her seat, and advancing towards Philipson, requested him, for courtesy, to pass at a greater distance, and not interfere with their amusement.

The traveller willingly complied with her request.

"I will ride, fair damsel," he said, "at whatever distance you please. And allow me, in guerdon, to ask, whether there is convent, castle, or good man's house, where a stranger, who is belated and weary, might receive a night's hospitality?"

The girl, whose face he had not yet distinctly seen, seemed to suppress some desire to laugh, as she replied, "Hath not yon castle, think you," pointing to the distant towers, "some corner which might accommodate a stranger in such extremity?"

"Space enough, certainly," said Arthur; "but perhaps little inclination to grant it."

"I myself," said the girl, "being one, and a formidable part of the garrison, will be answerable for your reception. But as you parley with me in such hostile fashion, it is according to martial order that I should put down my visor."

So saying, she concealed her face under one of those riding masks, which at that period women often wore when they went abroad, whether for protecting their complexion, or screening themselves from intrusive observation. But ere she could accomplish this operation, Arthur had detected the merry countenance of Annette Veilchen, a girl who, though her attendance on Anne of Geierstein was in a menial capacity, was held in high estimation at Geierstein. She was a bold wench, unaccustomed to the distinctions of rank, which were little regarded in the simplicity of the Helvetian hills, and she was ready to laugh, jest, and flirt with the young men of the Landamman's family. This attracted no attention, the mountain manners making little distinction between the degrees of attendant and mistress, further than that the mistress was a young woman who required help, and the maiden one who was in a situation to offer and afford it. This kind of familiarity would perhaps have been dangerous in other lands, but the simplicity of Swiss manners, and the turn of Annette's disposition, which was resolute and sensible, though rather bold and free, when compared to the manners of more civilized countries, kept all intercourse betwixt her and the young men of the family in the strict path of honour and innocence.

Arthur himself had paid considerable attention to Annette, being naturally, from his feelings towards Anne of Geierstein, heartily desirous to possess the good graces of her attendant; a point which was easily gained by the attentions of a handsome young man, and the generosity with which he heaped upon her small presents of articles of dress or ornament, which the damsel, however faithful, could find no heart to refuse.

The assurance that he was in Anne's neighbourhood, and that he was likely to pass the night under the same roof, both of which circumstances were intimated by the girl's presence and language, sent the blood in a hastier current through Arthur's veins; for though, since he had crossed the river, he had sometimes nourished hopes of again seeing her who had made so strong an impression on his imagination, yet his understanding had as often told him how slight was the chance of their meeting, and it was even now chilled by the reflection, that it could be followed only by the pain of a sudden and final separation. He yielded himself, however, to the prospect of promised pleasure, without attempting to ascertain what was to be its duration or its consequence. Desirous, in the meantime, to hear as much of Anne's circumstances as Annette chose to tell, he resolved not to let that merry maiden perceive that she was known by him, until she chose of her own accord to lay aside her mystery.

While these thoughts passed rapidly through his imagination, Annette bade the lad drop his nets, and directed him that, having taken two of the best fed partridges from the covey, and carried them into the kitchen, he was to set the rest at liberty.

"I must provide supper," said she to the traveller, "since I am bringing home unexpected company."

Arthur earnestly expressed his hope that his experiencing the hospitality of the castle would occasion no trouble to the inmates, and received satisfactory assurances upon the subject of his scruples.

"I would not willingly be the cause of inconvenience to your mistress," pursued the traveller.

"Look you there," said Annette Veilchen, "I have said nothing of master or mistress, and this poor forlorn traveller has already concluded in his own mind that he is to be harboured in a lady's bower!"

"Why, did you not tell me," said Arthur, somewhat confused at his blunder, "that you were the person of second importance in the place? A damsel, I judged, could only be an officer under a female governor."

"I do not see the justice of the conclusion," replied the maiden. "I have known ladies bear offices of trust in lords' families; nay, and over the lords themselves."

"Am I to understand, fair damsel, that you hold so predominant a situation in the castle which we are now approaching, and of which I pray you to tell me the name?"

"The name of the castle is Arnheim," said Annette.

"Your garrison must be a large one," said Arthur, looking at the extensive building, "if you are able to man such a labyrinth of walls and towers."

"In that point," said Annette, "I must needs own we are very deficient. At present, we rather hide in the castle than inhabit it; and yet it is well enough defended by the reports which frighten every other person who might disturb its seclusion."

"And yet you yourselves dare to reside in it?" said the Englishman, recollecting the tale which had been told by Rudolph Donnerhugel, concerning the character of the Barons of Arnheim, and the final catastrophe of the family.

"Perhaps," replied his guide, "we are too intimate with the cause of such fears to feel ourselves strongly oppressed with them—perhaps we have means of encountering the supposed terrors proper to ourselves—perhaps, and it is not the least likely conjecture, we have no choice of a better place of refuge. Such seems to be your own fate at present, sir, for the tops of the distant hills are gradually losing the lights of the evening; and if you rest not in Arnheim, well contented or not, you are likely to find no safe lodging for many a mile."

As she thus spoke she separated from Arthur, taking, with the fowler who attended her, a very steep but short footpath, which ascended straight up to the site of the castle; at the same time motioning to the young Englishman to follow a horse-track, which, more circuitous, led to the same point, and, though less direct, was considerably more easy.

He soon stood before the south front of Arnheim castle, which was a much larger building than he had conceived, either from Rudolph's description, or from the distant view. It had been erected at many different periods, and a considerable part of the edifice was less in the strict Gothic than in what has been termed the Saracenic style, in which the imagination of the architect is more florid than that which is usually indulged in the North,—rich in minarets, cupolas, and similar approximations to Oriental structures. This singular building bore a general appearance of desolation and desertion, but Rudolph had been misinformed when he declared that it had become ruinous. On the contrary, it had been maintained with considerable care; and when it fell into the hands of the Emperor, although no garrison was maintained within its precincts, care was taken to keep the building in repair; and though the prejudices of the country people prevented any one from passing the night within the fearful walls, yet it was regularly visited from time to time by a person having commission from the imperial chancery to that effect. The occupation of the domain around the castle was a valuable compensation for this official person's labour, and he took care not to endanger the loss of it by neglecting his duty. Of late this officer had been withdrawn, and now it appeared that the young Baroness of Arnheim had found refuge in the deserted towers of her ancestors.

The Swiss damsel did not leave the youthful traveller time to study particularly the exterior of the castle, or to construe the meaning of emblems and mottoes, seemingly of an Oriental character, with which the outside was inscribed, and which expressed in various modes, more or less directly, the attachment of the builders of this extensive pile to the learning of the Eastern sages. Ere he had time to take more than a general survey of the place, the voice of the Swiss maiden called him to an angle of the wall in which there was a projection, from whence a long plank extended over a dry moat, and was connected with a window in which Annette was standing.

"You have forgotten your Swiss lessons already," said she, observing that Arthur went rather timidly about crossing the temporary and precarious drawbridge.

The reflection that Anne, her mistress, might make the same observation, recalled the young traveller to the necessary degree of composure. He passed over the plank with the same *sang froid* with which he had learned to brave the far more terrific bridge, beneath the ruinous Castle of Geierstein. He had no sooner entered the window than Annette, taking off her mask, bade him welcome to Germany, and to old friends with new names.

"Anne of Geierstein," she said, "is no more; but you will presently see the Lady Baroness of Arnheim, who is extremely like her; and I, who was Annette Veilchen in Switzerland, the servant to a damsel who was not esteemed much greater than myself, am now the young Baroness's waiting-woman, and make everybody of less quality stand back."

"If, in such circumstances," said young Philipson, "you have the influence due to your consequence, let me beseech of you to tell the Baroness, since we must now call her so, that my present intrusion on her is occasioned by my ignorance."

"Away, away," said the girl, laughing, "I know better what to say in your behalf. You are not the first poor man and pedlar that has got the graces of a great lady; but I warrant you it was not by making humble apologies, and talking of unintentional intrusion. I will tell her of love, which all the Rhine cannot quench, and which has driven you hither, leaving you no other choice than to come or to perish!"

"Nay, but Annette, Annette——"

"Fie on you for a fool,—make a shorter name of it,—cry Anne, Anne! and there will be more prospect of your being answered."

So saying, the wild girl ran out of the room, delighted, as a mountaineer of her description was likely to be, with the thought of having done as she would desire to be done by, in her benevolent exertions to bring two lovers together, when on the eve of inevitable separation.

In this self-approving disposition, Annette sped up a narrow turnpike stair to a closet, or dressing-room, where her young mistress was seated, and exclaimed, with open mouth,—"Anne of Gei——, I mean my Lady Baroness, they are come—they are come!"

"The Philipsons?" said Anne, almost breathless as she asked the question.

"Yes—no—" answered the girl; "that is, yes,—for the best of them is come, and that is Arthur."

"What meanest thou, girl? Is not Seignor Philipson, the father, along with his son?"

"Not he, indeed," answered Veilchen, "nor did I ever think of asking about him. He was no friend of mine, nor of any one else, save the old Landamman; and well met they were for a couple of wise-acres, with eternal proverbs in their mouths, and care upon their brows."

"Unkind, inconsiderate girl, what hast thou done?" said Anne of Geierstein. "Did I not warn and charge thee to bring them both hither? and you have brought the young man alone to a place where we are nearly in solitude? What will he—what can he think of me?"

"Why, what should I have done?" said Annette, remaining firm in her argument. "He was alone, and should I have sent him down to the dorff to be murdered by the Rhingrave's Lanz-knechts? All is fish, I trow, that comes to their net; and how is he to get through this country, so beset with wandering soldiers, robber barons, (I beg your ladyship's pardon,) and roguish Italians, flocking to the Duke of Burgundy's standard?—Not to mention the greatest terror of all, that is never in one shape or other absent from one's eye or thought."

"Hush, hush, girl! add not utter madness to the excess of folly; but let us think what is to be done. For our sake, for his own, this unfortunate young man must leave this castle instantly."

"You must take the message yourself then, Anne —I beg pardon, most noble Baroness;—it may be very fit for a lady of high birth to send such a message, which, indeed, I have heard the Minne-singers tell in their romances; but I am sure it is not a meet one for me, or any frank-hearted Swiss girl, to carry. No more foolery; but remember, if you were born Baroness of Arnheim, you have been bred and brought up in the bosom of the Swiss hills, and should conduct yourself like an honest and well-meaning damsel."

"And in what does your wisdom reprehend my folly, good Mademoiselle Annette?" replied the Baroness.

"Ay, marry! now our noble blood stirs in our veins. But remember, gentle my lady, that it was a bargain between us, when I left yonder noble mountains, and the free air that blows over them, to coop myself up in this land of prisons and slaves, that I should speak my mind to you as freely as I did when our heads lay on the same pillow."

"Speak, then," said Anne, studiously averting her

face as she prepared to listen ; " but beware that you say nothing which it is unfit for me to hear."

" I will speak nature and common sense; and if your noble ears are not made fit to hear and understand these, the fault lies in them, and not in my tongue. Look you, you have saved this youth from two great dangers,—one at the earth-shoot at Geierstein, the other this very day, when his life was beset. A handsome young man he is, well spoken, and well qualified to gain deservedly a lady's favour. Before you saw him, the Swiss youth were at least not odious to you. You danced with them,—you jested with them,—you were the general object of their admiration,—and, as you well know, you might have had your choice through the Canton—Why, I think it possible a little urgency might have brought you to think of Rudolph Donnerhugel as your mate."

" Never, wench, never ! " exclaimed Anne.

" Be not so very positive, my lady. Had he recommended himself to the uncle in the first place, I think, in my poor sentiment, he might at some lucky moment have carried the niece. But since we have known this young Englishman, it has been little less than contemning, despising, and something like hating, all the men whom you could endure well enough before."

" Well, well," said Anne, " I will detest and hate thee more than any of them, unless you bring your matters to an end."

" Softly, noble lady, fair and easy go far. All this argues you love the young man, and let those say that you are wrong, who think there is anything wonderful in the matter. There is much to justify you, and nothing that I know against it."

"What, foolish girl! Remember my birth forbids me to love a mean man—my condition to love a poor man—my father's commands to love one whose addresses are without his consent—above all, my maidenly pride forbids me fixing my affections on one who cares not for me,—nay, perhaps, is prejudiced against me by appearances."

"Here is a fine homily!" said Annette; "but I can clear every point of it as easily as Father Francis does his text in a holiday sermon. Your birth is a silly dream, which you have only learned to value within these two or three days, when, having come to German soil, some of the old German weed, usually called family pride, has begun to germinate in your heart. Think of such folly as you thought when you lived at Geierstein, that is, during all the rational part of your life, and this great terrible prejudice will sink into nothing. By condition, I conceive you mean estate. But Philipson's father, who is the most freehearted of men, will surely give his son as many zechins as will stock a mountain farm. You have fire-wood for the cutting, and land for the occupying, since you are surely entitled to part of Geierstein, and gladly will your uncle put you in possession of it. You can manage the dairy, Arthur can shoot, hunt, fish, plough, harrow, and reap."

Anne of Geierstein shook her head, as if she greatly doubted her lover's skill in the last of the accomplishments enumerated.

"Well, well, he can learn, then," said Annette,

Veilchen; "and you will only live the harder the first year or so. Besides, Sigismund Biederman will aid him willingly, and he is a very horse at labour; and I know another besides, who is a friend——"

"Of thine own, I warrant," quoth the young Baroness.

"Marry, it is my poor friend, Martin Sprenger; and I'll never be so false-hearted as to deny my bachelor."

"Well, well, but what is to be the end of all this?" said the Baroness, impatiently.

"The end of it, in my opinion," said Annette, "is very simple. Here are priests and prayer-books within a mile—go down to the parlour, speak your mind to your lover, or hear him speak his mind to you; join hands, go quietly back to Geierstein in the character of man and wife, and get everything ready to receive your uncle on his return. This is the way that a plain Swiss wench would cut off the romance of a German Baroness——"

"And break the heart of her father," said the young lady, with a sigh.

"It is more tough than you are aware of," replied Annette; "he hath not lived without you so long, but that he will be able to spare you for the rest of his life, a great deal more easily than you, with all your new-fangled ideas of quality, will be able to endure his schemes of wealth and ambition, which will aim at making you the wife of some illustrious Count, like De Hagenbach, whom we saw not long since make such an edifying end, to the great example of all Robber-Chivalry upon the Rhine."

"Thy plan is naught, wench; a childish vision of a girl, who never knew more of life than she has heard told over her milking-pail. Remember that my uncle entertains the highest ideas of family discipline, and that, to act contrary to my father's will, would destroy us in his good opinion. Why else am I here? wherefore has he resigned his guardianship? and why am I obliged to change the habits that are dear to me, and assume the manners of a people that are strange, and therefore unpleasing to me?"

"Your uncle," said Annette, firmly, "is Landamman of the Canton of Unterwalden; respects its freedom, and is the sworn protector of its laws, of which, when you, a denizen of the Confederacy, claim the protection, he cannot refuse it to you."

"Even then," said the young Baroness, "I should forfeit his good opinion, his more than paternal affection; but it is needless to dwell upon this. Know, that although I could have loved the young man, whom I will not deny to be as amiable as your partiality paints him—know,"—she hesitated for a moment,—" that he has never spoken a word to me on such a subject as you, without knowing either his sentiments or mine, would intrude on my consideration."

"Is it possible?" answered Annette. "I thought —I believed, though I have never pressed on your confidence—that you must—attached as you were to each other—have spoken together, like true maid and true bachelor, before now. I have done wrong, when I thought to do for the best. — Is it possible! — such things have been heard of even in our Canton

—is it possible he can have harboured so unutterably base purposes, as that Martin of Brisach, who made love to Adela of the Sundgau, enticed her to folly—the thing, though almost incredible, is true—fled—fled—from the country and boasted of his villany, till her cousin Raymond silenced for ever his infamous triumph, by beating his brains out with his club, even in the very street of the villain's native town? By the Holy Mother of Einsiedlen! could I suspect this Englishman of meditating such treason, I would saw the plank across the moat till a fly's weight would break it, and it should be at six fathom deep that he should abye the perfidy which dared to meditate dishonour against an adopted daughter of Switzerland."

As Annette Veilchen spoke, all the fire of her mountain courage flashed from her eyes, and she listened reluctantly while Anne of Geierstein endeavoured to obliterate the dangerous impression which her former words had impressed on her simple but faithful attendant.

"On my word,"—she said, "on my soul—you do Arthur Philipson injustice—foul injustice, in intimating such a suspicion;—his conduct towards me has ever been upright and honourable—a friend to a friend—a brother to a sister—could not, in all he has done and said, have been more respectful, more anxiously affectionate, more undeviatingly candid. In our frequent interviews and intercourse he has indeed seemed very kind—very attached. But had I been disposed—at times I may have been too much so —to listen to him with endurance,"—the young lady here put her hand on her forehead, but the tears streamed through her slender fingers, — "he has never spoken of any love — any preference; if he indeed entertains any, some obstacle, insurmountable on his part, has interfered to prevent him."

"Obstacle?" replied the Swiss damsel. "Ay, doubtless—some childish bashfulness—some foolish idea about your birth being so high above his own—some dream of modesty pushed to extremity which considers as impenetrable the ice of a spring frost. This delusion may be broken by a moment's encouragement, and I will take the task on myself to spare your blushes, my dearest Anne."

"No, no; for Heaven's sake, no, Veilchen!" answered the Baroness, to whom Annette had so long been a companion and confidant, rather than a domestic. "You cannot anticipate the nature of the obstacles which may prevent his thinking on what you are so desirous to promote. Hear me—My early education, and the instructions of my kind uncle, have taught me to know something more of foreigners and their fashions, than I ever could have learned in our happy retirement of Geierstein; I am well-nigh convinced that these Philipsons are of rank, as they are of manners and bearing, far superior to the occupation which they appear to hold. The father is a man of deep observation, of high thoughts and pretension, and lavish of gifts, far beyond what consists with the utmost liberality of a trader."

"That is true," said Annette; "I will say for myself, that the silver chain he gave me weighs against ten silver crowns, and the cross which Arthur added to it, the day after the long ride we had together up towards Mons Pilatre, is worth, they tell me, as much more. There is not the like of it in the Cantons. Well, what then? They are rich, so are you. So much the better."

"Alas! Annette, they are not only rich, but noble. I am persuaded of this; for I have observed often, that even the father retreated, with an air of quiet and dignified contempt, from discussions with Donnerhugel and others, who, in our plain way, wished to fasten a dispute upon him. And when a rude observation or blunt pleasantry was pointed at the son, his eyes flashed, his cheek coloured, and it was only a glance from his father which induced him to repress the retort of no friendly character which rose to his lips."

"You have been a close observer," said Annette. "All this may be true, but I noted it not. But what then, I say once more? If Arthur has some fine noble name in his own country, are not you yourself Baroness of Arnheim? And I will frankly allow it as something of worth, if it smooths the way to a match, where I think you must look for happiness —I hope so, else I am sure it should have no encouragement from me."

"I do believe so, my faithful Veilchen; but, alas! how can you, in the state of natural freedom in which you have been bred, know, or even dream, of the various restraints which this gilded or golden chain of rank and nobility hangs upon those whom it fetters and encumbers, I fear, as much as it decorates? In every country, the distinction of rank binds men to certain duties. It may carry with it restrictions, which may prevent alliances in foreign countries—it often may prevent them from consulting their inclinations, when they wed in their own. It leads to alliances in which the heart is never consulted, to treaties of marriage, which are often formed when the parties are in the cradle, or in leading strings, but which are not the less binding on them in honour and faith. Such may exist in the present case. These alliances are often blended and mixed up with state policy; and if the interest of England, or what he deems such, should have occasioned the elder Philipson to form such an engagement, Arthur would break his own heart—the heart of any one else—rather than make false his father's word."

"The more shame to them that formed such an engagement!" said Annette. "Well, they talk of England being a free country; but if they can bar young men and women of the natural privilege to call their hands and hearts their own, I would as soon be a German serf.—Well, lady, you are wise, and I am ignorant. But what is to be done? I have brought this young man here, expecting, God knows, a happier issue to your meeting. But it is clear you cannot marry him without his asking you. Now, although I confess that, if I could think him willing to forfeit the hand of the fairest maid of the Cantons, either from want of manly courage to ask it, or from regard to some ridiculous engagement, formed betwixt his father and some other nobleman of their island of noblemen, I would not in either case grudge him a ducking in the moat; yet it is another question, whether we should send him down to be murdered among those cut-throats of the Rhingrave; and unless we do so, I know not how to get rid of him."

"Then let the boy William give attendance on him here, and do you see to his accommodation. It is best we do not meet."

"I will," said Annette; "yet what am I to say for you? Unhappily, I let him know that you were here."

"Alas, imprudent girl! Yet why should I blame thee," said Anne of Geierstein, "when the imprudence has been so great on my own side? It is myself, who, suffering my imagination to rest too long upon this young man and his merits, have led me into this entanglement. But I will shew thee that I can overcome this folly, and I will not seek in my own error a cause for evading the duties of hospitality. Go, Veilchen, get some refreshment ready. Thou shalt sup with us, and thou must not leave us. Thou shalt see me behave as becomes both a German lady and a Swiss maiden. Get me first a candle, however, my girl, for I must wash these tell-tales, my eyes, and arrange my dress."

To Annette this whole explanation had been one scene of astonishment, for, in the simple ideas of love and courtship in which she had been brought up amid the Swiss mountains, she had expected that the two lovers would have taken the first opportunity of the absence of their natural guardians, and have united themselves for ever; and she had even arranged a little secondary plot, in which she herself and Martin Sprenger, her faithful bachelor, were to reside with the young couple as friends and dependants. Silenced, therefore, but not satisfied, by the objections of her young mistress, the zealous Annette retreated murmuring to herself,—"That little hint about her dress is the only natural and sensible word she has said in my hearing. Please God, I will return and help her in the twinkling of an eye. That dressing my mistress is the only part of a waiting-lady's life that I have the least fancy for—it seems so natural for one pretty maiden to set off another—in faith we are but learning to dress ourselves at another time."

And with this sage remark Annette Veilchen tripped down stairs.

CASTLE OF HOHEN SYBURG.

CHAPTER THE TWENTY-SECOND.

Tell me not of it—I could ne'er abide
The mummery of all that forced civility.
"Pray, seat yourself, my lord." With cringing hams
The speech is spoken, and, with bended knee,
Heard by the smiling courtier.—" Before you, sir?
It must be on the earth then." Hang it all!
The pride which cloaks itself in such poor fashion
Is scarcely fit to swell a beggar's bosom.
                                        OLD PLAY.

UP stairs and down stairs tripped Annette Veilchen, the soul of all that was going on in the only habitable corner of the huge castle of Arnheim. She was equal to every kind of service, and therefore popped her head into the stable to be sure that William attended properly to Arthur's horse, looked into the kitchen to see that the old cook, Marthon, roasted the partridges in due time, (an interference for which she received little thanks,) rummaged out a flask or two of Rhine wine from the huge Dom Daniel of a cellar, and, finally, just peeped into the parlour to see how Arthur was looking; when, having the satisfaction to see he had in the best manner he could sedulously arranged his person, she assured him that he should shortly see her mistress, who was rather indisposed, yet could not refrain from coming down to see so valued an acquaintance.

Arthur blushed when she spoke thus, and seemed so handsome in the waiting-maid's eye, that she could not help saying to herself, as she went to her young lady's room—"Well, if true love cannot manage to bring that couple together, in spite of all the obstacles that they stand boggling at, I will never believe that there is such a thing as true love in the world, let Martin Sprenger say what he will, and swear to it on the gospels."

When she reached the young Baroness's apartment, she found, to her surprise, that, instead of having put on what finery she possessed, that young lady's choice had preferred the same simple kirtle which she had worn during the first day that Arthur had dined at Geierstein. Annette looked at first puzzled and doubtful, then suddenly recognised the good taste which had dictated the attire, and exclaimed— "You are right—you are right—it is best to meet him as a free-hearted Swiss maiden."

Anne also smiled as she replied—"But, at the same time, in the walls of Arnheim, I must appear in some respect as the daughter of my father.—Here, girl, aid me to put this gem upon the riband which binds my hair."

It was an aigrette, or plume, composed of two feathers of a vulture, fastened together by an opal, which changed to the changing light with a variability which enchanted the Swiss damsel, who had never seen any thing resembling it in her life.

"Now, Baroness Anne," said she, "if that pretty thing be really worn as a sign of your rank, it is the only thing belonging to your dignity that I should ever think of coveting; for it doth shimmer and change colour after a most wonderful fashion, even something like one's own cheek when one is fluttered."

"Alas, Annette!" said the Baroness, passing her hand across her eyes, "of all the gauds which the females of my house have owned, this perhaps hath been the most fatal to its possessors."

"And why then wear it?" said Annette. "Why wear it now, of all days in the year?"

"Because it best reminds me of my duty to my father and family. And now, girl, look thou sit with us at table, and leave not the apartment; and see thou fly not to and fro to help thyself or others with any thing on the board, but remain quiet and seated till William helps you to what you have occasion for."

"Well, that is a gentle fashion, which I like well enough," said Annette, "and William serves us so debonairly, that it is a joy to see him; yet, ever and anon, I feel as I were not Annette Veilchen herself, but only Annette Veilchen's picture, since I can neither rise, sit down, run about, nor stand still, without breaking some rule of courtly breeding. It is not so, I dare say, with you, who are always mannerly."

"Less courtly than thou seemest to think," said the high-born maiden; "but I feel the restraint more on the greensward, and under Heaven's free air, than when I undergo it closed within the walls of an apartment."

"Ah, true—the dancing," said Annette; "that was something to be sorry for indeed."

"But most am I sorry, Annette, that I cannot tell whether I act precisely right or wrong in seeing this young man, though it must be for the last time. Were my father to arrive?—Were Ital Schreckenwald to return——"

"Your father is too deeply engaged on some of his dark and mystic errands," said the flippant Swiss; "sailed to the mountains of the Brockenberg, where witches hold their sabbath, or gone on a hunting-party with the Wild Huntsman."

"Fie, Annette, how dare you talk thus of my father?"

"Why, I know little of him personally," said the damsel, "and you yourself do not know much more. And how should that be false which all men say is true?"

"Why, fool, what do they say?"

"Why, that the Count is a wizard—that your grandmother was a will-of-the-wisp, and old Ital

Schreckenwald a born devil incarnate; and there is some truth in that, whatever comes of the rest."

"Where is he?"

"Gone down to spend the night in the village, to see the Rhingrave's men quartered, and keep them in some order, if possible; for the soldiers are disappointed of pay which they had been promised; and when this happens, nothing resembles a Lanz-knecht except a chafed bear."

"Go we down then, girl; it is perhaps the last night which we may spend, for years, with a certain degree of freedom."

I will not pretend to describe the marked embarrassment with which Arthur Philipson and Anne of Geierstein met; neither lifted their eyes, neither spoke intelligibly, as they greeted each other, and the maiden herself did not blush more deeply than her modest visitor; while the good-humoured Swiss girl, whose ideas of love partook of the freedom of a more Arcadian country and its customs, looked on with eyebrows a little arched, much in wonder, and a little in contempt, at a couple, who, as she might think, acted with such unnatural and constrained reserve. Deep was the reverence and the blush with which Arthur offered his hand to the young lady, and her acceptance of the courtesy had the same character of extreme bashfulness, agitation, and embarrassment. In short, though little or nothing intelligible passed between this very handsome and interesting couple, the interview itself did not on that account lose any interest. Arthur handed the maiden, as was the duty of a gallant of the day, into the next room, where their repast was prepared; and Annette, who watched with singular attention everything which occurred, felt with astonishment, that the forms and ceremonies of the higher orders of society had such an influence, even over her free-born mind, as the rites of the Druids over that of the Roman general, when he said,

"I scorn them, yet they awe me."

"What can have changed them?" said Annette; "when at Geierstein, they looked but like another girl and bachelor, only that Anne is so very handsome; but now they move in time and manner as if they were leading a stately pavin, and behave to each other with as much formal respect as if he were Landamman of the Unterwalden, and she the first lady of Berne. 'Tis all very fine, doubtless, but it is not the way that Martin Sprenger makes love."

Apparently, the circumstances in which each of the young people were placed, recalled to them the habits of lofty, and somewhat formal courtesy, to which they might have been accustomed in former days; and while the Baroness felt it necessary to observe the strictest decorum, in order to qualify the reception of Arthur into the interior of her retreat, he, on the other hand, endeavoured to shew, by the profoundness of his respect, that he was incapable of misusing the kindness with which he had been treated. They placed themselves at table, scrupulously observing the distance which might become a "virtuous gentleman and maid." The youth William did the service of the entertainment with deftness and courtesy, as one well accustomed to such duty; and Annette, placing herself between them, and endeavouring as closely as she could to adhere to the ceremonies which she saw them observe, made practice of the civilities which were expected from the attendant of a baroness. Various, however, were the errors which she committed. Her demeanour in general was that of a greyhound in the slips, ready to start up every moment; and she was only withheld by the recollection that she was to ask for that which she had far more mind to help herself to.

Other points of etiquette were transgressed in their turn, after the repast was over, and the attendant had retired. The waiting damsel often mingled too unceremoniously in the conversation, and could not help calling her mistress by her Christian name of Anne, and, in defiance of all decorum, addressed her, as well as Philipson, with the pronoun *thou*, which then, as well as now, was a dreadful solecism in German politeness. Her blunders were so far fortunate, that by furnishing the young lady and Arthur with a topic foreign to the peculiarities of their own situation, they enabled them to withdraw their attentions from its embarrassments, and to exchange smiles at poor Annette's expense. She was not long of perceiving this, and half nettled, half availing herself of the apology to speak her mind, said, with considerable spirit, "You have both been very merry, forsooth, at my expense, and all because I wished rather to rise and seek what I wanted, than wait till the poor fellow, who was kept trotting between the board and beauffet, found leisure to bring it to me.

You laugh at me now, because I call you by your names, as they were given to you in the blessed church at your christening; and because I say to you *thee* and *thou*, addressing my Juncker and my Yungfrau as I would do if I were on my knees praying to Heaven. But for all your new-world fancies, I can tell you, you are but a couple of children, who do not know your own minds, and are jesting away the only leisure given you to provide for your own happiness. Nay, frown not, my sweet Mistress Baroness; I have looked at Mount Pilatre too often, to fear a gloomy brow."

"Peace, Annette," said her mistress, "or quit the room."

"Were I not more your friend than I am my own," said the headstrong and undaunted Annette, "I would quit the room, and the castle to boot, and leave you to hold your house here, with your amiable seneschal, Ital Schreckenwald."

"If not for love, yet for shame, for charity, be silent, or leave the room."

"Nay," said Annette, "my bolt is shot, and I have but hinted at what all upon Geierstein Green said, the night when the bow of Buttisholz was bended. You know what the old saw says——"

"Peace! peace, for Heaven's sake, or I must needs fly!" said the young Baroness.

"Nay, then," said Annette, considerably changing her tone, as if afraid that her mistress should actually retire, "if you must fly, necessity must have its course. I know no one who can follow. This mistress of mine, Seignor Arthur, would require for her attendant, not a homely girl of flesh and blood like myself, but a waiting-woman with substance composed of gossamer, and breath supplied by the spirit of ether. Would you believe it—It is seriously held by many, that she partakes of the race of spirits of the elements, which makes her so much more bashful than maidens of this everyday world."

Anne of Geierstein seemed rather glad to lead away the conversation from the turn which her wayward maiden had given to it, and to turn it on more indifferent subjects, though these were still personal to herself.

"Seignor Arthur," she said, "thinks, perhaps, he has some room to nourish some such strange suspicion as your heedless folly expresses, and some fools believe, both in Germany and Switzerland. Confess, Seignor Arthur, you thought strangely of me when I passed your guard upon the bridge of Graffs-lust, on the night last past."

The recollection of the circumstances which had so greatly surprised him at the time, so startled Arthur, that it was with some difficulty he commanded himself, so as to attempt an answer at all; and what he did say on the occasion was broken and unconnected.

"I did hear, I own—that is, Rudolph Donnerhugel reported—But that I believed that you, gentle lady, were other than a Christian maiden——"

"Nay, if Rudolph were the reporter," said Annette, "you would hear the worst of my lady and her lineage, that is certain. He is one of those prudent personages who depreciate and find fault with the goods he has thoughts of purchasing, in order to deter other offerers. Yes, he told you a fine goblin story, I warrant you, of my lady's grandmother; and truly, it so happened, that the circumstances of the case gave, I dare say, some colour in your eyes to——"

"Not so, Annette," answered Arthur; "whatever might be said of your lady that sounded uncouth and strange, fell to the ground as incredible."

"Not quite so much so, I fancy," interrupted Annette, without heeding sign or frown. "I strongly suspect I should have had much more trouble in dragging you hither to this castle, had you known you were approaching the haunt of the Nymph of the Fire, the Salamander, as they call her, not to mention the shock of again seeing the descendant of that Maiden of the Fiery Mantle."

"Peace, once more, Annette," said her mistress; "since Fate has occasioned this meeting, let us not neglect the opportunity to disabuse our English friend, of the absurd report he has listened to with doubt and wonder perhaps, but not with absolute incredulity.

"Seignor Arthur Philipson," she proceeded, "it is true my grandfather, by the mother's side, Baron Herman of Arnheim, was a man of great knowledge in abstruse sciences. He was also a presiding judge of a tribunal of which you must have heard, called the Holy Vehme. One night a stranger, closely pursued by the agents of that body, which (crossing herself) it is not safe even to name, arrived at the castle and craved his protection, and the rights of hospitality. My grandfather, finding the advance which the stranger had made to the rank of Adept, gave him his protection, and became bail to deliver him to answer the charge against him, for a year and a day, which delay he was, it seems, entitled to require on his behalf. They studied together during that term, and pushed their researches into the mysteries of nature, as far, in all probability, as men have the power of urging them. When the fatal day drew nigh on which the guest must part from his host, he asked permission to bring his daughter to the castle, that they might exchange a last farewell. She was introduced with much secrecy, and after some days, finding that her father's fate was so uncertain, the Baron, with the sage's consent, agreed to give the forlorn maiden refuge in his castle, hoping to obtain from her some additional information concerning the languages and the wisdom of the East. Dannischemend, her father, left this castle, to go to render himself up to the Vehmegericht at Fulda. The result is unknown; perhaps he was saved by Baron Arnheim's testimony, perhaps he was given up to the steel and the cord. On such matters, who dare speak?

"The fair Persian became the wife of her guardian and protector. Amid many excellences, she had one peculiarity allied to imprudence. She availed herself of her foreign dress and manners, as well as of a beauty, which was said to have been marvellous, and an agility seldom equalled, to impose upon and terrify the ignorant German ladies, who, hearing her speak Persian and Arabic, were already disposed to consider her as over closely connected with unlawful arts. She was of a fanciful and imaginative disposition, and delighted to place herself in such colours and circumstances as might confirm their most ridiculous suspicions, which she considered only as matter of sport. There was no end to the stories to which she gave rise. Her first appearance in the castle was said to be highly picturesque, and to have inferred something of the marvellous. With the levity of a child, she had some childish passions, and while she encouraged the growth and circulation of the most extraordinary legends amongst some of the neighbourhood, she entered into disputes with persons of her own quality concerning rank and precedence, on which the ladies of Westphalia have at all times set great store. This cost her her life; for, on the morning of the christening of my poor mother, the Baroness of Arnheim died suddenly, even while a splendid company was assembled in the castle chapel to witness the ceremony. It was believed that she died of poison, administered by the Baroness Steinfeldt, with whom she was engaged in a bitter quarrel, entered into chiefly on behalf of her friend and companion, the Countess Waldstetten."

"And the opal gem?—and the sprinkling with water?" said Arthur Philipson.

"Ah!" replied the young Baroness, "I see you desire to hear the real truth of my family history, of which you have yet learned only the romantic legend. —The sprinkling of water was necessarily had recourse to, on my ancestress's first swoon. As for the opal, I have heard that it did indeed grow pale, but only because it is said to be the nature of that noble gem, on the approach of poison. Some part of the quarrel with the Baroness Steinfeldt was about the right of the Persian maiden to wear this stone, which an ancestor in my family won in battle from the Soldan of Trebizond. All these things were confused in popular tradition, and the real facts turned into a fairy tale."

"But you have said nothing," suggested Arthur Philipson, "on—on——"

"On what?" said his hostess.

"On your appearance last night."

"Is it possible," said she, "that a man of sense, and an Englishman, cannot guess at the explanation which I have to give, though not, perhaps, very distinctly? My father, you are aware, has been a busy man in a disturbed country, and has incurred the hatred of many powerful persons. He is, therefore, obliged to move in secret, and avoid unnecessary observation. He was, besides, averse to meet his brother, the Landamman. I was therefore told, on our entering Germany, that I was to expect a signal where and when to join him,—the token was to be a small crucifix of bronze, which had belonged to my poor mother. In my apartment at Graffs-lust I found the token, with a note from my father, making me acquainted with a secret passage proper to such places, which, though it had the appearance of being blocked up, was in fact very slightly barricaded. By this I was instructed to pass to the gate, make my escape into the woods, and meet my father at a place appointed there."

"A wild and perilous adventure," said Arthur.

"I have never been so much shocked," continued the maiden, "as at receiving this summons, compelling me to steal away from my kind and affectionate uncle, and go I knew not whither. Yet compliance was absolutely necessary. The place of meeting was plainly pointed out. A midnight walk, in the neighbourhood of protection, was to me a trifle; but the precaution of posting sentinels at the gate might have interfered with my purpose, had I not mentioned it to some of my elder cousins, the Biedermans, who readily agreed to let me pass and repass unquestioned. But you know my cousins; honest and kind-hearted, they are of a rude way of thinking, and as incapable of feeling a generous delicacy as— some other persons."—(Here there was a glance towards Annette Veilchen.)—"They exacted from me, that I should conceal myself and my purpose from Sigismund; and as they are always making sport with the simple youth, they insisted that I should pass him in such a manner as might induce him to believe that I was a spiritual apparition, and out of his terrors for supernatural beings they expected to have much amusement. I was obliged to secure their connivance at my escape on their own terms; and, indeed, I was too much grieved at the prospect of quitting my kind uncle, to think much of anything else. Yet my surprise was considerable, when, contrary to expectation, I found you on the bridge as sentinel, instead of my cousin Sigismund. Your own ideas I ask not for."

"They were those of a fool," said Arthur, "of a

thrice-sodden fool. Had I been aught else, I would have offered my escort. My sword——"

"I could not have accepted your protection," said Anne, calmly. "My mission was in every respect a secret one. I met my father—some intercourse had taken place betwixt him and Rudolph Donnerhugel, which induced him to alter his purpose of carrying me away with him last night. I joined him, however, early this morning, while Annette acted for a time my part amongst the Swiss pilgrims. My father desired that it should not be known when or with whom I left my uncle and his escort. I need scarce remind you that I saw you in the dungeon."

"You were the preserver of my life," said the youth—"the restorer of my liberty."

"Ask me not the reason of my silence. I was then acting under the agency of others, not under mine own. Your escape was effected, in order to establish a communication betwixt the Swiss without the fortress and the soldiers within. After the alarm at La Ferette, I learned from Sigismund Biederman that a party of banditti were pursuing your father and you, with a view to pillage and robbery. My father had furnished me with the means of changing Anne of Geierstein into a German maiden of quality. I set out instantly, and glad I am to have given you a hint which might free you from danger."

"But my father?" said Arthur.

"I have every reason to hope he is well and safe," answered the young lady. "More than I were eager to protect both you and him—poor Sigismund amongst the first.—And now, my friend, these mysteries explained, it is time we part, and for ever."

"Part!—and for ever!" repeated the youth, in a voice like a dying echo.

"It is our fate," said the maiden. "I appeal to you if it is not your duty—I tell you it is mine. You will depart with early dawn to Strasburg—and—and —we never meet again."

With an ardour of passion which he could not repress, Arthur Philipson threw himself at the feet of the maiden, whose faltering tone had clearly expressed that she felt deeply in uttering the words. She looked round for Annette, but Annette had disappeared at this most critical moment; and her mistress for a second or two was not perhaps sorry for her absence.

"Rise," she said, "Arthur—rise. You must not give way to feelings that might be fatal to yourself and me."

"Hear me, lady, before I bid you adieu, and for ever—the word of a criminal is heard, though he plead the worst cause—I am a belted knight, and the son and heir of an Earl, whose name has been spread throughout England and France, and wherever valour has had fame."

"Alas!" said she, faintly, "I have but too long suspected what you now tell me—Rise, I pray you, rise."

"Never till you hear me," said the youth, seizing one of her hands, which trembled, but hardly could be said to struggle in his grasp.—"Hear me," he said, with the enthusiasm of first love, when the obstacles of bashfulness and diffidence are surmounted —"My father and I are—I acknowledge it—bound on a most hazardous and doubtful expedition. You will very soon learn its issue for good or bad. If it succeed, you shall hear of me in my own character— If I fall, I must—I will—I do claim a tear from Anne of Geierstein. If I escape, I have yet a horse, a lance, and a sword; and you shall hear nobly of him whom you have thrice protected from imminent danger."

"Arise—arise," repeated the maiden, whose tears began to flow fast, as, struggling to raise her lover, they fell thick upon his head and face. "I have heard enough—to listen to more were indeed madness, both for you and myself."

"Yet one single word," added the youth; "while Arthur has a heart, it beats for you—while Arthur can wield an arm, it strikes for you, and in your cause."

Annette now rushed into the room.

"Away, away!" she cried—"Schreckenwald has returned from the village with some horrible tidings, and I fear me he comes this way."

Arthur had started to his feet at the first signal of alarm.

"If there is danger near your lady, Annette, there is at least one faithful friend by her side."

Annette looked anxiously at her mistress.

"But Schreckenwald," she said—"Schreckenwald, your father's steward—his confidant.—O, think better of it—I can hide Arthur somewhere."

The noble-minded girl had already resumed her

composure, and replied with dignity—" I have done nothing," she said, "to offend my father. If Schreckenwald be my father's steward, he is my vassal. I bide no guest to conciliate him. Sit down," (addressing Arthur,) "and let us receive this man.— Introduce him instantly, Annette, and let us hear his tidings—and bid him remember, that when he speaks to me he addresses his mistress."

Arthur resumed his seat, still more proud of his choice from the noble and fearless spirit displayed by one who had so lately shewn herself sensible to the gentlest feelings of the female sex.

Annette, assuming courage from her mistress's dauntless demeanour, clapped her hands together as she left the room, saying, but in a low voice, " I see that after all it is something to be a Baroness, if one can assert her dignity conformingly. How could I be so frightened for this rude man!"

CHAPTER THE TWENTY-THIRD.

——— Affairs that walk
(As they say spirits do) at midnight, have
In them a wilder nature, than the business
That seeks despatch by day.
                    HENRY VIII., *Act V*.

THE approach of the steward was now boldly expected by the little party. Arthur, flattered at once and elevated by the firmness which Anne had shewn when this person's arrival was announced, hastily considered the part which he was to act in the approaching scene, and prudently determined to avoid all active and personal interference, till he should observe from the demeanour of Anne, that such was likely to be useful or agreeable to her. He resumed his place, therefore, at a distant part of the board, on which their meal had been lately spread, and remained there, determined to act in the manner Anne's behaviour should suggest as most prudent and fitting,— veiling, at the same time, the most acute internal anxiety, by an appearance of that deferential composure, which one of inferior rank adopts when admitted to the presence of a superior. Anne, on her part, seemed to prepare herself for an interview of interest. An air of conscious dignity succeeded the extreme agitation which she had so lately displayed, and, busying herself with some articles of female work, she also seemed to expect with tranquillity the visit, to which her attendant was disposed to attach so much alarm.

A step was heard upon the stair, hurried and unequal, as that of some one in confusion as well as haste; the door flew open, and Ital Schreckenwald entered.

This person, with whom the details given to the elder Philipson by the Landamman Biederman have made the reader in some degree acquainted, was a tall, well-made, soldierly-looking man. His dress, like that of persons of rank at the period in Germany, was more varied in colour, more cut and ornamented, slashed and jagged, than the habit worn in France and England. The never-failing hawk's feather decked his cap, secured with a medal of gold, which served as a clasp. His doublet was of buff, for defence, but *laid down*, as it was called in the tailor's craft, with rich lace on each seam, and displaying on the breast a golden chain, the emblem of his rank in the Baron's household. He entered with rather a hasty step, and busy and offended look, and said, somewhat rudely, — "Why, how now, young lady—wherefore this? Strangers in the castle at this period of night!"

Anne of Geierstein, though she had been long absent from her native country, was not ignorant of its habits and customs, and knew the haughty manner in which all who were noble exerted their authority over their dependants.

"Are you a vassal of Arnheim, Ital Schreckenwald, and do you speak to the Lady of Arnheim in her own castle with an elevated voice, a saucy look, and bonneted withal? Know your place; and, when you have demanded pardon for your insolence, and told your errand in such terms as befit your condition and mine, I may listen to what you have to say."

Schreckenwald's hand, in spite of him, stole to his bonnet, and uncovered his haughty brow.

"Noble lady," he said, in a somewhat milder tone, "excuse me if my haste be unmannerly, but the alarm is instant. The soldiery of the Rhingrave have mutinied, plucked down the banners of their master, and set up an independent ensign, which they call the pennon of Saint Nicholas, under which they declare that they will maintain peace with God, and war with all the world. This castle cannot escape them, when they consider that the first course to maintain themselves must be to take possession of some place of strength. You must up then, and ride with the very peep of dawn. For the present, they are busy with the wine-skins of the peasants; but when they wake in the morning, they will unquestionably march hither; and you may chance to fall into the hands of those who will think of the terrors of the castle of Arnheim as the figments of a fairy-tale, and laugh at its mistress's pretensions to honour and respect."

"Is it impossible to make resistance? The castle is strong," said the young lady, "and I am unwilling to leave the house of my fathers without attempting somewhat in our defence."

"Five hundred men," said Schreckenwald, "might

STREET IN STRASBURG.

garrison Arnheim, battlement and tower. With a less number it were madness to attempt to keep such an extent of walls; and how to get twenty soldiers together, I am sure I know not.—So, having now the truth of the story, let me beseech you to dismiss this guest,—too young, I think, to be the inmate of a lady's bower,—and I will point to him the nighest way out of the castle; for this is a strait in which we must all be contented with looking to our own safety."

"And whither is it that you propose to go?" said the Baroness, continuing to maintain, in respect to Ital Schreckenwald, the complete and calm assertion of absolute superiority, to which the seneschal gave way with such marks of impatience, as a fiery steed exhibits under the management of a complete cavalier.

"To Strasburg I propose to go,—that is, if it so please you,—with such slight escort as I can get hastily together by daybreak. I trust we may escape being observed by the mutineers; or, if we fall in with a party of stragglers, I apprehend but little difficulty in forcing my way."

"And wherefore do you prefer Strasburg as a place of asylum?"

"Because I trust we shall there meet your excellency's father, the noble Count Albert of Geierstein."

"It is well," said the young lady.—"You also, I think, Seignor Philipson, spoke of directing your course to Strasburg. If it consist with your convenience, you may avail yourself of the protection of my escort as far as that city, where you expect to meet your father."

It will readily be believed, that Arthur cheerfully bowed assent to a proposal which was to prolong their remaining in society together; and might possibly, as his romantic imagination suggested, afford him an opportunity, on a road beset with dangers, to render some service of importance.

Ital Schreckenwald attempted to remonstrate.

"Lady!—lady!"—he said, with some marks of impatience.

"Take breath and leisure, Schreckenwald," said Anne, "and you will be more able to express yourself with distinctness, and with respectful propriety."

The impatient vassal muttered an oath betwixt his teeth, and answered with forced civility,—" Permit me to state, that our case requires we should charge ourselves with the care of no one but you. We shall be few enough for your defence, and I cannot permit any stranger to travel with us."

"If," said Arthur, "I conceived that I was to be a useless encumbrance on the retreat of this noble young lady, worlds, Sir Squire, would not induce me to accept her offer. But I am neither child nor woman—I am a full-grown man, and ready to shew such good service as manhood may in defence of your lady."

"If we must not challenge your valour and ability, young sir," said Schreckenwald, "who shall answer for your fidelity?"

"To question that elsewhere," said Arthur, "might be dangerous."

But Anne interfered between them. "We must straight to rest, and remain prompt for alarm, perhaps even before the hour of dawn. Schreckenwald, I trust to your care for due watch and ward.—You have men enough at least for that purpose.—And hear and mark—It is my desire and command, that this gentleman be accommodated with lodgings here for this night, and that he travel with us tomorrow. For this I will be responsible to my father, and your part is only to obey my commands. I have long had occasion to know both the young man's father and himself, who were ancient guests of my uncle, the Landamman. On the journey you will keep the youth beside you, and use such courtesy to him as your rugged temper will permit."

Ital Schreckenwald intimated his acquiescence with a look of bitterness, which it were vain to attempt to describe. It expressed spite, mortification, humbled pride, and reluctant submission. He did submit, however, and ushered young Philipson into a decent apartment with a bed, which the fatigue and agitation of the preceding day rendered very acceptable.

Notwithstanding the ardour with which Arthur expected the rise of the next dawn, his deep repose, the fruit of fatigue, held him until the reddening of the east, when the voice of Schreckenwald exclaimed, "Up, Sir Englishman, if you mean to accomplish your boast of loyal service. It is time we were in the saddle, and we shall tarry for no sluggards."

Arthur was on the floor of the apartment, and dressed in almost an instant, not forgetting to put on his shirt of mail, and assume whatever weapons seemed most fit to render him an efficient part of the convoy. He next hastened to seek out the stable, to have his horse in readiness; and descending for that purpose into the under story of the lower mass of buildings, he was wandering in search of the way which led to the offices, when the voice of Annette Veilchen softly whispered, "This way, Seignor Philipson; I would speak with you."

The Swiss maiden, at the same time, beckoned him into a small room, where he found her alone.

"Were you not surprised," she said, "to see my lady queen it so over Ital Schreckenwald, who keeps every other person in awe with his stern looks and cross words? But the air of command seems so natural to her, that, instead of being a baroness, she might have been an empress. It must come of birth, I think, after all, for I tried last night to take state upon me, after the fashion of my mistress, and, would you think it, the brute Schreckenwald threatened to throw me out of the window? But if ever I see Martin Sprenger again, I'll know if there is strength in a Swiss arm, and virtue in a Swiss quarterstaff.—But here I stand prating, and my lady wishes to see you for a minute ere we take to horse."

"Your lady?" said Arthur, starting, "why did you lose an instant?—why not tell me before?"

"Because I was only to keep you here till she came, and—here she is."

Anne of Geierstein entered, fully attired for her journey. Annette, always willing to do as she would wish to be done by, was about to leave the apartment, when her mistress, who had apparently made up her mind concerning what she had to do or say, commanded her positively to remain.

"I am sure," she said, "Seignor Philipson will rightly understand the feelings of hospitality—I will say of friendship—which prevented my suffering him to be expelled from my castle last night, and which have determined me this morning to admit of his company on the somewhat dangerous road to Strasburg. At the gate of the town we part, I to join my father, you to place yourself under the direction of yours. From that moment intercourse between us ends, and our remembrance of each other must be as the thoughts which we pay to friends deceased."

"Tender recollections," said Arthur, passionately, "more dear to our bosoms than all we have surviving upon earth."

"Not a word in that tone," answered the maiden. "With night delusion should end, and reason awaken with dawning. One word more—Do not address me on the road; you may, by doing so, expose me to vexatious and insulting suspicion, and yourself to quarrels and peril.—Farewell, our party is ready to take horse."

She left the apartment, where Arthur remained for a moment deeply bewildered in grief and disappointment. The patience, nay, even favour, with which Anne of Geierstein had, on the previous night, listened to his passion, had not prepared him for the terms of reserve and distance which she now adopted towards him. He was ignorant that noble maids, if feeling or passion has for a moment swayed them from the strict path of principle and duty, endeavour to atone for it by instantly returning, and severely adhering, to the line from which they have made a momentary departure. He looked mournfully on Annette, who, as she had been in the room before Anne's arrival, took the privilege of remaining a minute after her departure; but he read no comfort in the glances of the confidant, who seemed as much disconcerted as himself.

"I cannot imagine what hath happened to her," said Annette; "to me she is kind as ever, but to every other person about her she plays countess and baroness with a witness; and now she is begun to tyrannize over her own natural feelings—and, if this be greatness, Annette Veilchen trusts always to remain the penniless Swiss girl; she is mistress of her own freedom, and at liberty to speak with her bachelor when she pleases, so as religion and maiden modesty suffer nothing in the conversation. Oh, a single daisy twisted with content into one's hair, is worth all the opals in India, if they bind us to torment ourselves and other people, or hinder us from speaking our mind, when our heart is upon our tongue. But never fear, Arthur; for if she has the cruelty to think of forgetting you, you may rely on one friend who, while she has a tongue, and Anne has ears, will make it impossible for her to do so."

So saying, away tripped Annette, having first indicated to Philipson the passage by which he would find the lower court of the castle. There his steed stood ready among about twenty others. Twelve of these were accoutred with war saddles and frontlets of proof, being intended for the use of as many cavaliers, or troopers, retainers of the family of Arnheim, whom the seneschal's exertions had been able to collect on the spur of the occasion. Two palfreys, somewhat distinguished by their trappings, were designed for Anne of Geierstein and her favourite female attendant. The other menials, chiefly boys and women servants, had inferior horses. At a signal made, the troopers took their lances and stood by their steeds, till the females and menials were mounted and in order; they then sprang into their saddles and began to move forward, slowly and with great precaution. Schreckenwald led the van, and kept Arthur Philipson close beside him. Anne and her attendant were in the centre of the little body, followed by the unwarlike train of servants, while two or three experienced cavaliers brought up the rear with strict orders to guard against surprise.

On their being put into motion, the first thing which surprised Arthur was, that the horses' hoofs no longer sent forth the sharp and ringing sound arising from the collision of iron and flint, and as the morning light increased, he could perceive, that the fetlock and hoof of every steed, his own included, had been carefully wrapped around with a sufficient quantity of wool, to prevent the usual noise which accompanied their motions. It was a singular thing to behold the passage of the little body of cavalry down the rocky road which led from the castle, unattended with the noise which we are disposed to consider as inseparable from the motions of horse, the absence of which seemed to give a peculiar and almost an unearthly appearance to the cavalcade.

They passed in this manner the winding path which led from the castle of Arnheim to the adjacent village, which, as was the ancient feudal custom, lay so near the fortress, that its inhabitants, when summoned by their lord, could instantly repair for its defence. But it was at present occupied by very different inhabitants, the mutinous soldiers of the Rhingrave. When the party from Arnheim approached the entrance of the village, Schreckenwald made a signal to halt, which was instantly obeyed by his followers. He then rode forward in person to reconnoitre, accompanied by Arthur Philipson, both moving with the utmost steadiness and precaution. The deepest silence prevailed in the deserted streets. Here and there a soldier was seen, seemingly designed for a sentinel, but uniformly fast asleep.

"The swinish mutineers!" said Schreckenwald; "a fair night-watch they keep, and a beautiful morning's rouse would I treat them with, were not the point to protect yonder peevish wench.—Halt thou here, stranger, while I ride back and bring them on—there is no danger."

Schreckenwald left Arthur as he spoke, who, alone in the street of a village filled with banditti, though they were lulled into temporary insensibility, had no reason to consider his case as very comfortable. The chorus of a wassel-song, which some reveller was trolling over in his sleep; or, in its turn, the growling of some village cur, seemed the signal for an hundred ruffians to start up around him. But in the space of two or three minutes, the noiseless cavalcade, headed by Ital Schreckenwald, again joined him, and followed their leader, observing the utmost precaution not to give an alarm. All went well till they reached the farther end of the village, where, although the Baaren-hauter * who kept guard was as drunk as his companions on duty, a large shaggy dog which lay beside him was more vigilant. As the little troop approached, the animal sent forth a ferocious yell, loud enough to have broken the rest of the Seven Sleepers, and which effectually dispelled the slumbers of its master. The soldier snatched up his carabine and fired, he knew not well at what, or for what reason. The ball, however, struck Arthur's horse under him, and, as the animal fell, the sentinel rushed forward to kill or make prisoner the rider.

"Haste on, haste on, men of Arnheim! care for nothing but the young lady's safety," exclaimed the leader of the band.

"Stay, I command you;—aid the stranger, on your lives!"—said Anne, in a voice which, usually gentle and meek, she now made heard by those around her, like the note of a silver clarion. "I will not stir till he is rescued."

Schreckenwald had already spurred his horse for flight; but, perceiving Anne's reluctance to follow him, he dashed back, and seizing a horse, which, bridled and saddled, stood picqueted near him, he threw the reins to Arthur Philipson; and pushing his own horse, at the same time, betwixt the En-

* *Baaren-hauter*—he of the Bear's hide—a nickname for a German private soldier.

VOL. II.—8

glishman and the soldier, he forced the latter to quit the hold he had on his person. In an instant Philipson was again mounted, when, seizing a battle-axe which hung at the saddle-bow of his new steed, he struck down the staggering sentinel, who was endeavouring again to seize upon him. The whole troop then rode off at a gallop, for the alarm began to grow general in the village; some soldiers were seen coming out of their quarters, and others were beginning to get upon horseback. Before Schreckenwald and his party had ridden a mile, they heard more than once the sound of bugles; and when they arrived upon the summit of an eminence commanding a view of the village, their leader, who, during the retreat, had placed himself in the rear of his company, now halted to reconnoitre the enemy they had left behind them. There was bustle and confusion in the street, but there did not appear to be any pursuit; so that Schreckenwald followed his route down the river, with speed and activity indeed, but with so much steadiness at the same time, as not to distress the slowest horse of his party.

When they had ridden two hours or more, the confidence of their leader was so much augmented, that he ventured to command a halt at the edge of a pleasant grove, which served to conceal their number, whilst both riders and horses took some refreshment, for which purpose forage and provisions had been borne along with them. Ital Schreckenwald having held some communication with the Baroness, continued to offer their travelling companion a sort of surly civility. He invited him to partake of his own mess, which was indeed little different from that which was served out to the other troopers, but was seasoned with a glass of wine from a more choice flask.

"To your health, brother," he said; "if you tell this day's story truly, you will allow that I was a true comrade to you two hours since, in riding through the village of Arnheim."

"I will never deny it, fair sir," said Philipson, "and I return you thanks for your timely assistance; alike, whether it sprang from your mistress's order, or your own good-will."

"Ho! ho! my friend," said Schreckenwald, laughing, "you are a philosopher, and can try conclusions while your horse lies rolling above you, and a Baarenhauter aims his sword at your throat?—Well, since your wit hath discovered so much, I care not if you know, that I should not have had much scruple to sacrifice twenty such smooth-faced gentlemen as yourself, rather than the young Baroness of Arnheim had incurred the slightest danger."

"The propriety of the sentiment," said Philipson, "is so undoubtedly correct, that I subscribe to it, even though it is something discourteously expressed towards myself."

In making this reply, the young man, provoked at the insolence of Schreckenwald's manner, raised his voice a little. The circumstance did not escape observation, for, on the instant, Annette Veilchen stood before them, with her mistress's commands on them both to speak in whispers, or rather to be altogether silent.

"Say to your mistress that I am mute," said Philipson.

"Our mistress, the Baroness, says," continued Annette, with an emphasis on the title, to which she began to ascribe some talismanic influence, — "the Baroness, I tell you, says, that silence much concerns our safety, for it were most hazardous to draw upon this little fugitive party the notice of any passengers who may pass along the road during the necessary halt; and so, sirs, it is the Baroness's request that you will continue the exercise of your teeth as fast as you can, and forbear that of your tongues till you are in a safer condition."

"My lady is wise," answered Ital Schreckenwald, "and her maiden is witty. I drink, Mistress Annette, in a cup of Rudersheimer, to the continuance of her sagacity, and of your amiable liveliness of disposition. Will it please you, fair mistress, to pledge me in this generous liquor?"

"Out, thou German wine-flask!—Out, thou eternal swill-flagon!—Heard you ever of a modest maiden who drank wine before she had dined?"

"Remain without the generous inspiration then," said the German, "and nourish thy satirical vein on sour cider or acid whey."

A short space having been allowed to refresh themselves, the little party again mounted their horses, and travelled with such speed, that long before noon they arrived at the strongly fortified town of Kehl, opposite to Strasburg, on the eastern bank of the Rhine.

It is for local antiquaries to discover, whether the

travellers crossed from Kehl to Strasburg by the celebrated bridge of boats which at present maintains the communication across the river, or whether they were wafted over by some other mode of transportation. It is enough that they passed in safety, and had landed on the other side, where—whether she dreaded that he might forget the charge she had given him, that here they were to separate, or whether she thought that something more might be said in the moment of parting—the young Baroness, before remounting her horse, once more approached Arthur Philipson, who too truly guessed the tenor of what she had to say.

"Gentle stranger," she said, "I must now bid you farewell. But first let me ask if you know whereabouts you are to seek your father?"

"In an inn called the Flying Stag," said Arthur, dejectedly; "but where that is situated in this large town, I know not."

"Do you know the place, Ital Schreckenwald?"

"I, young lady?—Not I—I know nothing of Strasburg and its inns. I believe most of our party are as ignorant as I am."

"You and they speak German, I suppose," said the Baroness, dryly, "and can make inquiry more easily than a foreigner? Go, sir, and forget not that humanity to the stranger is a religious duty."

With that shrug of the shoulders which testifies a displeased messenger, Ital went to make some inquiry, and, in his absence, brief as it was, Anne took an opportunity to say apart,—"Farewell!—Farewell! Accept this token of friendship, and wear it for my sake. May you be happy!"

Her slender fingers dropped into his hand a very small parcel. He turned to thank her, but she was already at some distance; and Schreckenwald, who had taken his place by his side, said in his harsh voice, "Come, Sir Squire, I have found out your place of rendezvous, and I have but little time to play the gentleman-usher."

He then rode on; and Philipson, mounted on his military charger, followed him in silence to the point where a large street joined, or rather crossed, that which led from the quay on which they had landed.

"Yonder swings the Flying Stag," said Ital, pointing to an immense sign, which, mounted on a huge wooden frame, crossed almost the whole breadth of the street. "Your intelligence can, I think, hardly abandon you, with such a guide-post in your eye."

So saying, he turned his horse without further farewell, and rode back to join his mistress and her attendants.

Philipson's eyes rested on the same group for a moment, when he was recalled to a sense of his situation by the thoughts of his father; and, spurring his jaded horse down the cross street, he reached the hostelrie of the Flying Stag.

CHAPTER THE TWENTY-FOURTH.

———I was, I must confess,
Great Albion's Queen in former golden days;
But now mischance hath trode my title down,
And with dishonour laid me on the ground;
Where I must take like seat unto my fortune,
And to my humble seat conform myself.
                                HENRY VI., *Part III.*

THE hostelrie of the Flying Stag, in Strasburg, was, like every inn in the empire at that period, conducted with much the same discourteous inattention to the wants and accommodation of the guests, as that of John Mengs. But the youth and good looks of Arthur Philipson, circumstances which seldom or never fail to produce some effect where the fair are concerned, prevailed upon a short, plump, dimpled, blue-eyed, fair-skinned yungfrau, the daughter of the landlord of the Flying Stag, (himself a fat old man, pinned to the oaken-chair in the *stubé*,) to carry herself to the young Englishman with a degree of condescension, which, in the privileged race to which she belonged, was little short of degradation. She not only put her light buskins and her pretty ankles in danger of being soiled by tripping across the yard to point out an unoccupied stable, but, on Arthur's inquiry after his father, condescended to recollect, that such a guest as he described had lodged in the house last night, and had said he expected to meet there a young person, his fellow-traveller.

"I will send him out to you, fair sir," said the little yungfrau, with a smile, which, if things of the kind are to be valued by their rare occurrence, must have been reckoned inestimable.

She was as good as her word. In a few instants the elder Philipson entered the stable, and folded his son in his arms.

"My son—my dear son!" said the Englishman, his usual stoicism broken down and melted by natural feeling and parental tenderness,—"Welcome to me at all times—welcome, in a period of doubt and danger—and most welcome of all, in a moment which forms the very crisis of our fate. In a few hours I shall know what we may expect from the Duke of Burgundy.—Hast thou the token?"

Arthur's hand first sought that which was nearest to his heart, both in the literal and allegorical sense, the small parcel, namely, which Anne had given him at parting. But he recollected himself in the instant, and presented to his father the packet, which had been so strangely lost and recovered at La Ferette.

"It hath run its own risk since you saw it," he observed to his father, "and so have I mine. I received hospitality at a castle last night, and behold a body of *lanz-knechts* in the neighbourhood began in the morning to mutiny for their pay. The inhabitants fled from the castle to escape their violence, and as we passed their leaguer in the grey of the morning, a drunken Baaren-hauter shot my poor horse, and I was forced, in the way of exchange, to take up with his heavy Flemish animal, with its steel-saddle, and its clumsy chaffron."

"Our road is beset with perils," said his father. "I too have had my share, having been in great danger." (he told not its precise nature) "at an inn, where I rested last night. But I left it in the morning, and proceeded hither in safety. I have at length, however, obtained a safe escort to conduct me to the Duke's camp near Dijon; and I trust to have an audience of him this evening. Then if our last hope should fail, we will seek the seaport of Marseilles, hoist sail for Candia or for Rhodes, and spend our lives in defence of Christendom, since we may no longer fight for England."

Arthur heard these ominous words without reply; but they did not the less sink upon his heart, deadly as the doom of the judge which secludes the criminal from society and all its joys, and condemns him to an eternal prison-house. The bells from the cathedral began to toll at this instant, and reminded the elder Philipson of the duty of hearing mass, which was said at all hours in some one or other of the separate chapels which are contained in that magnificent pile. His son followed, on an intimation of his pleasure.

In approaching the access to this superb cathedral, the travellers found it obstructed, as is usual in Catholic countries, by the number of mendicants of both sexes, who crowded round the entrance to give the worshippers an opportunity of discharging the duty of alms-giving, so positively enjoined as a chief observance of their church. The Englishmen extri-

STRASBURG CATHEDRAL.

cated themselves from their importunity by bestowing, as is usual on such occasions, a donative of small coin upon those who appeared most needy, or most deserving of their charity. One tall woman stood on the steps close to the door, and extended her hand to the elder Philipson, who, struck with her appearance, exchanged for a piece of silver the copper coins which he had been distributing amongst others.

"A marvel!" she said, in the English language, but in a tone calculated only to be heard by him alone, although his son also caught the sound and sense of what she said,—"Ay, a miracle!—An Englishman still possesses a silver piece, and can afford to bestow it on the poor!"

Arthur was sensible that his father started somewhat at the voice or words, which bore, even in his ear, something of deeper import than the observation of an ordinary mendicant. But after a glance at the female who thus addressed him, his father passed onwards into the body of the church, and was soon engaged in attending to the solemn ceremony of the mass, as it was performed by a priest at the altar of a chapel, divided from the main body of the splendid edifice, and dedicated, as it appeared from the image over the altar, to Saint George; that military Saint, whose real history is so obscure, though his popular legend rendered him an object of peculiar veneration during the feudal ages. The ceremony was begun and finished with all customary forms. The officiating priest, with his attendants, withdrew, and though some of the few worshippers who had assisted at this solemnity remained tell-ing their beads, and occupied with the performance of their private devotions, far the greater part left the chapel, to visit other shrines, or to return to the prosecution of their secular affairs.

But Arthur Philipson remarked, that whilst they dropped off one after another, the tall woman who had received his father's alms continued to kneel near the altar; and he was yet more surprised to see that his father himself, who, he had many reasons to know, was desirous to spend in the church no more time than the duties of devotion absolutely claimed, remained also on his knees, with his eyes resting on the form of the veiled devotee, (such she seemed from her dress,) as if his own motions were to be guided by hers. By no idea which occurred to him, was Arthur able to form the least conjecture as to his father's motives—he only knew that he was engaged in a critical and dangerous negotiation, liable to influence or interruption from various quarters; and that political suspicion was so generally awake both in France, Italy, and Flanders, that the most important agents were often obliged to assume the most impenetrable disguises, in order to insinuate themselves without suspicion into the countries where their services were required. Louis XI. in particular, whose singular policy seemed in some degree to give a character to the age in which he lived, was well known to have disguised his principal emissaries and envoys in the fictitious garbs of mendicant monks, minstrels, gipsies, and other privileged wanderers of the meanest description.

Arthur concluded, therefore, that it was not improbable that this female might, like themselves, be something more than her dress imported; and he resolved to observe his father's deportment towards her, and regulate his own actions accordingly. A bell at last announced that mass, upon a more splendid scale, was about to be celebrated before the high altar of the cathedral itself, and its sound withdrew from the sequestered chapel of Saint George the few who had remained at the shrine of the military saint, excepting the father and son, and the female penitent who kneeled opposite to them. When the last of the worshippers had retired, the female arose and advanced towards the elder Philipson, who, folding his arms on his bosom, and stooping his head, in an attitude of obeisance which his son had never before seen him assume, appeared rather to wait what she had to say, than to propose addressing her.

There was a pause. Four lamps, lighted before the shrine of the saint, cast a dim radiance on his armour and steed, represented as he was in the act of transfixing with his lance the prostrate dragon, whose outstretched wings and writhing neck were in part touched by their beams. The rest of the chapel was dimly illuminated by the autumnal sun, which could scarce find its way through the stained panes of the small lanceolated window, which was its only aperture to the open air. The light fell doubtful and gloomy, tinged with the various hues through which it passed, upon the stately, yet somewhat broken and dejected form of the female, and on those of the melancholy and anxious father, and his son, who, with all the eager interest of youth, suspected and anticipated extraordinary consequences from so singular an interview.

At length the female approached to the same side of the shrine with Arthur and his father, as if to be more distinctly heard, without being obliged to raise the slow solemn voice in which she had spoken.

"Do you here worship," she said, "the Saint George of Burgundy, or the Saint George of merry England, the flower of chivalry?"

"I serve," said Philipson, folding his hands humbly on his bosom, "the saint to whom this chapel is dedicated, and the Deity with whom I hope for his holy intercession, whether here or in my native country."

"Ay—you," said the female, "even you can forget —you, even you, who have been numbered among the mirror of knighthood—can forget that you have worshipped in the royal fane of Windsor—that you have there bent a *gartered* knee, where kings and princes kneeled around you—you can forget this, and make your orisons at a foreign shrine, with a heart undisturbed with the thoughts of what you have been, — praying, like some poor peasant, for bread and life during the day that passes over you."

"Lady," replied Philipson, "in my proudest hours, I was, before the Being to whom I preferred my prayers, but as a worm in the dust—In His eyes I am now neither less nor more, degraded as I may be in the opinion of my fellow-reptiles."

"How canst thou think thus?" said the devotee; "and yet it is well with thee that thou canst. But what have thy losses been, compared to mine!"

She put her hand to her brow, and seemed for a moment overpowered by agonizing recollections.

Arthur pressed to his father's side, and inquired, in a tone of interest which could not be repressed, "Father, who is this lady?—Is it my mother?"

"No, my son," answered Philipson;—"peace, for the sake of all you hold dear or holy!"

The singular female, however, heard both the question and answer, though expressed in a whisper.

"Yes," she said, "young man—I am—I should say I was—your mother; the mother, the protectress, of all that was noble in England—I am Margaret of Anjou."

Arthur sank on his knees before the dauntless widow of Henry the Sixth, who so long, and in such desperate circumstances, upheld, by unyielding courage and deep policy, the sinking cause of her feeble husband; and who, if she occasionally abused victory by cruelty and revenge, had made some atonement by the indomitable resolution with which she had supported the fiercest storms of adversity: Arthur had been bred in devoted adherence to the now dethroned line of Lancaster, of which his father was one of the most distinguished supporters; and his earliest deeds of arms, which, though unfortunate, were neither obscure nor ignoble, had been done in their cause. With an enthusiasm belonging to his age and education, he in the same instant flung his bonnet on the pavement, and knelt at the feet of his ill-fated sovereign.

Margaret threw back the veil which concealed those noble and majestic features, which even yet,—

ARTHUR PHILIPSON KNEELING TO QUEEN MARGARET.

though rivers of tears had furrowed her cheeks,—though care, disappointment, domestic grief, and humbled pride, had quenched the fire of her eye, and wasted the smooth dignity of her forehead,—even yet shewed the remains of that beauty which once was held unequalled in Europe. The apathy with which a succession of misfortunes and disappointed hopes had chilled the feelings of the unfortunate Princess, was for a moment melted by the sight of the fair youth's enthusiasm. She abandoned one hand to him, which he covered with tears and kisses, and with the other stroked with maternal tenderness his curled locks, as she endeavoured to raise him from the posture he had assumed. His father, in the meanwhile, shut the door of the chapel, and placed his back against it, withdrawing himself thus from the group, as if for the purpose of preventing any stranger from entering, during a scene so extraordinary.

"And thou, then," said Margaret, in a voice where female tenderness combated strangely with her natural pride of rank, and with the calm, stoical indifference induced by the intensity of her personal misfortunes; "thou, fair youth, art the last scion of the noble stem, so many fair boughs of which have fallen in our hapless cause. Alas, alas! what can I do for thee? Margaret has not even a blessing to bestow! So wayward is her fate, that her benedictions are curses, and she has but to look on you and wish you well, to ensure your speedy and utter ruin. I—I have been the fatal poison-tree, whose influence has blighted and destroyed all the fair plants that arose beside and around me, and brought death upon every one, yet am myself unable to find it!"

"Noble and royal mistress," said the elder Englishman, "let not your princely courage, which has borne such extremities, be dismayed, now that they are passed over, and that a chance at least of happier times is approaching to you and to England."

"To England, to *me*, noble Oxford!" said the forlorn and widowed Queen.—"If to-morrow's sun could place me once more on the throne of England, could it give back to me what I have lost? I speak not of wealth or power—they are as nothing in the balance —I speak not of the hosts of noble friends who have fallen in defence of me and mine—Somersets, Percys, Staffords, Cliffords—they have found their place in fame, in the annals of their country—I speak not of my husband, he has exchanged the state of a suffering saint upon earth for that of a glorified saint in Heaven—But O, Oxford! my son—my Edward!— Is it possible for me to look on this youth, and not remember that thy Countess and I on the same night gave birth to two fair boys? How oft we endeavoured to prophesy their future fortunes, and to persuade ourselves that the same constellation which shone on their birth, would influence their succeeding life, and hold a friendly and equal bias till they reached some destined goal of happiness and honour! Thy Arthur lives; but, alas! my Edward, born under the same auspices, fills a bloody grave!"

She wrapped her head in her mantle, as if to stifle the complaints and groans which maternal affection poured forth at these cruel recollections. Philipson, or the exiled Earl of Oxford, as we may now term him, distinguished in those changeful times by the steadiness with which he had always maintained his loyalty to the line of Lancaster, saw the imprudence of indulging his sovereign in her weakness.

"Royal mistress," he said, "life's journey is that of a brief winter's day, and its course will run on, whether we avail ourselves of its progress or no. My sovereign is, I trust, too much mistress of herself to suffer lamentation for what is passed to deprive her of the power of using the present time. I am here in obedience to your command; I am to see Burgundy forthwith, and if I find him pliant to the purpose to which we would turn him, events may follow which will change into gladness our present mourning. But we must use our opportunity with speed as well as zeal. Let me know then, madam, for what reason your Majesty hath come hither, disguised and in danger? Surely it was not merely to weep over this young man that the high-minded Queen Margaret left her father's court, disguised herself in mean attire, and came from a place of safety to one of doubt at least, if not of danger?"

"You mock me, Oxford," said the unfortunate Queen, "or you deceive yourself, if you think you still serve that Margaret whose word was never spoken without a reason, and whose slightest action was influenced by a motive. Alas! I am no longer the same firm and rational being. The feverish character of grief, while it makes one place hateful to me, drives me to another in very impotence and impatience of spirit. My father's residence, thou sayst, is safe; but is it tolerable for such a soul as mine? Can one who has been deprived of the noblest and richest kingdom of Europe—one who has lost hosts of noble friends—one who is a widowed consort, a childless mother—one upon whose head Heaven hath poured forth its last vial of unmitigated wrath—can she stoop to be the companion of a weak old man, who, in sonnets and in music, in mummery and folly, in harping and rhyming, finds a comfort for all that poverty has that is distressing; and what is still worse, even a solace in all that is ridiculous and contemptible?"

"Nay, with your leave, madam," said her counsellor, "blame not the good King René, because, persecuted by fortune, he has been able to find out for himself humbler sources of solace, which your prouder spirit is disposed to disdain. A contention among his minstrels, has for him the animation of a knightly combat; and a crown of flowers, twined by his troubadours, and graced by their sonnets, he accounts a valuable compensation for the diadems of Jerusalem, of Naples, and of both Sicilies, of which he only possesses the empty titles."

"Speak not to me of the pitiable old man," said Margaret; "sunk below even the hatred of his worst enemies, and never thought worthy of anything more than contempt. I tell thee, noble Oxford, I have been driven nearly mad with my forced residence at Aix, in the paltry circle which he calls his court. My ears, tuned as they now are only to sounds of affliction, are not so weary of the eternal tinkling of harps, and squeaking of rebecks, and snapping of castanets—my eyes are not so tired of the beggarly affectation of court ceremonial, which is only respectable when it implies wealth and expresses power—as my very soul is sick of the paltry ambition which can find pleasure in spangles, tassels, and trumpery, when the reality of all that is great and noble hath passed away. No, Oxford, if I am doomed to lose the last cast which fickle fortune seems to offer me, I will retreat into the meanest convent in the Pyrenean hills, and at least escape the insult of the idiot gaiety of my father.—Let him pass from our memory as from the page of history, in which his name will never be recorded. I have much of more importance both to hear and to tell.—And now, my Oxford, what news from Italy? Will the Duke of Milan afford us assistance with his counsels, or with his treasures?"

"With his counsels willingly, madam; but how you will relish them I know not, since he recommends to us submission to our hapless fate, and resignation to the will of Providence."

"The wily Italian! Will not, then, Galeasso advance any part of his hoards, or assist a friend, to whom he hath in his time full often sworn faith?"

"Not even the diamonds which I offered to deposit in his hands," answered the Earl, "could make him unlock his treasury to supply us with ducats for our enterprise. Yet he said, if Charles of Burgundy should think seriously of an exertion in our favour, such was his regard for that great prince, and his deep sense of your majesty's misfortunes, that he would consider what the state of his exchequer, though much exhausted, and the condition of his subjects, though impoverished by taxes and talliages, would permit him to advance in your behalf."

"The double-faced hypocrite!" said Margaret. "If the assistance of the princely Burgundy lends us a chance of regaining what is our own, then he will give us some paltry parcel of crowns, that our restored prosperity may forget his indifference to our adversity!—But what of Burgundy? I have ventured hither to tell you what I have learned, and to hear report of your proceedings—a trusty watch provides for the secrecy of our interview. My impatience to see you brought me hither in this mean disguise. I have a small retinue at a convent a mile beyond the town—I have had your arrival watched by the faithful Lambert—and now I come to know your hopes or your fears, and to tell you my own."

"Royal lady," said the Earl, "I have not seen the Duke. You know his temper to be wilful, sudden, haughty, and unpersuadable. If he can adopt the calm and sustained policy which the times require, I little doubt his obtaining full amends of Louis, his sworn enemy, and even of Edward, his ambitious brother-in-law. But if he continues to yield to extravagant fits of passion, with or without provocation, he may hurry into a quarrel with the poor but hardy Helvetians, and is likely to engage in a perilous contest, in which he cannot be expected to gain anything, while he undergoes a chance of the most serious losses."

"Surely," replied the Queen, "he will not trust

the usurper Edward, even in the very moment when he is giving the greatest proof of treachery to his alliance?"

"In what respect, madam?" replied Oxford. "The news you allude to has not reached me."

"How, my lord? Am I then the first to tell you, that Edward of York has crossed the sea with such an army, as scarce even the renowned Henry V., my father-in-law, ever transported from France to Italy?"

"So much I have indeed heard was expected," said Oxford; "and I anticipated the effect as fatal to our cause."

"Edward is arrived," said Margaret, "and the traitor and usurper hath sent defiance to Louis of France, and demanded of him the crown of that kingdom as his own right—that crown which was placed on the head of my unhappy husband, when he was yet a child in the cradle."

"It is then decided—the English are in France!" answered Oxford, in a tone expressive of the deepest anxiety.—"And whom brings Edward with him on this expedition?"

"All—all the bitterest enemies of our house and cause—The false, the traitorous, the dishonoured George, whom he calls Duke of Clarence—the blood-drinker, Richard—the licentious Hastings—Howard—Stanley—in a word, the leaders of all those traitors whom I would not name, unless by doing so my curses could sweep them from the face of the earth."

"And—I tremble to ask," said the Earl—"Does Burgundy prepare to join them as a brother of the war, and make common cause with this Yorkish host against King Louis of France?"

"By my advices," replied the Queen, "and the are both private and sure, besides that they are confirmed by the bruit of common fame—No, my good Oxford, no!"

"For that may the Saints be praised!" answered Oxford. "Edward of York—I will not malign even an enemy—is a bold and fearless leader—But he is neither Edward the Third, nor the heroic Black Prince—nor is he that fifth Henry of Lancaster, under whom I won my spurs, and to whose lineage the thoughts of his glorious memory would have made me faithful, had my plighted vows of allegiance ever permitted me to entertain a thought of varying, or of defection. Let Edward engage in war with Louis without the aid of Burgundy, on which he has reckoned. Louis is indeed no hero, but he is a cautious and skilful general, more to be dreaded, perhaps, in these politic days, than if Charlemagne could again raise the Oriflamme, surrounded by Roland and all his paladins. Louis will not hazard such fields as those of Cressy, of Poictiers, or of Agincourt. With a thousand lances from Hainault, and twenty thousand crowns from Burgundy, Edward shall risk the loss of England, while he is engaged in a protracted struggle for the recovery of Normandy and Guienne. But what are the movements of Burgundy?"

"He has menaced Germany," said Margaret, "and his troops are now employed in overrunning Lorraine, of which he has seized the principal towns and castles."

"Where is Ferrand de Vaudemont—a youth, it is said, of courage and enterprise, and claiming Lorraine in right of his mother, Yolande of Anjou, the sister of your grace?"

"Fled," replied the Queen, "into Germany or Helvetia."

"Let Burgundy beware of him," said the experienced Earl; "for should the disinherited youth obtain confederates in Germany, and allies among the hardy Swiss, Charles of Burgundy may find him a far more formidable enemy than he expects. We are strong for the present, only in the Duke's strength, and if it is wasted in idle and desultory efforts, our hopes, alas! vanish with his power, even if he should be found to have the decided will to assist us. My friends in England are resolute not to stir without men and money from Burgundy."

"It is a fear," said Margaret, "but not our worst fear. I dread more the policy of Louis, who, unless my espials have grossly deceived me, has even already proposed a secret peace to Edward, offering with large sums of money to purchase England to the Yorkists, and a truce of seven years."

"It cannot be," said Oxford. "No Englishman, commanding such an army as Edward must now lead, dares for very shame to retire from France without a manly attempt to recover his lost provinces."

"Such would have been the thoughts of a rightful prince," said Margaret, "who left behind him an obedient and faithful kingdom. Such may not be the thoughts of this Edward, misnamed Plantagenet, base perhaps in mind as in blood, since they say his real father was one Blackburn, an archer of Middleham—usurper, at least, if not bastard—such will not be his thoughts.* Every breeze that blows from England will bring with it apprehensions of defection amongst those over whom he has usurped authority. He will not sleep in peace till he returns to England with those cut-throats, whom he relies upon for the defence of his stolen crown. He will engage in no war with Louis, for Louis will not hesitate to soothe his pride by humiliation—to gorge his avarice and pamper his voluptuous prodigality by sums of gold—and I fear much we shall soon hear of the English army retiring from France with the idle boast, that they have displayed their banners once more, for a week or two, in the provinces which were formerly their own."

"It the more becomes us to be speedy in moving Burgundy to decision," replied Oxford; "and for that purpose I post to Dijon. Such an army as Edward's cannot be transported over the narrow seas in several weeks. The probability is, that they must winter in France, even if they should have truce with King Louis. With a thousand Hainault lances from the eastern part of Flanders, I can be soon in the North, where we have many friends, besides the assurance of help from Scotland. The faithful west will rise at a signal—a Clifford can be found, though the mountain mists have hid him from Edward's researches—the Welsh will assemble at the rallying word of Tudor—the Red Rose raises its head once more—and so, God save King Henry!"

* The Lancastrian party threw the imputation of bastardy, (which was totally unfounded,) upon Edward IV.

"Alas!" said the Queen—"But no husband—no friend of mine—the son but of my mother-in-law by a Welsh chieftain—cold, they say, and crafty—But be it so—let me only see Lancaster triumph, and obtain revenge upon York, and I will die contented!"

"It is then your pleasure that I should make the proffers expressed by your Grace's former mandates, to induce Burgundy to stir himself in our cause? If he learns the proposal of a truce betwixt France and England, it will sting sharper than aught I can say."

"Promise all, however," said the Queen. "I know his inmost soul—it is set upon extending the dominions of his House in every direction. For this he has seized Gueldres—for this he now overruns and occupies Lorraine—for this he covets such poor remnants of Provence as my father still calls his own. With such augmented territories, he proposes to exchange his ducal diadem for an arched crown of independent sovereignty. Tell the Duke, Margaret can assist his views—tell him, that my father René shall disown the opposition made to the Duke's seizure of Lorraine—He shall do more—he shall declare Charles his heir in Provence, with my ample consent—tell him, the old man shall cede his dominions to him upon the instant that his Hainaulters embark for England, some small pension deducted to maintain a concert of fiddlers, and a troop of morrice-dancers. These are René's only earthly wants. Mine are still fewer—Revenge upon York, and a speedy grave!—For the paltry gold which we may need, thou hast jewels to pledge—For the other conditions, security if required."

"For these, madam, I can pledge my knightly word, in addition to your royal faith; and if more is required, my son shall be a hostage with Burgundy."

"Oh, no—no!" exclaimed the dethroned Queen, touched by perhaps the only tender feeling, which repeated and extraordinary misfortunes had not chilled into insensibility,—"Hazard not the life of the noble youth—he that is the last of the loyal and faithful House of Vere—he that should have been the brother in arms of my beloved Edward—he that had so nearly been his companion in a bloody and untimely grave! Do not involve this poor child in these fatal intrigues, which have been so baneful to his family. Let him go with me. Him at least I will shelter from danger whilst I live, and provide for when I am no more."

"Forgive me, madam," said Oxford, with the firmness which distinguished him. "My son, as you deign to recollect, is a De Vere, destined, perhaps, to be the last of his name. Fall, he may, but it must not be without honour. To whatever dangers his duty and allegiance call him, be it from sword or lance, axe or gibbet, to these he must expose himself frankly, when his doing so can mark his allegiance. His ancestors have shewn him how to brave them all."

"True, true," exclaimed the unfortunate Queen, raising her arms wildly,—"All must perish—all that have honoured Lancaster—all that have loved Margaret, or whom she has loved! The destruction must be universal—the young must fall with the old—not a lamb of the scattered flock shall escape!"

"For God's sake, gracious madam," said Oxford,

"compose yourself! — I hear them knock on the chapel door."

"It is the signal of parting," said the exiled Queen, collecting herself. "Do not fear, noble Oxford, I am not often thus; but how seldom do I see those friends, whose faces and voices can disturb the composure of my despair! Let me tie this relic about thy neck, good youth, and fear not its evil influence, though you receive it from an ill-omened hand. It was my husband's, blessed by many a prayer, and sanctified by many a holy tear; even my unhappy hands cannot pollute it. I should have bound it on my Edward's bosom on the dreadful morning of Tewkesbury fight; but he armed early— went to the field without seeing me, and all my purpose was vain."

She passed a golden chain round Arthur's neck as she spoke, which contained a small gold crucifix of rich but barbarous manufacture. It had belonged, said tradition, to Edward the Confessor. The knock at the door of the chapel was repeated.

"We must not tarry," said Margaret; "let us part here—you for Dijon—I to Aix, my abode of unrest in Provence. Farewell—we may meet in a better hour—yet how can I hope it? Thus I said on the morning before the fight of Saint Albans—thus on the dark dawning of Towton—thus on the yet more bloody field of Tewkesbury — and what was the event? Yet hope is a plant which cannot be rooted out of a noble breast, till the last heart-string crack as it is pulled away."

So saying, she passed through the chapel door, and

mingled in the miscellaneous assemblage of personages who worshipped or indulged their curiosity, or consumed their idle hours amongst the aisles of the cathedral.

Philipson and his son, both deeply impressed with the singular interview which had just taken place, returned to their inn, where they found a pursuivant, with the Duke of Burgundy's badge and livery, who informed them, that if they were the English merchants who were carrying wares of value to the court of the Duke, he had orders to afford them the countenance of his escort and inviolable character. Under his protection they set out from Strasburg; but such was the uncertainty of the Duke of Burgundy's motions, and such the numerous obstacles which occurred to interrupt their journey, in a country disturbed by the constant passage of troops and preparation for war, that it was evening on the second day ere they reached the plain near Dijon, on which the whole, or great part of his power, lay encamped.

CHAPTER THE TWENTY-FIFTH.

Thus said the Duke—thus did the Duke infer.
RICHARD III.

THE eyes of the elder traveller were well accustomed to sights of martial splendour, yet even he was dazzled with the rich and glorious display of the Burgundian camp, in which, near the walls of Dijon, Charles, the wealthiest prince in Europe, had displayed his own extravagance, and encouraged his followers to similar profusion. The pavilions of the meanest officers were of silk and samite, while those of the nobility and great leaders glittered with cloth of silver, cloth of gold, variegated tapestry, and other precious materials, which in no other situation would have been employed as a cover from the weather, but would themselves have been thought worthy of the most careful protection. The horsemen and infantry who mounted guard, were arrayed in the richest and most gorgeous armour. A beautiful and very numerous train of artillery was drawn up near the entrance of the camp, and in its commander, Philipson (to give the Earl the travelling name to which our readers are accustomed) recognized Henry Colvin, an Englishman of inferior birth, but distinguished for his skill in conducting these terrible engines, which had of late come into general use in war. The banners and pennons which were displayed by every knight, baron, and man of rank, floated before their tents, and the owners of these transitory dwellings sat at the door half-armed, and enjoyed the military contests of the soldiers, in wrestling, pitching the bar, and other athletic exercises.

Long rows of the noblest horses were seen at picquet, prancing and tossing their heads, as impatient of the inactivity to which they were confined, or were heard neighing over the provender, which was spread plentifully before them. The soldiers formed joyous groups around the minstrels and strolling jugglers, or were engaged in drinking parties at the sutlers' tent; others strolled about with folded arms, casting their eyes now and then to the sinking sun, as if desirous that the hour should arrive which would put an end to a day unoccupied, and therefore tedious.

At length the travellers reached, amidst the dazzling varieties of this military display, the pavilion of the Duke himself, before which floated heavily in the evening breeze, the broad and rich banner, in which glowed the armorial bearings and quarterings of a prince, Duke of six provinces, and Count of fifteen counties, who was, from his power, his disposition, and the success which seemed to attend his enterprises, the general dread of Europe. The pursuivant made himself known to some of the household, and the Englishmen were immediately received with courtesy, though not such as to draw attention upon them, and conveyed to a neighbouring tent, the residence of a general officer, which they were given to understand was destined for their accommodation, and where their packages were accordingly deposited, and refreshments offered them.

"As the camp is filled," said the domestic who waited upon them, "with soldiers of different nations and uncertain dispositions, the Duke of Burgundy, for the safety of your merchandise, has ordered you the protection of a regular sentinel. In the meantime be in readiness to wait on his Highness, seeing you may look to be presently sent for."

Accordingly, the elder Philipson was shortly after summoned to the Duke's presence, introduced by a back entrance into the ducal pavilion, and into that part of it which, screened by close curtains and wooden barricades, formed Charles's own separate apartment. The plainness of the furniture, and the coarse apparatus of the Duke's toilet, formed a strong contrast to the appearance of the exterior of the pavilion; for Charles, whose character was, in that as in other things, far from consistent, exhibited in his own person during war an austerity, or rather coarseness of dress, and sometimes of manners also, which was more like the rudeness of a German lanz knecht, than the bearing of a prince of exalted rank; while, at the same time, he encouraged and enjoined a great splendour of expense and display amongst his vassals and courtiers, as if to be rudely attired, and to despise every restraint, even of ordinary ceremony, were a privilege of the sovereign alone. Yet when it pleased him to assume state in person and manners, none knew better than Charles of Burgundy how he ought to adorn and demean himself.

Upon his toilet appeared brushes and combs,

which might have claimed dismissal as past the term of service, over-worn hats and doublets, dog-leashes, leather-belts, and other such paltry articles; amongst which lay at random, as it seemed, the great diamond called Sanci,—the three rubies termed the Three Brothers of Antwerp,—another great diamond called the Lamp of Flanders, and other precious stones of scarcely inferior value and rarity. This extraordinary display somehow resembled the character of the Duke himself, who mixed cruelty with justice, magnanimity with meanness of spirit, economy with extravagance, and liberality with avarice; being, in fact, consistent in nothing excepting in his obstinate determination to follow the opinion he had once formed, in every situation of things, and through all variety of risks.

In the midst of the valueless and inestimable articles of his wardrobe and toilet, the Duke of Burgundy called out to the English traveller, "Welcome, Herr Philipson—welcome, you of a nation whose traders are princes, and their merchants the mighty ones of the earth. What new commodities have you brought to gull us with? You merchants, by Saint George, are a wily generation."

"Faith, no new merchandise I, my lord," answered the elder Englishman; "I bring but the commodities which I shewed your Highness the last time I communicated with you, in the hope of a poor trader, that your Grace may find them more acceptable upon a review, than when you first saw them."

"It is well, Sir—Philipville, I think they call you? —you are a simple trader, or you take me for a silly purchaser, that you think to gull me with the same wares which I fancied not formerly. Change of fashion, man—novelty—is the motto of commerce; your Lancaster wares have had their day, and I have bought of them like others, and was like enough to have paid dear for them too. York is all the vogue now."

"It may be so among the vulgar," said the Earl of Oxford; "but for souls like your Highness, faith, honour, and loyalty, are jewels which change of fancy or mutability of taste, cannot put out of fashion."

"Why, it may be, noble Oxford," said the Duke, "that I preserve in my secret mind some veneration for these old-fashioned qualities, else how should I have such regard for your person, in which they have ever been distinguished? But my situation is painfully urgent, and should I make a false step at this crisis, I might break the purposes of my whole life. Observe me, Sir Merchant. Here has come over your old competitor, Blackburn, whom some call Edward of York and of London, with a commodity of bows and bills such as never entered France since King Arthur's time; and he offers to enter into joint adventure with me, or, in plain speech, to make common cause with Burgundy, till we smoke out of his earths the old fox Louis, and nail his hide to the stable-door. In a word, England invites me to take part with him against my most wily and inveterate enemy, the King of France; to rid myself of the chain of vassalage, and to ascend into the rank of independent princes;—how think you, noble Earl, can I forego this seducing temptation?"

"You must ask this of some of your counsellors of Burgundy," said Oxford; "it is a question fraught too deeply with ruin to my cause, for me to give a fair opinion on it."

"Nevertheless," said Charles, "I ask thee as an honourable man, what objections you see to the course proposed to me? Speak your mind, and speak it freely."

"My lord, I know it is in your Highness's nature to entertain no doubts of the facility of executing any thing which you have once determined shall be done. Yet, though this prince-like disposition may in some cases prepare for its own success, and has often done so, there are others, in which persisting in our purpose, merely because we have once willed it, leads not to success, but to ruin. Look, therefore, at this English army; winter is approaching, where are they to be lodged? how are they to be victualled? by whom are they to be paid? Is your Highness to take all the expense and labour of fitting them for the summer campaign? for, rely on it, an English army never was, nor will be, fit for service, till they have been out of their own island long enough to accustom them to military duty. They are men, I grant, the fittest for soldiers in the world; but they are not soldiers as yet, and must be trained to become such at your Highness's expense."

"Be it so," said Charles; "I think the Low Countries can find food for the beef-consuming knaves for a few weeks, and villages for them to lie in, and officers to train their sturdy limbs to war, and provost-marshals enough to reduce their refractory spirit to discipline."

"What happens next?" said Oxford. "You march to Paris, add to Edward's usurped power another kingdom; restore to him all the possessions which England ever had in France, Normandy, Maine, Anjou, Gascony, and all besides.—Can you trust this Edward when you shall have thus fostered his strength, and made him far stronger than this Louis whom you have united to pull down?"

"By Saint George, I will not dissemble with you! It is in that very point that my doubts trouble me. Edward is indeed my brother-in-law, but I am a man little inclined to put my head under my wife's girdle."

"And the times," said Philipson, "have too often shewn the inefficiency of family alliances to prevent the most gross breaches of faith."

"You say well, Earl. Clarence betrayed his father-in-law; Louis poisoned his brother—Domestic affections, pshaw! they sit warm enough by a private man's fireside, but they cannot come into fields of battle, or princes' halls, where the wind blows cold. No, my alliance with Edward by marriage were little succour to me in time of need. I would as soon ride an unbroken horse, with no better bridle than a lady's garter. But what then is the result? He wars on Louis; whichever gains the better, I, who must be strengthened in their mutual weakness, receive the advantage—The Englishmen slay the French with their cloth-yard shafts, and the Frenchmen, by skirmishes, waste, weaken, and destroy the English. With spring I take the field with an army superior to both, and then, Saint George for Burgundy!"

"And if, in the meanwhile, your Highness will deign to assist, even in the most trifling degree, a cause the most honourable that ever knight laid lance in rest for,—a moderate sum of money, and a small body of Hainault lances, who may gain both fame and fortune by the service, may replace the injured heir of Lancaster in the possession of his native and rightful dominion."

"Ay, marry, Sir Earl," said the Duke, "you come roundly to the point; but we have seen, and indeed partly assisted at, so many turns betwixt York and Lancaster, that we have some doubt which is the side to which Heaven has given the right, and the inclinations of the people the effectual power; we are surprised into absolute giddiness by so many extraordinary revolutions of fortune as England has exhibited."

"A proof, my lord, that these mutations are not yet ended, and that your generous aid may give to the better side an effectual turn of advantage."

"And lend my cousin, Margaret of Anjou, my arm to dethrone my wife's brother? Perhaps he deserves small good-will at my hands, since he and his insolent nobles have been urging me with remonstrances, and even threats, to lay aside all my own important affairs, and join Edward, forsooth, in his knight-errant expedition against Louis. I will march against Louis at my own time, and not sooner; and, by Saint George! neither island king, nor island noble, shall dictate to Charles of Burgundy. You are fine conceited companions, you English of both sides, that think the matters of your own bedlam island are as interesting to all the world as to yourselves. But neither York nor Lancaster; neither brother Blackburn, nor cousin Margaret of Anjou, not with John de Vere to back her, shall gull me. Men lure no hawks with empty hands."

Oxford, familiar with the Duke's disposition, suffered him to exhaust himself in chafing, that any one should pretend to dictate his course of conduct, and, when he was at length silent, replied with calmness —" Do I live to hear the noble Duke of Burgundy, the mirror of European chivalry, say, that no reason has been shewn to him for an adventure where a helpless queen is to be redressed—a royal house raised from the dust? Is there not immortal *los* and honour—the trumpet of fame to proclaim the sovereign, who, alone in a degenerate age, has united the duties of a generous knight with those of a princely sovereign——"

The Duke interrupted him, striking him at the same time on the shoulder—" And King René's five hundred fiddlers to tune their cracked violins in my praise! and King René himself to listen to them, and say 'Well fought Duke—well played fiddler!' I tell thee, John of Oxford, when thou and I wore maiden armour, such words as fame, honour, *los*, knightly glory, lady's love, and so forth, were good mottoes for our snow-white shields, and a fair enough argument for splintering lances—Ay, and in tilt-yard, though somewhat old for these fierce follies, I would jeopard my person in such a quarrel yet, as becomes a knight of the order. But when we come to paying down of crowns, and embarking of large squadrons, we must have to propose to our subjects some substantial excuse for plunging them in war; some proposal for the public good—or, by Saint George! for our own private advantage, which is the same thing. This is the course the world runs, and Oxford, to tell the plain truth, I mean to hold the same bias."

"Heaven forbid that I should expect your Highness to act otherwise than with a view to your subjects' welfare—the increase, that is, as your Grace happily expresses it, of your own power and dominion. The money we require is not in benevolence, but in loan; and Margaret is willing to deposit these jewels, of which I think your Grace knows the value, till she shall repay the sum which your friendship may advance in her necessity."

"Ha, ha!" said the Duke, "would our cousin make a pawnbroker of us, and have us deal with her like a Jewish usurer with his debtor?—Yet, in faith, Oxford, we may need the diamonds, for if this business were otherwise feasible, it is possible that I myself must become a borrower to aid my cousin's necessities. I have applied to the States of the Duchy, who are now sitting, and expect, as is reasonable, a large supply But there are restless heads and close hands among them, and they may be niggardly—So place the jewels on the table in the meanwhile.—Well, say I am to be no sufferer in purse by this feat of knight-errantry which you propose to me, still princes enter not into war without some view of advantage?"

"Listen to me, noble sovereign. You are naturally bent to unite the great estates of your father, and those you have acquired by your own arms, into a compact and firm dukedom——"

"Call it kingdom," said Charles; "it is the worthier word."

"Into a kingdom, of which the crown shall sit as fair and even on your Grace's brow as that of France on your present suzerain, Louis."

"It needs not such shrewdness as yours to descry that such is my purpose," said the Duke; "else, wherefore am I here with helm on my head, and sword by my side? And wherefore are my troops seizing on the strong places in Lorraine, and chasing before them the beggarly De Vaudemont, who has the insolence to claim it as his inheritance? Yes, my friend, the aggrandizement of Burgundy is a theme for which the duke of that fair province is bound to fight, while he can put foot in stirrup."

"But think you not," said the English Earl, "since you allow me to speak freely with your Grace, on the footing of old acquaintanceship, think you not that in this chart of your dominions, otherwise so fairly bounded, there is something on the southern frontier which might be arranged more advantageously for a King of Burgundy?"

"I cannot guess whither you would lead me," said the Duke, looking at a map of the Duchy and his other possessions, to which the Englishman had pointed his attention, and then turning his broad keen eye upon the face of the banished Earl.

"I would say," replied the latter, "that, to so

powerful a prince as your Grace, there is no safe neighbour but the sea. Here is Provence, which interferes betwixt you and the Mediterranean; Provence, with its princely harbours, and fertile cornfields and vineyards. Were it not well to include it in your map of sovereignty, and thus touch the middle sea with one hand, while the other rested on the sea-coast of Flanders?"

"Provence, said you?" — replied the Duke, eagerly; "why, man, my very dreams are of Provence. I cannot smell an orange but it reminds me of its perfumed woods and bowers, its olives, citrons, and pomegranates. But how to frame pretensions to it? Shame it were to disturb René, the harmless old man, nor would it become a near relation. Then he is the uncle of Louis; and most probably, failing his daughter Margaret, or perhaps in preference to her, he hath named the French King his heir."

"A better claim might be raised up in your Grace's own person," said the Earl of Oxford, "if you will afford Margaret of Anjou the succour she requires by me."

"Take the aid thou requirest," replied the Duke; "take double the amount of it in men and money! Let me but have a claim upon Provence, though thin as a single thread of thy Queen Margaret's hair, and let me alone for twisting it into the tough texture of a quadruple cable.—But I am a fool to listen to the dreams of one, who, ruined himself, can lose little by holding forth to others the most extravagant hopes."

Charles breathed high, and changed complexion as he spoke.

"I am not such a person, my Lord Duke," said the Earl. "Listen to me—René is broken with years, fond of repose, and too poor to maintain his rank with the necessary dignity; too good-natured, or too feeble-minded, to lay farther imposts on his subjects; weary of contending with bad fortune, and desirous to resign his territories——"

"His territories!" said Charles.

"Yes, all he actually possesses; and the much more extensive dominions which he has claim to, but which have passed from his sway."

"You take away my breath!" said the Duke. "René resign Provence! and what says Margaret—the proud, the high-minded Margaret—will she subscribe to so humiliating a proceeding?"

"For the chance of seeing Lancaster triumph in England, she would resign, not only dominion, but life itself. And in truth the sacrifice is less than it may seem to be. It is certain that, when René dies, the King of France will claim the old man's county of Provence as a male fief, and there is no one strong enough to back Margaret's claim of inheritance, however just it may be."

"It is just," said Charles; "it is undeniable! I will not hear of its being denied or challenged—that is, when once it is established in our own person. It is the true principle of the war for the public good, that none of the great fiefs be suffered to revert again to the crown of France, least of all while it stands on a brow so astucious and unprincipled as that of Louis. Burgundy joined to Provence—a dominion from the German Ocean to the Mediterranean! Oxford—thou art my better angel!"

"Your Grace must, however, reflect," said Oxford, "that honourable provision must be made for King René."

"Certainly, man, certainly; he shall have a score of fiddlers and jugglers to play, roar, and recite to him from morning till night. He shall have a court of Troubadours, who shall do nothing but drink, flute, and fiddle to him, and pronounce *arrests* of *love*, to be confirmed or reversed by an appeal to himself, the supreme *Roi d'Amour*. And Margaret shall also be honourably sustained, in the manner you may point out."

"That will be easily settled," answered the English Earl. "If our attempts on England succeed, she will need no aid from Burgundy. If she fails, she retires into a cloister, and it will not be long that she will need the honourable maintenance which, I am sure, your Grace's generosity will willingly assign her."

"Unquestionably," answered Charles; "and on a scale which will become us both;—but, by my halidome, John of Vere, the abbess into whose cloister Margaret of Anjou shall retire, will have an ungovernable penitent under her charge. Well do I know her; and, Sir Earl, I will not clog our discourse by expressing any doubts, that, if she pleases, she can compel her father to resign his estates to whomsoever she will. She is like my brache, Gorgon, who compels whatsoever hound is coupled with her to go the way she chooses, or she strangles him if he resists. So has Margaret acted with her simple-minded husband, and I am aware that her father, a fool of a different cast, must of necessity be equally tractable. I think *I* could have matched her,—though my very neck aches at the thought of the struggles we should have had for mastery. But you look grave, because I jest with the pertinacious temper of my unhappy cousin."

"My lord," said Oxford, "whatever are or have been the defects of my mistress, she is in distress, and almost in desolation. She is my sovereign, and your Highness's cousin not the less."

"Enough said, Sir Earl," answered the Duke. "Let us speak seriously. Whatever we may think of the abdication of King René, I fear we shall find it difficult to make Louis XI. see the matter as favourably as we do. He will hold that the county of Provence is a male fief, and that neither the resignation of René, nor the consent of his daughter, can prevent its reverting to the crown of France, as the King of Sicily, as they call him, hath no male issue."

"That, may it please your Grace, is a question for battle to decide; and your Highness has successfully braved Louis for a less important stake. All I can say is, that if your Grace's active assistance enables the young Earl of Richmond to succeed in his enterprise, you shall have the aid of three thousand English archers, if old John of Oxford, for want of a better leader, were to bring them over himself."

"A noble aid," said the Duke; "graced still more

by him who promises to lead them. Thy succour, noble Oxford, were precious to me, did you but come with your sword by your side, and a single page at your back. I know you well, both heart and head. But let us to this gear; exiles, even the wisest, are privileged in promises, and sometimes—excuse me, noble Oxford—impose on themselves as well as on their friends. What are the hopes on which you desire me again to embark on so troubled and uncertain an ocean, as these civil contests of yours?"

The Earl of Oxford produced a schedule, and explained to the Duke the plan of his expedition, to be backed by an insurrection of the friends of Lancaster, of which it is enough to say, that it was bold to the verge of temerity; but yet so well compacted and put together, as to bear in those times of rapid revolution, and under a leader of Oxford's approved military skill and political sagacity, a strong appearance of probable success.

While Duke Charles mused over the particulars of an enterprise attractive and congenial to his own disposition,—while he counted over the affronts which he had received from his brother-in-law, Edward IV., the present opportunity for taking a signal revenge, and the rich acquisition which he hoped to make in Provence by the cession in his favour of René of Anjou and his daughter, the Englishman failed not to press on his consideration the urgent necessity of suffering no time to escape.

"The accomplishment of this scheme," he said, "demands the utmost promptitude. To have a chance of success, I must be in England, with your Grace's auxiliary forces, before Edward of York can return from France with his army."

"And, having come hither," said the Duke, "our worthy brother will be in no hurry to return again. He will meet with black-eyed French women and ruby-coloured French wine, and brother Blackburn is no man to leave such commodities in a hurry."

"My Lord Duke, I will speak truth of my enemy. Edward is indolent and luxurious when things are easy around him, but let him feel the spur of necessity, and he becomes as eager as a pampered steed. Louis, too, who seldom fails in finding means to accomplish his ends, is bent upon determining the English King to re-cross the sea—therefore speed, noble Prince—speed is the soul of your enterprise."

"Speed!" said the Duke of Burgundy,—"Why, I will go with you and see the embarkation myself; and tried, approved soldiers you shall have, such as are nowhere to be found save in Artois and Hainault."

"But pardon yet, noble Duke, the impatience of a drowning wretch urgently pressing for assistance.— When shall we to the coast of Flanders, to order this important measure?"

"Why, in a fortnight, or perchance a week, or, in a word, so soon as I shall have chastised to purpose a certain gang of thieves and robbers, who, as the scum of the caldron will always be uppermost, have got up into the fastnesses of the Alps, and from thence annoy our frontiers by contraband traffic, pillage, and robbery."

"Your Highness means the Swiss Confederates?"

"Ay, the peasant churls give themselves such a name. They are a sort of manumitted slaves of Austria, and, like a ban-dog, whose chain is broken, they avail themselves of their liberty to annoy and rend whatever comes in their way."

"I travelled through their country from Italy," said the exiled Earl, "and I heard it was the purpose of the Cantons to send envoys to solicit peace of your Highness."

"Peace!" exclaimed Charles.—"A proper sort of peaceful proceedings those of their embassy have been! Availing themselves of a mutiny of the burghers of La Ferette, the first garrison town which they entered, they stormed the walls, seized on Archibald de Hagenbach, who commanded the place on my part, and put him to death in the marketplace. Such an insult must be punished, Sir John de Vere; and if you do not see me in the storm of passion which it well deserves, it is because I have already given orders to hang up the base runagates who call themselves ambassadors."

"For God's sake, noble Duke," said the Englishman, throwing himself at Charles's feet—"for your own character, for the sake of the peace of Christendom, revoke such an order if it is really given!"

"What means this passion?" said Duke Charles. —"What are these men's lives to thee, excepting that the consequences of a war may delay your expedition for a few days?"

"May render it altogether abortive," said the Earl; "nay, *must* needs do so.—Hear me, Lord Duke. I was with these men on a part of their journey."

"You!" said the Duke—"you a companion of the paltry Swiss peasants? Misfortune has sunk the pride of English nobility to a low ebb, when you selected such associates."

"I was thrown amongst them by accident," said the Earl. "Some of them are of noble blood, and are, besides, men for whose peaceable intentions I ventured to constitute myself their warrant."

"On my honour, my Lord of Oxford, you graced them highly, and me no less, in interfering between the Swiss and myself! Allow me to say that I condescend, when, in deference to past friendship, I permit you to speak to me of your own English affairs. Methinks you might well spare me your opinion upon topics with which you have no natural concern."

"My Lord of Burgundy," replied Oxford, "I followed your banner to Paris, and had the good luck to rescue you in the fight at Mont L'Hery, when you were beset by the French men-at-arms——"

"We have not forgot it," said Duke Charles; "and it is a sign that we keep the action in remembrance, that you have been suffered to stand before us so long, pleading the cause of a set of rascals, whom we are required to spare from the gallows, that groans for them, because, forsooth, they have been the fellow-travellers of the Earl of Oxford!"

"Not so, my lord. I ask their lives, only because they are upon a peaceful errand, and the leaders amongst them, at least, have no accession to the crime of which you complain."

The Duke traversed the apartment with unequal steps in much agitation, his large eyebrows drawn down over his eyes, his hands clenched, and his teeth set, until at length he seemed to take a resolution. He rung a hand-bell of silver, which stood upon his table.

"Here, Contay," he said to the gentleman of his chamber who entered, "are these mountain fellows yet executed?"

"No, may it please your Highness; but the executioner waits them so soon as the priest hath confessed them."

"Let them live," said the Duke. "We will hear to-morrow in what manner they propose to justify their proceedings towards us."

Contay bowed and left the apartment; then turning to the Englishman, the Duke said, with an indescribable mixture of haughtiness with familiarity and even kindness, but having his brows cleared and his looks composed,—" We are now clear of obligation, my Lord of Oxford—you have obtained life for life—nay, to make up some inequality which there may be betwixt the value of the commodities bestowed, you have obtained six lives for one. I will, therefore, pay no more attention to you, should you again upbraid me with the stumbling horse at Mont L'Hery, or your own achievements on that occasion. Most princes are contented with privately hating such men as have rendered them extraordinary services—I feel no such disposition—I only detest being reminded of having had occasion for them.—Pshaw! I am half-choked with the effort of foregoing my own fixed resolution.—So ho! who waits there? Bring me to drink."

An usher entered, bearing a large silver flagon, which, instead of wine, was filled with tisanne, slightly flavoured by aromatic herbs.

"I am so hot and choleric by nature," said the Duke, "that our leeches prohibit me from drinking wine. But you, Oxford, are bound by no such regimen. Get thee to thy countryman, Colvin, the general of our artillery. We commend thee to his custody and hospitality till to-morrow, which must be a busy day, since I expect to receive the answer of these wiseacres of the Dijon assembly of estates; and have also to hear (thanks to your lordship's interference) these miserable Swiss envoys, as they call themselves. Well, no more on't.—Good-night. You may communicate freely with Colvin, who is, like yourself, an old Lancastrian.—But hark ye, not a word respecting Provence—not even in your sleep.—Contay, conduct this English gentleman to Colvin's tent. He knows my pleasure respecting him."

"So please your Grace," answered Contay, "I left the English gentleman's son with Monsieur de Colvin."

"What! thine own son, Oxford? And with thee here? Why did you not tell me of him? Is he a true scion of the ancient tree?"

"It is my pride to believe so, my lord. He has been the faithful companion of all my dangers and wanderings."

"Happy man!" said the Duke with a sigh. "You,

Oxford, have a son to share your poverty and distress—I have none to be partner and successor to my greatness."

"You have a daughter, my lord," said the noble De Vere, "and it is to be hoped she will one day wed some powerful prince, who may be the stay of your Highness's house."

"Never! By Saint George, never!" answered the Duke, sharply and shortly. "I will have no son-in-law, who may make the daughter's bed a stepping-stone to reach the father's crown. Oxford, I have spoken more freely than I am wont, perhaps more freely than I ought—but I hold some men trustworthy, and believe you, Sir John de Vere, to be one of them."

The English nobleman bowed, and was about to leave his presence, but the Duke presently recalled him.

"There is one thing more, Oxford.—The cession of Provence is not quite enough. René and Margaret must disavow this hot-brained Ferrand de Vaudemont, who is making some foolish stir in Lorraine, in right of his mother Yolande."

"My lord," said Oxford, "Ferrand is the grandson of King René, the nephew of Queen Margaret; but yet——"

"But yet, by Saint George, his rights, as he calls them, on Lorraine, must positively be disowned. You talk of their family feelings, while you are urging me to make war on my own brother-in-law!"

"René's best apology for deserting his grandson," answered Oxford, "will be his total inability to support and assist him. I will communicate your Grace's condition, though it is a hard one."

So saying, he left the pavilion.

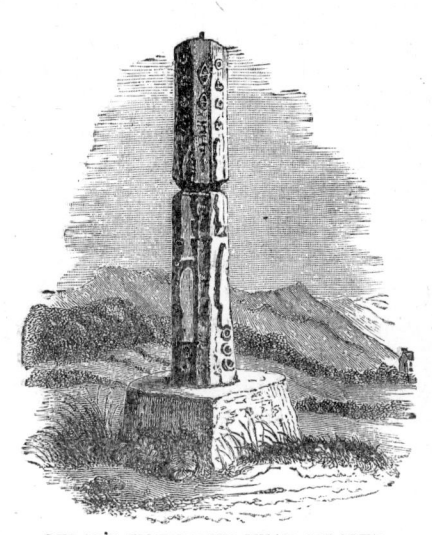

PERCY'S MONUMENT NEAR WOOLER.

CHAPTER THE TWENTY-SIXTH.

*I humbly thank your Highness;
And am right glad to catch this good occasion
Most thoroughly to be winnow'd, where my chaff
And corn shall fly asunder.*

KING HENRY VIII.

COLVIN, the English officer, to whom the Duke of Burgundy, with splendid pay and appointments, committed the charge of his artillery, was owner of the tent assigned for the Englishman's lodging, and received the Earl of Oxford with the respect due to his rank, and to the Duke's especial orders upon that subject. He had been himself a follower of the Lancaster faction, and of course was well disposed towards one of the very few men of distinction whom he had known personally, and who had constantly adhered to that family through the train of misfortunes by which they seemed to be totally overwhelmed. A repast, of which his son had already partaken, was offered to the Earl by Colvin, who omitted not to recommend, by precept and example, the good wine of Burgundy, from which the sovereign of the province was himself obliged to refrain.

"His Grace shews command of passion in that," said Colvin. "For, sooth to speak, and only conversing betwixt friends, his temper grows too headlong to bear the spur which a cup of cordial beverage gives to the blood, and he, therefore, wisely restricts himself to such liquid as may cool rather than inflame his natural fire of disposition."

"I can perceive as much," said the Lancastrian noble. "When I first knew the noble Duke, who was then Earl of Charolois, his temper, though always sufficiently fiery, was calmness to the impetuosity which he now displays on the smallest contradiction. Such is the course of an uninterrupted flow of prosperity. He has ascended, by his own courage and the advantage of circumstances, from the doubtful place of a feudatory and tributary prince, to rank with the most powerful sovereigns in Europe, and to assume independent majesty. But I trust the noble starts of generosity, which atoned for his wilful and wayward temper, are not more few than formerly?"

"I have good right to say that they are not," replied the soldier of fortune, who understood generosity in the restricted sense of liberality. "The Duke is a noble and open-handed master."

"I trust his bounty is conferred on men who are as faithful and steady in their service as you, Colvin, have ever been. But I see a change in your army. I know the banners of most of the old houses in Burgundy—How is it that I observe so few of them in the Duke's camp? I see flags, and pennons, and pennoncelles; but even to me, who have been so many years acquainted with the nobility both of France and Flanders, their bearings are unknown."

"My noble Lord of Oxford," answered the officer, "it ill becomes a man who lives on the Duke's pay to censure his conduct; but his Highness hath of late trusted too much, as it seems to me, to the hired arms of foreign levies, and too little to his own native subjects and retainers. He holds it better to take into his pay large bands of German and Italian mercenary soldiers, than to repose confidence in the knights and squires, who are bound to him by allegiance and feudal faith. He uses the aid of his own subjects but as the means of producing him sums of money, which he bestows on his hired troops. The Germans are honest knaves enough while regularly paid; but Heaven preserve me from the Duke's Italian bands, and that Campo-Basso their leader, who waits but the highest price to sell his Highness like a sheep for the shambles!"

"Think you so ill of him?" demanded the Earl.

"So very ill indeed, that I believe," replied Colvin, "there is no sort of treachery which the heart can devise, or the arm perpetrate, that hath not ready reception in his breast, and prompt execution at his hand. It is painful, my lord, for an honest Englishman like me to serve in an army where such traitors have command. But what can I do, unless I could once more find me a soldier's occupation in my native country? I often hope it will please merciful Heaven again to awaken those brave civil wars in my own dear England, where all was fair fighting, and treason was unheard of."

Lord Oxford gave his host to understand, that there was a possibility that his pious wish of living and dying in his own country, and in the practice of his profession, was not to be despaired of. Meantime he requested of him, that early on the next morning he would procure him a pass and an escort for his son, whom he was compelled to despatch forthwith to Nancy, the residence of King René.

"What!" said Colvin, "is my young Lord of Oxford to take a degree in the Court of Love, for no other business is listened to at King René's capital, save love and poetry?"

"I am not ambitious of such distinction for him, my good host," answered Oxford; "but Queen Margaret is with her father, and it is but fitting that the youth should kiss her hand."

"Enough spoken," said the veteran Lancastrian. "I trust, though winter is fast approaching, the Red Rose may bloom in spring."

He then ushered the Earl of Oxford to the partition of the tent which he was to occupy, in which there was a couch for Arthur also—their host, as Colvin might be termed, assuring them, that, with peep of day, horses and faithful attendants should be ready to speed the youth on his journey to Nancy.

"And now, Arthur," said his father, "we must part once more. I dare give thee, in this land of danger, no written communication to my mistress, Queen Margaret; but say to her, that I have found the Duke of Burgundy wedded to his own views of interest, but not averse to combine them with hers. Say, that I have little doubt that he will grant us the required aid, but not without the expected resignation in his favour by herself and King René. Say, I would never have recommended such a sacrifice for the precarious chance of overthrowing the House of York, but that I am satisfied that France and Burgundy are hanging like vultures over Provence, and that the one or other, or both princes, are ready, on her father's demise, to pounce on such possessions as they have reluctantly spared to him during his life. An accommodation with Burgundy may therefore, on the one hand, ensure his active co-operation in the attempt on England; and, on the other, if our high-spirited princess complies not with the Duke's request, the justice of her cause will give no additional security to her hereditary claims on her father's dominions. Bid Queen Margaret, therefore, unless she should have changed her views, obtain King Rene's formal deed of cession, conveying his estates to the Duke of Burgundy, with her Majesty's consent. The necessary provisions to the King and to herself may be filled up at her Grace's pleasure, or they may be left blank. I can trust to the Duke's generosity to their being suitably arranged. All that I fear is, that Charles may embroil himself——"

"In some silly exploit, necessary for his own honour and the safety of his dominions," answered a voice behind the lining of the tent; "and, by doing so, attend to his own affairs more than to ours? Ha, Sir Earl!"

At the same time the curtain was drawn aside, and a person entered, in whom, though clothed with the jerkin and bonnet of a private soldier of the Walloon guard, Oxford instantly recognised the Duke of Burgundy's harsh features and fierce eyes, as they sparkled from under the fur and feather with which the cap was ornamented.

Arthur, who knew not the Prince's person, started

THE INTERVIEW WITH CHARLES THE BOLD.

at the intrusion, and laid his hand on his dagger; but his father made a signal which stayed his hand, and he gazed with wonder on the solemn respect with which the Earl received the intrusive soldier. The first word informed him of the cause.

"If this masking be done in proof of my faith, noble Duke, permit me to say it is superfluous."

"Nay, Oxford," answered the Duke, "I was a courteous spy; for I ceased to play the eaves-dropper, at the very moment when I had reason to expect you were about to say something to anger me."

"As I am a true Knight, my Lord Duke, if you had remained behind the arras, you would only have heard the same truths which I am ready to tell in your Grace's presence, though it may have chanced they might have been more bluntly expressed."

"Well, speak them then, in whatever phrase thou wilt—they lie in their throats that say Charles of Burgundy was ever offended by advice from a well-meaning friend."

"I would then have said," replied the English Earl, "that all which Margaret of Anjou had to apprehend, was that the Duke of Burgundy, when buckling on his armour to win Provence for himself, and to afford to her his powerful assistance to assert her rights in England, was likely to be withdrawn from such high objects by an imprudently eager desire to avenge himself of imaginary affronts, offered to him, as he supposed, by certain confederacies of Alpine mountaineers, over whom it is impossible to gain any important advantage, or acquire reputation, while, on the contrary, there is a risk of losing both.

These men dwell amongst rocks and deserts which are almost inaccessible, and subsist in a manner so rude, that the poorest of your subjects would starve if subjected to such diet. They are formed by nature to be the garrison of the mountain fortresses in which she has placed them; — for Heaven's sake meddle not with them, but follow forth your own nobler and more important objects, without stirring a nest of hornets, which, once in motion, may sting you into madness."

The Duke had promised patience, and endeavoured to keep his word; but the swollen muscles of his face, and his flashing eyes, shewed how painful to him it was to suppress his resentment.

"You are misinformed, my lord," he said; "these men are not the inoffensive herdsmen and peasants you are pleased to suppose them. If they were, I might afford to despise them. But, flushed with some victories over the sluggish Austrians, they have shaken off all reverence for authority, assume airs of independence, form leagues, make inroads, storm towns, doom and execute men of noble birth at their pleasure.—Thou art dull, and look'st as if thou dost not apprehend me. To rouse thy English blood, and make thee sympathise with my feelings to these mountaineers, know that these Swiss are very Scots to my dominions in their neighbourhood; poor, proud, ferocious; easily offended, because they gain by war; ill to be appeased, because they nourish deep revenge; ever ready to seize the moment of advantage, and attack a neighbour when he is engaged in other affairs. The same unquiet, perfidious, and inveterate enemies that the Scots are to England, are the Swiss to Burgundy and to my allies. What say you? Can I undertake anything of consequence till I have crushed the pride of such a people? It will be but a few days' work. I will grasp the mountain-hedgehog, prickles and all, with my steel-gauntlet."

"Your Grace will then have shorter work with them," replied the disguised nobleman, "than our English Kings have had with Scotland. The wars there have lasted so long, and proved so bloody, that wise men regret we ever began them."

"Nay," said the Duke, "I will not dishonour the Scots by comparing them in all respects to these mountain-churls of the Cantons. The Scots have blood and gentry among them, and we have seen many examples of both; these Swiss are a mere brood of peasants, and the few gentlemen of birth they can boast must hide their distinction in the dress and manners of clowns. They will, I think, scarce stand against a charge of Hainaulters."

"Not if the Hainaulters find ground to ride upon. But——"

"Nay, to silence your scruples," said the Duke, interrupting him, "know, that these people encourage, by their countenance and aid, the formation of the most dangerous conspiracies in my dominions. Look here—I told you that my officer, Sir Archibald de Hagenbach, was murdered when the town of Brisach was treacherously taken by these harmless Switzers of yours. And here is a scroll of parchment, which announces that my servant was murdered by doom of the Vehme-gericht, a band of secret assassins, whom I will not permit to meet in any part of my dominions. O, could I but catch them above ground as they are found lurking below, they should know what the life of a nobleman is worth. Then, look at the insolence of their attestation."

The scroll bore, with the day and date adjected, that judgment had been done on Archibald de Hagenbach, for tyranny, violence, and oppression, by order of the Holy Vehme, and that it was executed by their officials, who were responsible for the same to their tribunal alone. It was countersigned in red ink, with the badges of the Secret Society, a coil of ropes and a drawn dagger.

"This document I found stuck to my toilet with a knife," said the Duke; "another trick by which they give mystery to their murderous jugglery."

The thought of what he had undergone in John Mengs's house, and reflections upon the extent and omnipresence of these Secret Associations, struck even the brave Englishman with an involuntary shudder.

"For the sake of every saint in Heaven," he said, "forbear, my lord, to speak of these tremendous societies, whose creatures are above, beneath, and around us. No man is secure of his life, however guarded, if it be sought by a man who is careless of his own. You are surrounded by Germans, Italians, and other strangers—How many amongst these may be bound by the secret ties which withdraw men from every other social bond, to unite them together in one inextricable, though secret compact? Beware, noble Prince, of the situation on which your throne is placed, though it still exhibits all the splendour of power, and all the solidity of foundation that belongs to so august a structure. I—the friend of thy house —were it with my dying breath—must needs tell thee, that the Swiss hang like an avalanche over thy head; and the Secret Associations work beneath thee like the first throes of the coming earthquake. Provoke not the contest, and the snow will rest undisturbed on the mountain-side—the agitation of the subterranean vapours will be hushed to rest; but a single word of defiance, or one flash of indignant scorn, may call their terrors into instant action."

"You speak," said the Duke, "with more awe of a pack of naked churls, and a band of midnight assassins, than I have seen you shew for real danger. Yet I will not scorn your counsel—I will hear the Swiss envoys patiently, and I will not, if I can help it, shew the contempt with which I cannot but regard their pretensions to treat as independent states. On the Secret Associations I will be silent, till time gives me the means of acting in combination with the Emperor, the Diet, and the Princes of the Empire, that they may be driven from all their burrows at once.—Ha, Sir Earl, said I well?"

"It is well thought, my lord, but it may be unhappily spoken. You are in a position, where one word overheard by a traitor, might produce death and ruin."

"I keep no traitors about me," said Charles. "If I thought there were such in my camp, I would rather die by them at once, than live in perpetual terror and suspicion."

"Your Highness's ancient followers and servants," said the Earl, "speak unfavourably of the Count of Campo-Basso, who holds so high a rank in your confidence."

"Ay," replied the Duke, with composure, "it is easy to decry the most faithful servant in a court by the unanimous hatred of all the others. I warrant me your bull-headed countryman, Colvin, has been railing against the Count like the rest of them, for Campo-Basso sees nothing amiss in any department, but he reports it to me without fear or favour. And then his opinions are cast so much in the same mould with my own, that I can hardly get him to enlarge upon what he best understands, if it seems in any respect different from my sentiments. Add to this, a noble person, grace, gaiety, skill in the exercises of war, and in the courtly arts of peace—such is Campo-Basso; and being such, is he not a gem for a prince's cabinet?"

"The very materials out of which a favourite is formed," answered the Earl of Oxford, "but something less adapted for making a faithful counsellor."

"Why, thou mistrustful fool," said the Duke, "must I tell thee the very inmost secret respecting this man, Campo-Basso, and will nothing short of it stay these imaginary suspicions which thy new trade of an itinerant merchant hath led thee to entertain so rashly?"

"If your Highness honours me with your confidence," said the Earl of Oxford, "I can only say that my fidelity shall deserve it."

"Know then, thou misbelieving mortal, that my

good friend and brother, Louis of France, sent me private information, through no less a person than his famous barber, Oliver le Diable, that Campo-Basso had for a certain sum offered to put my person into his hands, alive or dead.—You start!"

"I do indeed—recollecting your Highness's practice of riding out lightly armed, and with a very small attendance, to reconnoitre the ground, and visit the outposts, and therefore how easily such a treacherous device might be carried into execution."

"Pshaw!" answered the Duke.—"Thou seest the danger as if it were real, whereas nothing can be more certain than that, if my cousin of France had ever received such an offer, he would have been the last person to have put me on my guard against the attempt. No—he knows the value I set on Campo-Basso's services, and forged the accusation to deprive me of them."

"And yet, my lord," replied the English Earl, "your Highness, by my counsel, will not unnecessarily or impatiently fling aside your armour of proof, or ride without the escort of some score of your trusty Walloons."

"Tush, man, thou wouldst make a carbonado of a fever-stirred wretch like myself, betwixt the bright iron and the burning sun. But I will be cautious though I jest thus—and you, young man, may assure my cousin, Margaret of Anjou, that I will consider her affairs as my own. And remember, youth, that the secrets of princes are fatal gifts, if he to whom they are imparted blaze them abroad; but if duly treasured up, they enrich the bearer. And thou shalt have cause to say so, if thou canst bring back with thee from Aix the deed of resignation, of which thy father hath spoken.—Good-night—good-night!"

He left the apartment.

"You have just seen," said the Earl of Oxford to his son, "a sketch of this extraordinary prince, by his own pencil. It is easy to excite his ambition or thirst of power, but well-nigh impossible to limit him to the just measures by which it is most likely to be gratified. He is ever like the young archer, startled from his mark by some swallow crossing his eye, even careless as he draws the string. Now irregularly and offensively suspicious—now unreservedly lavish of his confidence—not long since the enemy of the line of Lancaster, and the ally of her deadly foe — now its last and only stay and hope. God mend all!—It is a weary thing to look on the game and see how it might be won, while we are debarred by the caprice of others from the power of playing it according to our own skill. How much must depend on the decision of Duke Charles upon the morrow, and how little do I possess the power of influencing him, either for his own safety or our advantage! Good-night, my son, and let us trust events to Him who alone can control them."

CHAPTER THE TWENTY-SEVENTH.

>My blood hath been too cold and temperate,
>Unapt to stir at those indignities,
>And you have found me ; for, accordingly,
>You tread upon my patience.
>
>HENRY IV.

THE dawn of morning roused the banished Earl of Oxford and his son, and its lights were scarce abroad on the eastern heaven, ere their host, Colvin, entered with an attendant, bearing some bundles, which he placed on the floor of the tent, and instantly retired. The officer of the Duke's ordnance then announced, that he came with a message from the Duke of Burgundy.

" His Highness," he said, " has sent four stout yeomen, with a commission of credence to my young master of Oxford, and an ample purse of gold, to furnish his expenses to Aix, and while his affairs may detain him there. Also a letter of credence to King René, to ensure his reception, and two suits of honour for his use, as for an English gentleman, desirous to witness the festive solemnities of Provence, and in whose safety the Duke deigns to take deep interest. His farther affairs there, if he hath any, his Highness recommends to him to manage with prudence and secrecy. His Highness hath also sent a couple of horses for his use—one an ambling jennet for the road, and another a strong barbed horse of Flanders, in case he hath aught to do. It will be fitting that my young master change his dress, and assume attire more near his proper rank. His attendants know the road, and have power, in case of need, to summon, in the Duke's name, assistance from all faithful Burgundians. I have but to add, the sooner the young gentleman sets forward, it will be the better sign of a successful journey."

"I am ready to mount, the instant that I have changed my dress," said Arthur.

"And I," said his father, "have no wish to detain him on the service in which he is now employed. Neither he nor I will say more than God be with you. How and where we are to meet again, who can tell?"

"I believe," said Colvin, "that must rest on the motions of the Duke, which, perchance, are not yet determined upon; but his Highness depends upon your remaining with him, my noble lord, till the affairs of which you come to treat may be more fully decided. Something I have for your lordship's private ear, when your son hath parted on his journey."

While Colvin was thus talking with his father, Arthur, who was not above half-dressed when he entered the tent, had availed himself of an obscure corner, in which he exchanged the plain garb belonging to his supposed condition as a merchant, for such a riding suit as became a young man of some quality attached to the Court of Burgundy. It was not without a natural sensation of pleasure, that the youth resumed an apparel suitable to his birth, and which no one was personally more fitted to become; but it was with much deeper feeling that he hastily, and as secretly as possible, flung round his neck, and concealed under the collar and folds of his ornamented doublet, a small thin chain of gold, curiously linked in what was called Morisco work. This was the contents of the parcel which Anne of Geierstein had indulged his feelings, and perhaps her own, by putting into his hands as they parted. The chain was secured by a slight plate of gold, on which a bodkin, or a point of a knife, had traced on the one side, in distinct though light characters, ADIEU FOR EVER! while, on the reverse, there was much more obscurely traced, the word REMEMBER!—A. VON G.

All who may read this are, have been, or will be, lovers; and there is none, therefore, who may not be able to comprehend why this token was carefully suspended around Arthur's neck, so that the inscription might rest on the region of his heart, without the interruption of any substance which could prevent the pledge from being agitated by every throb of that busy organ.

This being hastily ensured, a few minutes completed the rest of his toilet; and he kneeled before his father to ask his blessing, and his further commands for Aix.

His father blessed him almost inarticulately, and then said, with recovered firmness, that he was already possessed of all the knowledge necessary for success on his mission.

"When you can bring me the deeds wanted," he whispered with more firmness, "you will find me near the person of the Duke of Burgundy."

They went forth of the tent in silence, and found before it the four Burgundian yeomen, tall and active-looking men, ready mounted themselves, and holding two saddled horses—the one accoutred for war, the other a spirited jennet, for the purposes of the journey. One of them led a sumpter-horse, on which Colvin informed Arthur he would find the change of habit necessary when he should arrive at Aix; and at the same time delivered to him a heavy purse of gold.

"Thiebault," he continued, pointing out the eldest of the attendant troopers, "may be trusted—I will be warrant for his sagacity and fidelity. The other three are picked men, who will not fear their skin-cutting."

Arthur vaulted into the saddle with a sensation of pleasure, which was natural to a young cavalier who had not for many months felt a spirited horse beneath him. The lively jennet reared with impatience. Arthur, sitting firm on his seat, as if he had been a part of the animal, only said, "Ere we are long acquainted, thy spirit, my fair roan, will be something more tamed."

"One word more, my son," said his father, and whispered in Arthur's ear, as he stooped from the saddle; "if you receive a letter from me, do not think yourself fully acquainted with the contents till the paper has been held opposite to a hot fire."

Arthur bowed, and motioned to the elder trooper to lead the way, when all, giving rein to their horses, rode off through the encampment at a round pace, the young leader signing an adieu to his father and Colvin.

The Earl stood like a man in a dream, following his son with his eyes, in a kind of reverie, which was only broken when Colvin said, "I marvel not, my lord, that you are anxious about my young master; he is a gallant youth, well worth a father's caring for, and the times we live in are both false and bloody."

"God and Saint Mary be my witness," said the Earl, "that if I grieve, it is not for my own house only;—if I am anxious, it is not for the sake of my own son alone;—but it is hard to risk a last stake in a cause so perilous.—What commands brought you from the Duke?"

"His Grace," said Colvin, "will get on horseback after he has breakfasted. He sends you some garments, which, if not fitting your quality, are yet nearer to suitable apparel than those you now wear, and he desires that, observing your incognito as an English merchant of eminence, you will join him in his cavalcade to Dijon, where he is to receive the answer of the Estates of Burgundy concerning matters submitted to their consideration, and thereafter give public audience to the Deputies from Switzerland. His Highness has charged me with the care of finding you suitable accommodation during the ceremonies of the day, which, he thinks, you will, as a stranger, be pleased to look upon. But he probably told you all this himself, for I think you saw him last night in disguise—Nay, look as strange as you will—the Duke plays that trick too often to be able to do it with secrecy; the very horse-boy know him while he traverses the tents of the common soldiery, and sutler women give him the name of the spied spy. If it were only honest Harry Colvin who knew this, it should not cross his lips. But it is practised too openly, and too widely known. Come, noble lord, though I must teach my tongue to forego that courtesy, will you along to breakfast?"

The meal, according to the practice of the time, was a solemn and solid one; and a favoured officer of the great Duke of Burgundy lacked no means, it may be believed, of rendering due hospitality to a guest having claims of such high respect. But ere the breakfast was over, a clamorous flourish of trumpets announced that the Duke, with his attendants and retinue, were sounding to horse. Philipson, as he was still called, was, in the name of the Duke, presented with a stately charger, and with his host mingled in the splendid assembly which began to gather in front of the Duke's pavilion. In a few minutes, the Prince himself issued forth, in the superb dress of the Order of the Golden Fleece, of which his father Philip had been the founder, and Charles was himself the patron and sovereign. Several of his courtiers were dressed in the same magnificent robes, and with their followers and attendants displayed so much wealth and splendour of appearance, as to warrant the common saying, that the Duke of Burgundy maintained the most magnificent court in Christendom. The officers of his household attended in their order, together with heralds and pursuivants, the grotesque richness of whose habits had a singular effect among those of the high clergy in their albes and dalmatiques, and of the knights and crown vassals who were arrayed in armour. Among these last, who were variously equipped, according to the different character of their service, rode Oxford, but in a peaceful habit, neither so plain as to be out of place amongst such splendour, nor so rich as to draw on him a special or particular degree of attention. He rode by the side of Colvin, his tall muscular figure and deep-marked features forming a strong contrast to the rough, almost ignoble, cast of countenance, and stout thick-set form, of the less distinguished soldier of fortune.

Ranged into a solemn procession, the rear of which was closed by a guard of two hundred picked arquebusiers, a description of soldiers who were just then coming into notice, and as many mounted men-at-arms; the Duke and his retinue, leaving the barriers of the camp, directed their march to the town, or rather city, of Dijon, in those days the capital of all Burgundy.

It was a town well secured with walls and ditches, which last were filled by means of a small river, named Dousche, which combines its waters for that purpose with a torrent called Suson. Four gates, with appropriate barbicans, outworks, and drawbridges, corresponded nearly to the cardinal points of the compass, and gave admission to the city. The number of towers, which stood high above its walls, and defended them at different angles, was thirty-three; and the walls themselves, which exceeded in most places the height of thirty feet, were built of stones hewn and squared, and were of great thickness. This stately city was surrounded on the outside with hills covered with vineyards, while from within its walls rose the towers of many noble buildings, both public and private, as well as the steeples of magnificent churches, and of well-endowed convents, attesting the wealth and devotion of the House of Burgundy.

When the trumpets of the Duke's procession had summoned the burgher guard at the gate of Saint Nicholas, the drawbridge fell, the portcullis rose, the people shouted joyously, the windows were hung with tapestry, and as, in the midst of his retinue, Charles himself came riding on a milk-white steed, attended only by six pages under fourteen years old, with each a gilded partisan in his hand, the acclamations with which he was received on all sides, shewed that, if some instances of misrule had diminished his popularity, enough of it remained to render his reception into his capital decorous at least, if not enthusiastic. It is probable that the veneration attached to his father's memory counteracted for a long time the unfavourable effect which some of his own actions were calculated to produce on the public mind.

The procession halted before a large Gothic building in the centre of Dijon. This was then called Maison du Duc, as, after the union of Burgundy with France, it was termed Maison du Roy. The Maire of Dijon attended on the steps before this palace, accompanied by his official brethren, and escorted by a hundred able-bodied citizens, in black velvet cloaks, bearing half pikes in their hands. The Maire kneeled to kiss the stirrup of the Duke, and at the moment when Charles descended from his horse, every bell in the city commenced so thundering a peal, that they might almost have awakened the dead who slept in the vicinity of the steeples, which rocked with their clangour. Under the influence of this stunning peal of welcome, the Duke entered the great hall of the building, at the upper end of which were erected a throne for the sovereign, seats for his more distinguished officers of state and higher vassals, with benches behind for persons of less note. On one of these, but in a spot from which he might possess a commanding view of the whole assembly, as well as of the Duke himself, Colvin placed the noble Englishman; and Charles, whose quick stern eye glanced rapidly over the party when they were seated, seemed, by a nod so slight as to be almost imperceptible to those around him, to give his approbation of the arrangement adopted.

When the Duke and his assistants were seated and in order, the Maire, again approaching, in the most humble manner, and kneeling on the lowest step of the ducal throne, requested to know if his Highness's leisure permitted him to hear the inhabitants of his capital express their devoted zeal to his person, and to accept the benevolence which, in the shape of a silver cup filled with gold pieces, he had the distinguished honour to place before his feet, in name of the citizens and community of Dijon.

Charles, who at no time affected much courtesy,

answered, briefly and bluntly, with a voice which was naturally harsh and dissonant, "All things in their order, good Master Maire. Let us first hear what the Estates of Burgundy have to say to us; we will then listen to the burghers of Dijon."

The Maire rose and retired, bearing in his hand the silver cup, and experiencing probably some vexation, as well as surprise, that its contents had not secured an instant and gracious acceptance.

"I expected," said Duke Charles, " to have met at this hour and place our Estates of the duchy of Burgundy, or a deputation of them, with an answer to our message conveyed to them three days since by our chancellor. Is there no one here on their part?"

The Maire, as none else made any attempt to answer, said that the members of the Estates had been in close deliberation the whole of that morning, and doubtless would instantly wait upon his Highness, when they heard that he had honoured the town with his presence.

"Go, Toison d'Or," said the Duke to the herald of the Order of the Golden Fleece,* "bear to these gentlemen the tidings that we desire to know the end of their deliberations; and that neither in courtesy nor in loyalty can they expect us to wait long. Be round with them, Sir Herald, or we shall be as round with you."

While the herald was absent on his mission, we may remind our readers, that in all feudalized countries, (that is to say, in almost all Europe during the

* The chief order of knighthood in the state of Burgundy.

PARLIAMENT OF CHARLES THE BOLD. FROM AN OLD PRINT.

middle ages,) an ardent spirit of liberty pervaded the constitution; and the only fault that could be found was, that the privileges and freedom for which the great vassals contended did not sufficiently descend to the lower orders of society, or extend protection to those who were most likely to need it. The two first ranks in the state, the nobles and clergy, enjoyed high and important privileges; and even the third estate, or citizens, had this immunity in peculiar, that no new duties, customs, or taxes of any kind, could be exacted from them save by their own consent.

The memory of Duke Philip, the father of Charles, was dear to the Burgundians; for during twenty years that sage prince had maintained his rank amongst the sovereigns of Europe with much dignity, and had accumulated treasure without exacting or receiving any great increase of supplies from the rich countries which he governed. But the extravagant schemes and immoderate expense of Duke Charles had already excited the suspicion of his Estates; and the mutual good-will betwixt the prince and people began to be exchanged for suspicion and distrust on the one side, and defiance on the other. The refractory disposition of the Estates had of late increased; for they had disapproved of various wars in which their Duke had needlessly embarked; and from his levying such large bodies of mercenary troops, they came to suspect he might finally employ the wealth voted to him by his subjects, for the undue extension of his royal prerogative, and the destruction of the liberties of the people.

At the same time, the Duke's uniform success in enterprises which appeared desperate as well as difficult, esteem for the frankness and openness of his character, and dread of the obstinacy and headstrong tendency of a temper which could seldom bear persuasion, and never endured opposition, still threw awe and terror around the throne, which was materially aided by the attachment of the common people to the person of the present Duke, and to the memory of his father. It had been understood, that upon the present occasion there was strong opposition amongst the Estates to the system of taxation proposed on the part of the Duke, and the issue was expected with considerable anxiety by the Duke's counsellors, and with fretful impatience by the sovereign himself.

After a space of about ten minutes had elapsed, the Chancellor of Burgundy, who was Archbishop of Vienne, and a prelate of high rank, entered the hall with his train; and passing behind the ducal throne to occupy one of the most distinguished places in the assembly, he stopped for a moment to urge his master to receive the answer of his Estates in a private manner, giving him at the same time to understand, that the result of the deliberations had been by no means satisfactory.

"By Saint George of Burgundy, my Lord Archbishop," answered the Duke, sternly and aloud, "we are not a prince of a mind so paltry that we need to shun the moody looks of a discontented and insolent faction. If the Estates of Burgundy send a disobedient and disloyal answer to our paternal message, let them deliver it in open court, that the assembled people may learn how to decide between their Duke and those petty yet intriguing spirits, who would interfere with our authority."

The Chancellor bowed gravely, and took his seat; while the English Earl observed, that most of the members of the assembly, excepting such as in doing so could not escape the Duke's notice, passed some observations to their neighbours, which were received with a half-expressed nod, shrug, or shake of the head, as men treat a proposal upon which it is dangerous to decide. At the same time, Toison d'Or, who acted as master of the ceremonies, introduced into the hall a committee of the Estates, consisting of twelve members, four from each branch of the Estates, announced as empowered to deliver the answer of that assembly to the Duke of Burgundy.

When the deputation entered the hall, Charles arose from his throne, according to ancient custom, and taking from his head his bonnet, charged with a huge plume of feathers, "Health and welcome," he said, "to my good subjects of the Estates of Burgundy!" All the numerous train of courtiers rose and uncovered their heads with the same ceremony. The members of the states then dropped on one knee, the four ecclesiastics, among whom Oxford recognised the Black Priest of Saint Paul's, approaching nearest to the Duke's person, the nobles kneeling behind them, and the burgesses in the rear of the whole.

"Noble Duke," said the Priest of Saint Paul's, "will it best please you to hear the answer of your good and loyal Estates of Burgundy by the voice of one member speaking for the whole, or by three persons, each delivering the sense of the body to which he belongs?"

"As you will," said the Duke of Burgundy.

"A priest, a noble, and a free burgher," said the churchman, still on one knee, "will address your Highness in succession. For though, blessed be the God who leads brethren to dwell together in unity! we are agreed in the general answer, yet each body of the Estates may have special and separate reasons to allege for the common opinion."

"We will hear you separately," said Duke Charles, casting his hat upon his head, and throwing himself carelessly back into his seat. At the same time, all who were of noble blood, whether in the committee or amongst the spectators, vouched their right to be peers of their sovereign by assuming their bonnets; and a cloud of waving plumes at once added grace and dignity to the assembly.

When the Duke resumed his seat, the deputation arose from their knees, and the Black Priest of Saint Paul's, again stepping forth, addressed him in these words:—

"My Lord Duke, your loyal and faithful clergy have considered your Highness's proposal to lay a talliage on your people, in order to make war on the Confederate Cantons in the country of the Alps. The quarrel, my liege lord, seems to your clergy an unjust and oppressive one on your Highness's part; nor can they hope that God will bless those who arm in it. They are therefore compelled to reject your Highness's proposal."

The Duke's eye lowered gloomily on the deliverer of this unpalatable message. He shook his head with one of those stern and menacing looks which the harsh composition of his features rendered them peculiarly qualified to express. "You have spoken, Sir Priest," was the only reply which he deigned to make.

One of the four nobles, the Sire de Myrebeau, then expressed himself thus:—

"Your Highness has asked of your faithful nobles to consent to new imposts and exactions, to be levied through Burgundy, for the raising of additional bands of hired soldiers for the maintenance of the quarrels of the state. My lord, the swords of the Burgundian nobles, knights, and gentlemen, have been ever at your Highness's command, as those of our ancestors have been readily wielded for your predecessors. In your Highness's just quarrel we will go farther, and fight firmer, than any hired fellows who can be procured, whether from France, or Germany, or Italy. We will not give our consent that the people should be taxed for paying mercenaries to discharge that military duty which it is alike our pride and our exclusive privilege to render."

"You have spoken, Sire de Myrebeau," were again the only words of the Duke's reply. He uttered them slowly and with deliberation, as if afraid lest some phrase of imprudent violence should escape along with what he purposed to say. Oxford thought he cast a glance towards him before he spoke, as if the consciousness of his presence was some additional restraint on his passion. "Now, Heaven grant," he said to himself, "that this opposition may work its proper effect, and induce the Duke to renounce an imprudent attempt, so hazardous and so unnecessary!"

While he muttered these thoughts, the Duke made a sign to one of the *tiers état*, or commons, to speak in his turn. The person who obeyed the signal was Martin Block, a wealthy butcher and grazier of Dijon. His words were these;—"Noble Prince, our fathers were the dutiful subjects of your predecessors; we are the same to you; our children will be alike the liegemen of your successors. But touching the request your chancellor has made to us, it is such as our ancestors never complied with; such as we are determined to refuse, and such as will never be conceded by the Estates of Burgundy, to any prince whatsoever, even to the end of time."

Charles had borne with impatient silence the speeches of the two former orators, but this blunt and hardy reply of the third Estate excited him beyond what his nature could endure. He gave way to the impetuosity of his disposition, stamped on the floor till the throne shook, and the high vault rung over their heads, and overwhelmed the bold burgher with reproaches. "Beast of burden," he said, "am I to be stunned with thy braying, too? The nobles may claim leave to speak, for they can fight; the clergy may use their tongues, for it is their trade; but thou, that hast never shed blood, save that of bullocks, less stupid than thou art thyself—must thou and thy herd come hither, privileged, forsooth, to bellow at a prince's footstool? Know, brute as thou art, that steers are never introduced into temples but to be sacrificed, or butchers and mechanics brought before their sovereign, save that they may have the honour to supply the public wants from their own swelling hoards!"

A murmur of displeasure, which even the terror of the Duke's wrath could not repress, ran through the audience at these words; and the burgher of Dijon, a sturdy plebeian, replied, with little reverence, —"Our purses, my Lord Duke, are our own—we will not put the strings of them into your Highness's hands, unless we are satisfied with the purposes to which the money is to be applied; and we know well how to protect our persons and our goods against foreign ruffians and plunderers."

Charles was on the point of ordering the deputy to be arrested, when, having cast his eye towards the Earl of Oxford, whose presence, in despite of himself, imposed a certain degree of restraint upon him, he exchanged that piece of imprudence for another.

"I see," he said, addressing the committee of Estates, "that you are all leagued to disappoint my purposes, and doubtless to deprive me of all the power of a sovereign, save that of wearing a coronet, and being served on the knee like a second Charles the Simple, while the Estates of my kingdom divide the power among them. But you shall know that you have to do with Charles of Burgundy, a prince, who, though he has deigned to consult you, is fully able to fight battles without the aid of his nobles, since they refuse him the assistance of their swords—to defray the expense without the help of his sordid burghers—and, it may be, to find out a path to Heaven without the assistance of an ungrateful priesthood. I will shew all that are here present, how little my mind is affected, or my purpose changed, by your seditious reply to the message with which I honoured you.—Here, Toison d'Or, admit into our presence these men from the confederated towns and cantons, as they call themselves, of Switzerland."

Oxford, and all who really interested themselves in the Duke's welfare, heard, with the utmost apprehension, his resolution to give an audience to the Swiss Envoys, prepossessed as he was against them, and in the moment when his mood was chafed to the uttermost by the refusal of the Estates to grant him supplies. They were aware that obstacles opposed to the current of his passion were like rocks in the bed of a river, whose course they cannot interrupt, while they provoke it to rage and foam. All were sensible that the die was cast, but none who were not endowed with more than mortal prescience could have imagined how deep was the pledge which depended upon it. Oxford, in particular, conceived that the execution of his plan of a descent upon England was the principal point compromised by the Duke in his rash obstinacy; but he suspected not—he dreamed not of supposing—that the life of Charles himself, and the independence of Burgundy as a separate kingdom, hung quivering in the same scales.

CHAPTER THE TWENTY-EIGHTH.

>Why, 'tis a boisterous and cruel style,
>A style for challengers. Why, she defies us,
>Like Turk to Christian.
>
>AS YOU LIKE IT.

THE doors of the hall were now opened to the Swiss Deputies, who for the preceding hour had been kept in attendance on the outside of the building, without receiving the slightest of those attentions, which among civilized nations are universally paid to the representatives of a foreign state. Indeed, their very appearance, dressed in coarse grey frocks, like mountain hunters or shepherds, in the midst of an assembly blazing with divers-coloured garments, gold and silver lace, embroidery, and precious stones, served to confirm the idea that they could only have come hither in the capacity of the most humble petitioners.

Oxford, however, who watched closely the deportment of his late fellow-travellers, failed not to observe that they retained each in his own person the character of firmness and indifference which formerly distinguished them. Rudolph Donnerhugel preserved his bold and haughty look; the Banneret the military indifference which made him look with apparent apathy on all around him; the burgher of Soleure was as formal and important as ever; nor did any of the three shew themselves affected in the slightest degree by the splendour of the scene around them, or embarrassed by the consideration of their own comparative inferiority of appointments. But the noble Landamman, on whom Oxford chiefly bent his attention, seemed overwhelmed with a sense of the precarious state in which his country was placed; fearing from the rude and unhonoured manner in which they were received, that war was unavoidable, while, at the same time, like a good patriot, he mourned over the consequences of ruin to the freedom of his country by defeat, or injury to her simplicity and virtuous indifference of wealth, by the introduction of foreign luxuries and the evils attending on conquest.

Well acquainted with the opinions of Arnold Biederman, Oxford could easily explain his sadness, while his comrade Bonstetten, less capable of comprehending his friend's feelings, looked at him with the expression which may be seen in the countenance of a faithful dog, when the creature indicates sympathy with his master's melancholy, though unable to ascertain or appreciate its cause. A look of wonder now and then glided around the splendid assembly on the part of all the forlorn group, excepting Donnerhugel and the Landamman; for the indomitable pride of the one, and the steady patriotism of the other, could not for even an instant be diverted by external objects from their own deep and stern reflections.

After a silence of nearly five minutes, the Duke spoke, with the haughty and harsh manner which he might imagine belonged to his place, and which certainly expressed his character.

"Men of Berne, of Schwitz, or of whatever hamlet and wilderness you may represent, know that we had not honoured you, rebels as you are to the dominion of your lawful superiors, with an audience in our own presence, but for the intercession of a well-esteemed friend, who has sojourned among your mountains, and whom you may know by the name of Philipson, an Englishman, following the trade of a merchant, and charged with certain valuable matters of traffic to our court. To his intercession we have so far given way, that instead of commanding you, according to your demerits, to the gibbet and the wheel in the Place de Morimont, we have condescended to receive you into our own presence, sitting in our *cour plénière*, to hear from you such submission as you can offer for your outrageous storm of our town of La Ferette, the slaughter of many of our liegemen, and the deliberate murder of the noble knight, Archibald of Hagenbach, executed in your presence, and by your countenance and device. Speak—if you can say aught in defence of your felony and treason, either to deprecate just punishment, or crave undeserved mercy."

The Landamman seemed about to answer; but Rudolph Donnerhugel, with his characteristic boldness and hardihood, took the task of reply on himself. He confronted the proud Duke with an eye unappalled, and a countenance as stern as his own.

"We came not here," he said, "to compromise our

own honour, or the dignity of the free people whom we represent, by pleading guilty in their name, or our own, to crimes of which we are innocent. And when you term us rebels, you must remember, that a long train of victories, whose history is written in the noblest blood of Austria, has restored to the confederacy of our communities the freedom, of which an unjust tyranny in vain attempted to deprive us. While Austria was a just and beneficent mistress, we served her with our lives;—when she became oppressive and tyrannical, we assumed independence. If she has aught yet to claim from us, the descendants of Tell, Faust, and Staufbaucher, will be as ready to assert their liberties as their fathers were to gain them. Your Grace—if such be your title—has no concern with any dispute betwixt us and Austria. For your threats of gibbet and wheel, we are here defenceless men, on whom you may work your pleasure; but we know how to die, and our countrymen know how to avenge us."

The fiery Duke would have replied by commanding the instant arrest, and probably the immediate execution, of the whole deputation. But his chancellor, availing himself of the privilege of his office, rose, and doffing his cap with a deep reverence to the Duke, requested leave to reply to the misproud young man, who had, he said, so greatly mistaken the purpose of his Highness's speech.

Charles, feeling perhaps at the moment too much irritated to form a calm decision, threw himself back in his chair of state, and with an impatient and angry nod, gave his chancellor permission to speak.

"Young man," said that high officer, "you have mistaken the meaning of the high and mighty sovereign, in whose presence you stand. Whatever be the lawful rights of Austria over the revolted villages which have flung off their allegiance to their native superior, we have no call to enter on that argument. But that for which Burgundy demands your answer, is, wherefore, coming here in the guise, and with the character, of peaceful envoys, on affairs touching your own communities and the rights of the Duke's subjects, you have raised war in our peaceful dominions, stormed a fortress, massacred its garrison, and put to death a noble knight, its commander?—all of them actions contrary to the law of nations, and highly deserving of the punishment with which you have been justly threatened, but with which I hope our gracious sovereign will dispense, if you express some sufficient reason for such outrageous insolence, with an offer of due submission to his Highness's pleasure, and satisfactory reparation for such a high injury."

"You are a priest, grave sir?" answered Rudolph Donnerhugel, addressing the Chancellor of Burgundy. "If there be a soldier in this assembly who will avouch your charge, I challenge him to the combat, man to man. We did not storm the garrison of La Ferrette—we were admitted into the gates in a peaceful manner, and were there instantly surrounded by the soldiers of the late Archibald de Hagenbach, with the obvious purpose of assaulting and murdering us on our peaceful mission. I promise you there had been news of more men dying than us.

But an uproar broke out among the inhabitants of the town, assisted, I believe, by many neighbours, to whom the insolence and oppression of Archibald de Hagenbach had become odious, as to all who were within his reach. We rendered them no assistance; and, I trust, it was not expected that we should interfere in the favour of men who had stood prepared to do the worst against us. But not a pike or sword belonging to us or our attendants was dipped in Burgundian blood. Archibald de Hagenbach perished, it is true, on a scaffold, and I saw him die with pleasure, under a sentence pronounced by a competent court, such as is recognised in Westphalia, and its dependencies on this side of the Rhine. I am not obliged to vindicate their proceedings; but I aver, that the Duke has received full proof of his regular sentence; and, in fine, that it was amply deserved by oppression, tyranny, and foul abuse of his authority, I will uphold against all gainsayers, with the body of a man. There lies my glove."

And, with an action suited to the language he used, the stern Swiss flung his right-hand glove on the floor of the hall. In the spirit of the age, with the love of distinction in arms which it nourished, and perhaps with the desire of gaining the Duke's favour, there was a general motion among the young Burgundians to accept the challenge, and more than six or eight gloves were hastily doffed by the young knights present, those who were more remote flinging them over the heads of the nearest, and each proclaiming his name and title as he proffered the gage of combat.

"I set at all," said the daring young Swiss, gathering the gauntlets as they fell clashing around him. "More, gentlemen, more! a glove for every finger! come on, one at once—fair lists, equal judges of the field, the combat on foot, and the weapons two-handed swords, and I will not budge for a score of you."

"Hold, gentlemen; on your allegiance, hold!" said the Duke, gratified at the same time, and somewhat appeased, by the zeal which was displayed in his cause—moved by the strain of reckless bravery evinced by the challenger, with a hardihood akin to his own—perhaps also not unwilling to display, in the view of his *cour plénière*, more temperance than he had been at first capable of. "Hold, I command you all. — Toison d'Or, gather up these gauntlets, and return them each to its owner. God and Saint George forbid that we should hazard the life of even the least of our noble Burgundian gentry against such a churl as this Swiss peasant, who never so much as mounted a horse, and knows not a jot of knightly courtesy, or the grace of chivalry.—Carry your vulgar brawls elsewhere, young man, and know that, on the present occasion, the Place Morimont were your only fitting lists, and the hangman your meet antagonist. And you, sirs, his companions—whose behaviour in suffering this swaggerer to take the lead amongst you, seems to shew that the laws of nature, as well as of society, are inverted, and that age is preferred to youth, as gentry to peasants—you whitebearded men, I say, is there none of you who can speak your errand in such language as it becomes a sovereign prince to listen to?"

"God forbid else," said the Landamman, stepping forward and silencing Rudolph Donnerhugel, who was commencing an answer of defiance—"God forbid," he said, "Noble Duke, that we should not be able to speak so as to be understood before your Highness, since, I trust, we shall speak the language of truth, peace, and justice. Nay, should it incline your Highness to listen to us the more favourably for our humility, I am willing to humble myself rather than you should shun to hear us. For my own part, I can truly say, that though I have lived, and by free choice have resolved to die, a husbandman and a hunter on the Alps of the Unterwald, I may claim by birth the hereditary right to speak before Dukes and Kings, and the Emperor himself. There is no one, my Lord Duke, in this proud assembly, who derives his descent from a nobler source than Geierstein."

"We have heard of you," said the Duke. "Men call you the peasant-count. Your birth is your shame; or perhaps your mother's, if your father had happened to have a handsome ploughman, the fitting father of one who has become a willing serf."

"No serf, my lord," answered the Landamman, "but a freeman, who will neither oppress others, nor be himself tyrannized over. My father was a noble lord, my mother a most virtuous lady. But I will not be provoked, by taunt or scornful jest, to refrain from stating with calmness what my country has given me in charge to say. The inhabitants of the bleak and inhospitable regions of the Alps desire, mighty sir, to remain at peace with all their neighbours, and to enjoy the government they have chosen, as best fitted to their condition and habits, leaving all other states and countries to their free-will in the same respects. Especially, they desire to remain at peace and in unity with the princely House of Burgundy, whose dominions approach their possessions on so many points. My lord, they desire it, they entreat it, they even consent to pray for it. We have been termed stubborn, intractable, and insolent contemners of authority, and headers of sedition and rebellion. In evidence of the contrary, my Lord Duke, I, who never bent a knee but to Heaven, feel no dishonour in kneeling before your Highness, as before a sovereign prince in the *cour plénière* of his dominions, where he has a right to exact homage from his subjects out of duty, and from strangers out of courtesy. No vain pride of mine," said the noble old man, his eyes swelling with tears, as he knelt on one knee, " shall prevent me from personal humiliation, when peace—that blessed peace, so dear to God, so inappreciably valuable to man—is in danger of being broken off."

The whole assembly, even the Duke himself, were affected by the noble and stately manner in which the brave old man made a genuflexion, which was obviously dictated by neither meanness nor timidity. "Arise, sir," said Charles; "if we have said aught which can wound your private feelings, we retract it as publicly as the reproach was spoken, and sit prepared to hear you as a fair-meaning envoy."

"For that, my noble Lord, thanks; and I shall hold it a blessed day, if I can find words worthy of the cause I have to plead. My Lord, a schedule in your Highness's hands has stated the sense of many injuries received at the hand of your Highness's officers, and those of Romont, Count of Savoy, your strict ally and adviser, we have a right to suppose, under your Highness's countenance. For Count Romont—he has already felt with whom he has to contend; but we have as yet taken no measures to avenge injuries, affronts, interruptions to our commerce, from those who have availed themselves of your Highness's authority to intercept our countrymen, spoil our goods, impress their persons, and even, in some instances, take their lives. The affray at La Ferette—I can vouch for what I saw—had no origin or abettance from us; nevertheless, it is impossible an independent nation can suffer the repetition of such injuries, and free and independent we are determined to remain, or to die in defence of our rights. What then must follow, unless your Highness listens to the terms which I am commissioned to offer? War, a war to extermination; for so long as one of our Confederacy can wield a halberd, so long, if this fatal strife once commences, there will be war betwixt your powerful realms and our poor and barren states. And what can the noble Duke of Burgundy gain by such a strife?—is it wealth and plunder? Alas, my Lord, there is more gold and silver on the very bridle-bits of your Highness's household troops, than can be found in the public treasures or private hoards of our whole Confederacy. Is it fame and glory you aspire to? There is little honour to be won by a numerous army over a few scattered bands, by men clad in mail over half-armed husbandmen and shepherds—of such conquest small were the glory. But if, as all Christian men believe, and as it is the constant trust of my countrymen, from memory of the times of our fathers,—if the Lord of Hosts should cast the balance in behalf of the fewer numbers and worse-armed party, I leave it with your Highness to judge, what would in that event, be the diminution of worship and fame. Is it extent of vassalage and dominion your Highness desires, by warring with your mountain neighbours? Know that you may, if it be God's will, gain our barren and rugged mountains; but, like our ancestors of old, we will seek refuge in wilder and more distant solitudes, and when we have resisted to the last, we will starve in the icy wastes of the glaciers. Ay, men, women, and children, we will be frozen into annihilation together, ere one free Switzer will acknowledge a foreign master."

The speech of the Landamman made an obvious impression on the assembly. The Duke observed it, and his hereditary obstinacy was irritated by the general disposition which he saw entertained in favour of the ambassador. This evil principle overcame some impression which the address of the noble Biederman had not failed to make upon him. He answered with a lowering brow, interrupting the old man as he was about to continue his speech,— "You argue falsely, Sir Count, or Sir Landamman, or by whatever name you call yourself, if you think we war on you from any hope of spoil, or any desire of glory. We know as well as you can tell us, that there is neither profit nor fame to be achieved by conquering you. But sovereigns, to whom Heaven has given the power, must root out a band of robbers, though there is dishonour in measuring swords with them; and we hunt to death a herd of wolves, though their flesh is carrion, and their skins are nought."

The Landamman shook his grey head, and replied, without testifying emotion, and even with something approaching to a smile,—"I am an older woodsman than you, my Lord Duke—and, it may be, a more experienced one. The boldest, the hardiest hunter, will not safely drive the wolf to his den. I have shewn your Highness the poor chance of gain, and the great risk of loss, which even you, powerful as you are, must incur by risking a war with determined and desperate men. Let me now tell what we are willing to do to secure a sincere and lasting peace with our powerful neighbour of Burgundy. Your Grace is in the act of engrossing Lorraine, and it seems probable, under so vigorous and enterprising a Prince, your authority may be extended to the shores of the Mediterranean—be our noble friend and sincere ally, and our mountains, defended by warriors familiar with victory, will be your barriers against Germany and Italy. For your sake we will admit the Count of Savoy to terms, and restore to him our conquests, on such conditions as your Highness shall yourself judge reasonable. Of past subjects of offence on the part of your lieutenants and governors upon the frontier, we will be silent, so we have assurance of no such aggressions in future.

Nay, more, and it is my last and proudest offer, we will send three thousand of our youth to assist your Highness in any war which you may engage in, whether against Louis of France, or the Emperor of Germany. They are a different set of men—proudly and truly may I state it—from the scum of Germany and Italy, who form themselves into mercenary bands of soldiers. And, if Heaven should decide your Highness to accept our offer, there will be one corps in your army which will leave their carcasses on the field ere a man of them break their plighted troth."

A swarthy, but tall and handsome man, wearing a corslet richly engraved with arabesque work, started from his seat with the air of one provoked beyond the bounds of restraint. This was the Count de Campo-Basso, commander of Charles's Italian mercenaries, who possessed, as has been alluded to, much influence over the Duke's mind, chiefly obtained by accommodating himself to his master's opinions and prejudices, and placing before the Duke specious arguments to justify him for following his own way.

"This lofty presence must excuse me," he said, "if I speak in defence of my honour, and those of my bold lances, who have followed my fortunes from Italy to serve the bravest Prince in Christendom. I might, indeed, pass over without resentment the outrageous language of this grey-haired churl, whose words cannot affect a knight and a nobleman more than the yelling of a peasant's mastiff. But when I hear him propose to associate his bands of mutinous misgoverned ruffians, with your Highness's troops,

I must let him know that there is not a horse-boy in my ranks who would fight in such fellowship. No, even I myself, bound by a thousand ties of gratitude, could not submit to strive abreast with such comrades. I would fold up my banners, and lead five thousand men to seek,—not a nobler master, for the world has none such,—but wars in which we might not be obliged to blush for our assistants."

"Silence, Campo-Basso," said the Duke, "and be assured you serve a prince who knows your worth too well to exchange it for the untried and untrustful services of those, whom we have only known as vexatious and malignant neighbours."

Then addressing himself to Arnold Biederman, he said coldly and sternly, "Sir Landamman, we have heard you fairly. We have heard you, although you come before us with hands dyed deep in the blood of our servant, Sir Archibald de Hagenbach; for, supposing he was murdered by a villanous association,—which, by Saint George! shall never, while we live and reign, raise its pestilential head on this side of the Rhine,—yet it is not the less undeniable and undenied, that you stood by in arms, and encouraged the deed the assassins performed under your countenance. Return to your mountains, and be thankful that you return in life. Tell those who sent you that I will be presently on their frontiers. A deputation of your most notable persons, who meet me with halters round their necks, torches in their left hands, in their right their swords held by the point, may learn on what conditions we will grant you peace."

"Then farewell peace, and welcome war," said the

Landamman; "and be its plagues and curses on the heads of those who choose blood and strife rather than peace and union. We will meet you on our frontiers with our naked swords, but the hilts, not their points, shall be in our grasp. Charles of Burgundy, Flanders, and Lorraine, Duke of seven dukedoms, Count of seventeen earldoms, I bid you defiance; and declare war against you in the name of the Confederated Cantons, and such others as shall adhere to them. There," he said, "are my letters of defiance."

The herald took from Arnold Biederman the fatal denunciation.

"Read it not, Toison d'Or!" said the haughty Duke. "Let the executioner drag it through the streets at his horse's tail, and nail it to the gibbet, to shew in what account we hold the paltry scroll, and those who sent it.—Away, sirs," speaking to the Swiss, "trudge back to your wildernesses with such haste as your feet can use. When we next meet, you shall better know whom you have offended.—Get our horse ready—the council is broken up."

The Maire of Dijon, when all were in motion to leave the hall, again approached the Duke, and timidly expressed some hopes that his Highness would deign to partake of a banquet which the magistracy had prepared, in expectation he might do them such an honour.

"No, by Saint George of Burgundy, Sir Maire," said Charles, with one of the withering glances, by which he was wont to express indignation mixed with contempt,—"you have not pleased us so well with our breakfast as to induce us to trust our dinner to the loyalty of our good town of Dijon."

So saying, he rudely turned off from the mortified chief magistrate, and, mounting his horse, rode back to his camp, conversing earnestly on the way with the Count of Campo-Basso.

"I would offer you dinner, my Lord of Oxford," said Colvin to that nobleman, when he alighted at his tent, "but I foresee, ere you could swallow a mouthful, you will be summoned to the Duke's presence; for it is our Charles's way, when he has fixed on a wrong course, to wrangle with his friends and counsellors, in order to prove it is a right one. Marry, he always makes a convert of yon supple Italian."

Colvin's augury was speedily realised; for a page almost immediately summoned the English merchant, Philipson, to attend the Duke. Without waiting an instant, Charles poured forth an incoherent tide of reproaches against the Estates of his dukedom, for refusing him their countenance in so slight a matter, and launched out into explanations of the necessity which he alleged there was for punishing the audacity of the Swiss. "And thou, too, Oxford," he concluded, "art such an impatient fool as to wish me to indulge in a distant war with England, and transport forces over the sea, when I have such insolent mutineers to chastise on my own frontiers?"

When he was at length silent, the English Earl laid before him, with respectful earnestness, the danger that appeared to be involved in engaging with a people, poor indeed, but universally dreaded, from their discipline and courage, and that under the eye of so dangerous a rival as Louis of France, who was sure to support the Duke's enemies under hand, if he did not join them openly. On this point the Duke's resolution was immovable. "It shall never," he said, "be told of me, that I uttered threats which I dared not execute. These boors have declared war against me, and they shall learn whose wrath it is that they have wantonly provoked; but I do not, therefore, renounce thy scheme, my good Oxford. If thou canst procure me this same cession of Provence, and induce old René to give up the cause of his grandson, Ferrand of Vaudemont, in Lorraine, thou wilt make it well worth my while to send thee brave aid against my brother Blackburn, who, while he is drinking healths pottle-deep in France, may well come to lose his lands in England. And be not impatient because I cannot at this very instant send men across the seas. The march which I am making towards Neufchatel, which is, I think, the nearest point where I shall find these churls, will be but like a morning's excursion. I trust you will go with us, old companion. I should like to see if you have forgotten, among yonder mountains, how to back a horse and lay a lance in rest."

"I will wait on your Highness," said the Earl, "as is my duty, for my motions must depend upon your pleasure. But I will not carry arms, especially against those people of Helvetia, from whom I have experienced hospitality, unless it be for my own personal defence."

"Well," replied the Duke, "e'en be it so; we shall have in you an excellent judge, to tell us who best discharges his devoir against the mountain clowns."

At this point in the conversation there was a knocking at the entrance of the pavilion, and the Chancellor of Burgundy presently entered in great haste and anxiety. "News, my lord — news of France and England," said the prelate, and then observing the presence of a stranger, he looked at the Duke, and was silent.

"It is a faithful friend, my Lord Bishop," said the Duke; "you may tell your news before him."

"It will soon be generally known," said the chancellor — "Louis and Edward are fully accorded." Both the Duke and the English Earl started.

"I expected this," said the Duke, "but not so soon."

"The Kings have met," answered his minister.

"How—in battle?" said Oxford, forgetting himself in his extreme eagerness.

The chancellor was somewhat surprised, but as the Duke seemed to expect him to give an answer, he replied, "No, Sir Stranger, not in battle, but upon appointment, and in peace and amity."

"The sight must have been worth seeing," said the Duke; "when the old fox Louis, and my brother Black—I mean my brother Edward—met. Where held they their rendezvous?"

"On a bridge over the Seine, at Picquigny."

"I would thou hadst been there," said the Duke, looking to Oxford, "with a good axe in thy hand, to strike one fair blow for England, and another for

Burgundy. My grandfather was treacherously slain at just such a meeting, at the Bridge of Montereau, upon the Yonne."

"To prevent a similar chance," said the chancellor, "a strong barricade, such as closes the cages in which men keep wild beasts, was raised in the midst of the bridge, and prevented the possibility of their even touching each other's hands."

"Ha, ha! By Saint George, that smells of Louis's craft and caution; for the Englishman, to give him his due, is as little acquainted with fear as with policy. But what terms have they made? Where do the English army winter? What towns, fortresses, and castles, are surrendered to them, in pledge, or in perpetuity?"

"None, my liege," said the chancellor. "The English army returns into England, as fast as shipping can be procured to transport them; and Louis will accommodate them with every sail and oar in his dominions, rather than they should not instantly evacuate France."

"And by what concessions has Louis bought a peace so necessary to his affairs?"

"By fair words," said the chancellor, "by liberal presents, and by some five hundred tuns of wine."

"Wine!" exclaimed the Duke—"Heardst thou ever the like, Seignor Philipson? Why, your countrymen are little better than Esau, who sold his birthright for a mess of pottage. Marry, I must confess I never saw an Englishman who loved a dry-lipped bargain."

"I can scarce believe this news," said the Earl of Oxford. "If this Edward were content to cross the sea with fifty thousand Englishmen merely to return again, there are in his camp both proud nobles and haughty commons enough to resist his disgraceful purpose."

"The money of Louis," said the statesman, "has found noble hands willing to clutch it. The wine of France has flooded every throat in the English army—the riot and uproar was unbounded—and at one time the town of Amiens, where Louis himself resided, was full of so many English archers, all of them intoxicated, that the person of the King of France was almost in their hands. Their sense of national honour has been lost in the universal revel, and those amongst them who would be more dignified and play the wise politicians say, that having come to France by connivance of the Duke of Burgundy, and that prince having failed to join them with his forces, they have done well, wisely, and gallantly, considering the season of the year, and the impossibility of obtaining quarters, to take tribute of France, and return home in triumph."

"And leave Louis," said Oxford, "at undisturbed freedom to attack Burgundy with all his forces?"

"Not so, friend Philipson," said Duke Charles; "know, that there is a truce betwixt Burgundy and France for the space of seven years, and had not this been granted and signed, it is probable that we might have found some means of marring the treaty betwixt Edward and Louis, even at the expense of affording those voracious islanders beef and beer during the winter months.—Sir Chancellor, you may leave us, but be within reach of a hasty summons."

When his minister lest the pavilion, the Duke, who, with his rude and imperious character united much kindness, if it could not be termed generosity of disposition, came up to the Lancastrian lord, who stood like one at whose feet a thunderbolt had just broken, and who is still appalled by the terrors of the shock.

"My poor Oxford," he said, "thou art stupefied by this news, which thou canst not doubt must have a fatal effect on the plan which thy brave bosom cherishes with such devoted fidelity. I would for thy sake I could have detained the English a little longer in France; but had I attempted to do so, there were an end of my truce with Louis, and of course to my power to chastise these paltry Cantons, or send forth an expedition to England. As matters stand, give me but a week to punish these mountaineers, and you shall have a larger force than your modesty has requested of me for your enterprise; and, in the meanwhile, I will take care that Blackburn and his cousin-archers have no assistance of shipping from Flanders. Tush, man, never fear it— thou wilt be in England long ere they; and, once more, rely on my assistance—always, thou knowest, the cession of Provence being executed, as in reason. Our cousin Margaret's diamonds we must keep for a time; and perhaps they may pass as a pledge, with some of our own, for the godly purpose of setting at freedom the imprisoned angels of our Flemish usurers, who will not lend even to their sovereign, unless on good current security. To such straits has the disobedient avarice of our estates for the moment reduced us."

"Alas! my Lord," said the dejected nobleman, "I were ungrateful to doubt the sincerity of your good intentions. But who can presume on the events of war, especially when time presses for instant decision? You are pleased to trust me. Let your Highness extend your confidence thus far: I will take my horse and ride after the Landamman, if he hath already set forth. I have little doubt to make such an accommodation with him that you may be secure on all your south-eastern frontiers. You may then with security work your will in Lorraine and Provence."

"Do not speak of it," said the Duke, sharply; "thou forget'st thyself and me, when thou supposest that a prince, who has pledged his word to his people, can recall it like a merchant chaffering for his paltry wares. Go to—we will assist you, but we will be ourselves judge of the time and manner. Yet, having both kind will to our distressed cousin of Anjou, and being your good friend, we will not linger in the matter. Our host have orders to break up this evening and direct their march against Neufchatel, where these proud Swiss shall have a taste of the fire and sword which they have provoked."

Oxford sighed deeply, but made no further remonstrance; in which he acted wisely, since it was likely to have exasperated the fiery temper of the sovereign to whom it was addressed, while it was certain that it would not in the slightest degree alter his resolution.

He took farewell of the Duke, and returned to Colvin, whom he found immersed in the business of his department, and preparing for the removal of the artillery, an operation which the clumsiness of the ordnance, and the execrable state of the roads, rendered at that time a much more troublesome operation than at present, though it is even still one of the most laborious movements attending the march of an army. The Master of the Ordnance welcomed Oxford with much glee, and congratulated himself on the distinguished honour of enjoying his company during the campaign, and acquainted him, that, by the especial command of the Duke, he had made fitting preparations for his accommodation, suitable to the disguised character which he meant to maintain, but in every other respect as convenient as a camp could admit of.

CHAPTER THE TWENTY-NINTH.

A mirthful man he was—the snows of age
Fell, but they did not chill him. Gaiety,
Even in life's closing, touch'd his teeming brain
With such wild visions as the setting sun
Raises in front of some hoar glacier,
Painting the bleak ice with a thousand hues.
OLD PLAY.

LEAVING the Earl of Oxford in attendance on the stubborn Duke of Burgundy during an expedition, which the one represented as a brief excursion, more resembling a hunting party than a campaign, and which the other considered in a much graver and more perilous light, we return to Arthur De Vere, or the younger Philipson, as he continued to be called, who was conducted by his guide with fidelity and success, but certainly very slowly, upon his journey into Provence.

The state of Lorraine, overrun by the Duke of Burgundy's army, and infested at the same time by different scattered bands, who took the field, or held out the castles, as they alleged, for the interest of Count Ferrand de Vaudemont, rendered journeying so dangerous, that it was often necessary to leave the main road, and to take circuitous tracks, in order to avoid such unfriendly encounters as travellers might otherwise have met with.

Arthur, taught by sad experience to distrust strange guides, found himself, nevertheless, in this eventful and perilous journey, disposed to rest considerable confidence in his present conductor, Thiebault, a Provençal by birth, intimately acquainted with the roads which they took, and, as far as he could judge, disposed to discharge his office with fidelity. Prudence alike, and the habits which he had acquired in travelling, as well as the character of a merchant which he still sustained, induced him to wave the *morgue*, or haughty superiority of a knight and noble towards an inferior personage, especially as he rightly conjectured that free intercourse with this man, whose acquirements seemed of a superior cast, was likely to render him a judge of his opinions and disposition towards him. In return for his condescension, he obtained a good deal of information concerning the province which he was approaching.

As they drew near the boundaries of Provence, the communications of Thiebault became more fluent and interesting. He could not only tell the name and history of each romantic castle which they passed, in their devious and doubtful route, but had at his command the chivalrous history of the noble knights and barons to whom they now pertained, or had belonged in earlier days, and could recount their exploits against the Saracens, by repelling their attacks upon Christendom, or their efforts to recover the Holy Sepulchre from Pagan hands. In the course of such narrations, Thiebault was led to speak of the Troubadours, a race of native poets of Provençal origin, differing widely from the minstrels of

Normandy, and the adjacent provinces of France, with whose tales of chivalry, as well as the numerous translations of their works into Norman-French and English, Arthur, like most of the noble youth of his country, was intimately acquainted and deeply imbued. Thiebault boasted that his grandsire, of humble birth indeed, but of distinguished talent, was one of this gifted race, whose compositions produced so great an effect on the temper and manners of their age and country. It was, however, to be regretted, that inculcating as the prime duty of life a fantastic spirit of gallantry, which sometimes crossed the Platonic bound prescribed to it, the poetry of the Troubadours was too frequently used to soften and seduce the heart, and corrupt the principles.*

* The smoothness of the Provençal dialect, partaking strongly of the Latin, which had been spoken for so many ages in what was called for distinction's sake the Roman Province of Gaul, and the richness and fertility of a country abounding in all that could delight the senses and soothe the imagination, naturally disposed the inhabitants to cultivate the art of poetry, and to value and foster the genius of those who distinguished themselves by attaining excellence in it. Troubadours, that is, *finders* or *inventors*, equivalent to the northern term of *makers*, arose in every class, from the lowest to the highest, and success in their art dignified men of the meanest rank, and added fresh honours to those who were born in the Patrician file of society. War and love, more especially the latter, were dictated to them by the chivalry of the times as the especial subjects of their verse. Such, too, were the themes of our northern minstrels. But whilst the latter confined themselves in general to those well-known metrical histories in which scenes of strife and combat mingled with adventures of enchantment, and fables of giants and monsters subdued by valiant champions, such as

Arthur's attention was called to this peculiarity, by Thiebault singing, which he could do with good skill, the history of a Troubadour, named William Cabestainy, who loved, *par amours,* a noble and beautiful lady, Margaret, the wife of a baron called Raymond de Roussillon. The jealous husband obtained proof of his dishonour, and having put Cabestainy to death by assassination, he took his heart from his bosom, and causing it to be dressed like that of an animal, ordered it to be served up to his lady; and when she had eaten of the horrible mess, told her of what her banquet was composed. The lady replied that since she had been made to partake of food so precious, no coarser morsel should ever after cross her lips. She persisted in her resolution, and thus

best attracted the ears of the somewhat duller and more barbarous warriors of northern France, of Britain, and of Germany— the more lively Troubadours produced poems which turned on human passion, and on love, affection, and dutiful observance, with which the faithful knight was bound to regard the object of his choice, and the honour and respect with which she was bound to recompense his faithful services.

Thus far it cannot be disputed, that the themes selected by the Troubadours were those on which poetry is most naturally exerted, and with the best chance of rising to excellence. But it usually happens, that when any one of the fine arts is cultivated exclusively, the taste of those who practise and admire its productions loses sight of nature, simplicity, and true taste, and the artist endeavours to discover, while the public learn to admire, some more complicated system, in which pedantry supersedes the dictates of natural feeling, and metaphysical ingenuity is used instead of the more obvious qualifications of simplicity and good sense. Thus, with the unanimous approbation of their hearers, the Troubadours framed for themselves a spe-

starved herself to death. The Troubadour who celebrated this tragic history, had displayed in his composition a good deal of poetic art. Glossing over the error of the lovers as the fault of their destiny, dwelling on their tragical fate with considerable pathos, and finally, execrating the blind fury of the husband, with the full fervour of poetical indignation, he recorded, with vindictive pleasure, how every bold knight and true lover in the south of France assembled to besiege the baron's castle, stormed it by main force, left not one stone upon another, and put the tyrant himself to an ignominious death. Arthur was interested in the melancholy tale, which even beguiled him of a few tears; but as he thought further on its purport, he dried his eyes, and said, with some sternness—" Thiebault, sing me no more such lays. I have heard my father say, that the readiest

cies of poetry describing and inculcating a system of metaphysical affection, as inconsistent with nature as the minstrel's tales of magicians and monsters; with this evil to society, that it was calculated deeply to injure its manners and its morals. Every Troubadour, or good Knight, who took the maxims of their poetical school for his rule, was bound to choose a lady-love, the fairest and noblest to whom he had access, to whom he dedicated at once his lyre and his sword, and who, married or single, was to be the object to whom his life, words, and actions, were to be devoted. On the other hand, a lady thus honoured and distinguished, was bound, by accepting the services of such a gallant, to consider him as her lover, and on all due occasions to grace him as such with distinguished marks of personal favour. It is true, that according to the best authorities, the intercourse betwixt her lover and herself was to be entirely of a Platonic character, and the loyal swain was not to remode to corrupt a Christian man, is to bestow upon vice the pity and the praise which are due only to virtue. Your Baron of Roussillon is a monster of cruelty; but your unfortunate lovers were not the less guilty. It is by giving fair names to foul actions, that those who would start at real vice are led to practise its lessons, under the disguise of virtue."

"I would you knew, Seignor," answered Thiebault, "that this Lay of Cabestainy, and the Lady Margaret of Roussillon, is reckoned a masterpiece of the joyous science. Fie, sir, you are too young to be so strict a censor of morals. What will you do when your head is grey, if you are thus severe when it is scarcely brown?"

"A head which listens to folly in youth, will hardly be honourable in old age," answered Arthur.

quire, or the chosen lady to grant, anything beyond the favour she might in strict modesty bestow. Even under this restriction, the system was like to make wild work with the domestic peace of families, since it permitted, or rather enjoined, such familiarity betwixt the fair dame and her poetical admirer; and very frequently human passions, placed in such a dangerous situation, proved too strong to be confined within the metaphysical bounds prescribed to them by so fantastic and perilous a system. The injured husbands on many occasions avenged themselves with severity, and even with dreadful cruelty, on the unfaithful ladies, and the musical skill and chivalrous character of the lover proved no protection to his person. But the real spirit of the system was seen in this, that in the poems of the other Troubadours, by whom such events are recorded, their pity is all bestowed on the hapless lovers, while, without the least allowance for just provocation, the injured husband is held up to execration.

Thiebault had no mind to carry the dispute farther.

"It is not for me to contend with your worship. I only think, with every true son of chivalry and song, that a knight without a mistress is like a sky without a star."

"Do I not know that?" answered Arthur; "but yet better remain in darkness than be guided by such false lights as shower down vice and pestilence."

"Nay, it may be your seignorie is right," answered the guide. "It is certain, that even in Provence here we have lost much of our keen judgment on matters of love,—its difficulties, its intricacies, and its errors, since the Troubadours are no longer regarded as usual, and since the High and Noble Parliament of Love * has ceased to hold its sittings."

"But in these latter days," continued the Provençal, "kings, dukes, and sovereigns, instead of being the foremost and most faithful vassals of the Court of Cupid, are themselves the slaves of selfishness, and love of gain. Instead of winning hearts by breaking lances in the lists, they are breaking the hearts of their impoverished vassals by the most

* In Provence, during the flourishing time of the Troubadours, Love was esteemed so grave and formal a part of the business of life, that a Parliament or High Court of Love was appointed for deciding such questions. This singular tribunal was, it may be supposed, conversant with more of imaginary than of real suits; but it is astonishing with what cold and pedantic ingenuity the Troubadours of whom it consisted set themselves to plead and to decide, upon reasoning which was not less singular and able than out of place, the absurd questions which their own fantastic imaginations had previously devised.

cruel exactions—instead of attempting to deserve the smile and favours of their lady-loves, they are meditating how to steal castles, towns, and provinces from their neighbours. But long life to the good and venerable King René! While he has an acre of land left, his residence will be the resort of valiant knights, whose only aim is praise in arms, of true lovers, who are persecuted by fortune, and of high-toned harpers, who know how to celebrate faith and valour."

Arthur, interested in learning something more precise than common fame had taught him on the subject of this prince, easily induced the talkative Provençal to enlarge upon the virtues of his old sovereign's character, as just, joyous, and debonair, a friend to the most noble exercises of the chase and the tilt-yard, and still more so to the joyous science of Poetry and Music; who gave away more revenue than he received, in largesses to knights-errant and itinerant musicians, with whom his petty court was crowded, as one of the very few in which the ancient hospitality was still maintained.

Such was the picture which Thiebault drew of the

There, for example, is a reported case of much celebrity, where a lady sitting in company with three persons, who were her admirers, listened to one with the most favourable smiles, while she pressed the hand of the second, and touched with her own the foot of the third. It was a case much agitated and keenly contested in the Parliament of Love, which of these rivals had received the distinguishing mark of the lady's favour. Much ingenuity was wasted on this and similar cases, of which there is a collection, in all judicial form of legal proceedings, under the title of *Arrêts d'Amour* (Adjudged Cases of the Court of Love).

A TOURNAMENT, FROM AN ANCIENT DRAWING BY KING RENÉ.

last minstrel monarch; and though the eulogium was exaggerated, perhaps the facts were not overcharged.

Born of royal parentage, and with high pretensions, René had at no period of his life been able to match his fortunes to his claims. Of the kingdoms to which he asserted right, nothing remained in his possession but the county of Provence itself, a fair and fertile principality, but diminished by the many claims which France had acquired upon portions of it by advances of money to supply the personal expenses of its master, and by other portions, which Burgundy, to whom René had been a prisoner, held in pledge for his ransom. In his youth he engaged in more than one military enterprise, in the hope of attaining some part of the territory of which he was styled sovereign. His courage is not impeached, but fortune did not smile on his military adventures; and he seems at last to have become sensible, that the power of admiring and celebrating warlike merit, is very different from possessing that quality. In fact, René was a prince of very moderate parts, endowed with a love of the fine arts, which he carried to extremity, and a degree of good-humour, which never permitted him to repine at fortune, but rendered its possessor happy, when a prince of keener feelings would have died of despair. This insouciant, light-tempered, gay, and thoughtless disposition, conducted René, free from all the passions which embitter life, and often shorten it, to a hale and mirthful old age. Even domestic losses, which often affect those who are proof against mere reverses of fortune, made no deep impression on the feelings of this cheerful old monarch. Most of his children had died young; René took it not to heart. His daughter Margaret's marriage with the powerful Henry of England was considered a connection much above the fortunes of the King of the Troubadours. But in the issue, instead of René deriving any splendour from the match, he was involved in the misfortunes of his daughter, and repeatedly obliged to impoverish himself to supply her ransom. Perhaps in his private soul the old king did not think these losses so mortifying, as the necessity of receiving Margaret into his court and family. On fire when reflecting on the losses she had sustained, mourning over friends slain and kingdoms lost, the proudest and most passionate of princesses was ill suited to dwell with the gayest and best-humoured of sovereigns, whose pursuits she contemned, and whose lightness of temper, for finding comfort in such trifles, she could not forgive. The discomfort attached to her presence, and vindictive recollections, embarrassed the good-humoured old monarch, though it was unable to drive him beyond his equanimity.

Another distress pressed him more sorely.—Yolande, a daughter of his first wife, Isabella, had succeeded to his claims upon the Duchy of Lorraine, and transmitted them to her son, Ferrand, Count of Vaudemont, a young man of courage and spirit, engaged at this time in the apparently desperate undertaking of making his title good against the Duke of Burgundy, who, with little right, but great power, was seizing upon and overrunning this rich Duchy, which he laid claim to as a male fief. And to conclude, while the aged king on one side beheld his dethroned daughter in hopeless despair, and on the other his disinherited grandson, in vain attempting to recover part of their rights, he had the additional misfortune to know, that his nephew, Louis of France, and his cousin, the Duke of Burgundy, were secretly contending which should succeed him in that portion of Provence which he still continued to possess; and that it was only jealousy of each other which prevented his being despoiled of this last remnant of his territory. Yet amid all this distress, René feasted and received guests, danced, sung, composed poetry, used the pencil or brush with no small skill, devised and conducted festivals and processions, and studying to promote, as far as possible, the immediate mirth and good-humour of his subjects, if he could not materially enlarge their more permanent prosperity, was never mentioned by them, excepting as *Le bon Roi René*, a distinction conferred on him down to the present day, and due to him certainly by the qualities of his heart, if not by those of his head.

Whilst Arthur was receiving from his guide a full account of the peculiarities of King René, they entered the territories of that merry monarch. It was late in the autumn, and about the period when the south-eastern counties of France rather shew to least advantage. The foliage of the olive-tree is then decayed and withered, and as it predominates in the landscape, and resembles the scorched complexion of the soil itself, an ashen and arid hue is given to the whole. Still, however, there were scenes in the hilly and pastoral parts of the country, where the quantity of evergreens relieved the eye even in this dead season.

The appearance of the country, in general, had much in it that was peculiar.

The travellers perceived at every turn some marks of the King's singular character. Provence, as the part of Gaul which first received Roman civilisation, and as having been still longer the residence of the Grecian colony who founded Marseilles, is more full of the splendid relics of ancient architecture than any other country in Europe, Italy and Greece excepted. The good taste of the King René had dictated some attempts to clear out and restore these memorials of antiquity. Was there a triumphal arch, or an ancient temple—huts and hovels were cleared away from its vicinity, and means were used at least to retard the approach of ruin. Was there a marble fountain, which superstition had dedicated to some sequestered naiad—it was surrounded by olives, almond, and orange trees—its cistern was repaired, and taught once more to retain its crystal treasures. The huge amphitheatres, and gigantic colonnades, experienced the same anxious care, attesting that the noblest specimens of the fine arts found one admirer and preserver in King René, even during the course of those which are termed the dark and barbarous ages.

A change of manners could also be observed in passing from Burgundy and Lorraine, where society relished of German bluntness, into the pastoral country of Provence, where the influence of a fine climate and melodious language, joined to the pursuits of the romantic old monarch, with the universal taste for music and poetry, had introduced a civilisation of manners, which approached to affectation. The shepherd literally marched abroad in the morning, piping his flocks forth to the pasture, with some love sonnet, the composition of an amorous Troubadour; and his "fleecy care" seemed actually to be under the influence of his music, instead of being ungraciously insensible to its melody, as is the case in colder climates. Arthur observed, too, that the Provençal sheep, instead of being driven before the shepherd, regularly followed him, and did not disperse to feed until the swain, by turning his face round to them, remaining stationary, and executing variations on the air which he was playing, seemed to remind them that it was proper to do so. While in motion, his huge dog, of a species which is trained to face the wolf, and who is respected by the sheep as their guardian, and not feared as their tyrant, followed his master with his ears pricked, like the chief critic and prime judge of the performance, at some tones of which he seldom failed to intimate disapprobation; while the flock, like the generality of an audience, followed in unanimous though silent applause. At the hour of noon, the shepherd had sometimes acquired an augmentation to his audience, as some comely matron or blooming maiden, with whom he had rendezvoused by such a fountain as we have described, and who listened to the husband's or lover's chalumeau, or mingled her voice with his in the duets, of which the songs of the Troubadours have left so many examples. In the cool of the evening, the dance on the village green, or the concert before the hamlet door; the little repast of fruits, cheese, and bread, which the traveller was readily invited to share, gave new charms to the illusion, and seemed in earnest to point out Provence as the Arcadia of France.

But the greatest singularity was, in the eyes of Arthur, the total absence of armed men and soldiers in this peaceful country. In England, no man stirred without his long - bow, sword, and buckler. In France, the hind wore armour even when he was betwixt the stilts of his plough. In Germany, you could not look along a mile of highway, but the eye was encountered by clouds of dust, out of which were seen, by fits, waving feathers and flashing armour. Even in Switzerland, the peasant, if he had a journey to make, though but of a mile or two, cared not to travel without his halberd and two-handed sword. But in Provence all seemed quiet and peaceful, as if the music of the land had lulled to sleep all its wrathful passions. Now and then a mounted cavalier might pass them, the harp at whose saddle-bow, or carried by one of his attendants, attested the character of a Troubadour, which was affected by men of all ranks; and then only a short sword on his left thigh, borne for show rather than use, was a necessary and appropriate part of his equipment.

"Peace," said Arthur, as he looked around him, "is an inestimable jewel; but it will be soon snatched from those who are not prepared with heart and hand to defend it."

The sight of the ancient and interesting town of Aix, where King René held his court, dispelled reflections of a general character, and recalled to the young Englishman the peculiar mission on which he was engaged.

He then required to know from the Provençal, Thiebault, whether his instructions were to leave him, now that he had successfully attained the end of his journey.

"My instructions," answered Thiebault, "are to remain in Aix while there is any chance of your seignorie's continuing there, to be of such use to you as you may require, either as a guide or an attendant, and to keep these men in readiness to wait upon you when you have occasion for messengers or guards. With your approbation, I will see them disposed of in fitting quarters, and receive my farther instructions from your seignorie wherever you please to appoint me. I propose this separation, because I understand it is your present pleasure to be private."

"I must go to court," answered Arthur, "without any delay. Wait for me in half an hour by that fountain in the street, which projects into the air such a magnificent pillar of water, surrounded, I would almost swear, by a vapour like steam, serving as a shroud to the jet which it envelopes."

"The jet is so surrounded," answered the Provençal, "because it is supplied by a hot-spring rising from the bowels of the earth, and the touch of frost on this autumn morning makes the vapour more distinguishable than usual.—But if it is good King René whom you seek, you will find him at this time walking in his chimney. Do not be afraid of approaching him, for there never was a monarch so easy of access, especially to good-looking strangers like your seignorie."

"But his ushers," said Arthur, "will not admit me into his hall."

"His hall!" repeated Thiebault—"Whose hall?"

"Why, King René's, I apprehend. If he is walking in a chimney, it can only be in that of his hall, and a stately one it must be to give him room for such exercise."

"You mistake my meaning," said the guide, laughing.—"What we call King René's chimney is the narrow parapet yonder; it extends between these two towers, has an exposure to the south, and is sheltered in every other direction. Yonder it is his pleasure to walk and enjoy the beams of the sun, on such cool mornings as the present. It nurses, he says, his poetical vein. If you approach his promenade he will readily speak to you, unless, indeed, he is in the very act of a poetical composition."

Arthur could not forbear smiling at the thoughts of a king, eighty years of age, broken down with misfortunes and beset with dangers, who yet amused himself with walking in an open parapet, and composing poetry in presence of all such of his loving subjects as chose to look on.

"If you will walk a few steps this way," said Thiebault, " you may see the good King, and judge whether or not you will accost him at present. I will dispose of the people, and await your orders at the fountain in the Corso."

Arthur saw no objection to the proposal of his guide, and was not unwilling to have an opportunity of seeing something of the good King René, before he was introduced to his presence.

PORTRAIT OF KING RENÉ.

CHAPTER THE THIRTIETH.

> Ay, this is he who wears the wreath of bays
> Wove by Apollo and the Sisters Nine,
> Which Jove's dread lightning scathes not.   He hath doft
> The cumbrous helm of steel, and flung aside
> The yet more galling diadem of gold;
> While, with a leafy circlet round his brows,
> He reigns the King of Lovers and of Poets.

A CAUTIOUS approach to the chimney, that is, the favourite walk of the King, who is described by Shakspeare as bearing—

ANNE OF GEIERSTEIN. 241

> ——the style of King of Naples,
> Of both the Sicilies, and Jerusalem,
> Yet not so wealthy as an English yeoman,

gave Arthur the perfect survey of his Majesty in person. He saw an old man, with locks and beard, which, in amplitude and whiteness, nearly rivalled those of the envoy from Schwitz, but with a fresh and ruddy colour in his cheek, and an eye of great vivacity. His dress was showy to a degree almost inconsistent with his years; and his step, not only firm but full of alertness and vivacity, while occupied in traversing the short and sheltered walk, which he had chosen, rather for comfort than privacy, shewed juvenile vigour, still animating an aged frame. The old King carried his tablets and a pencil in his hand, seeming totally abstracted in his own thoughts, and indifferent to being observed by several persons from the public street beneath his elevated promenade.

Of these, some, from their dress and manner, seemed themselves Troubadours; for they held in their hands rebecks, rotes, small portable harps, and other indications of their profession. Such appeared to be stationary, as if engaged in observing and recording their remarks on the meditations of their Prince. Other passengers, bent on their own more serious affairs, looked up to the King as to some one whom they were accustomed to see daily, but never passed without doffing their bonnets, and expressing, by a suitable obeisance, a respect and affection towards his person, which appeared to make up in cordiality of feeling what it wanted in deep and solemn deference.

René, in the meanwhile, was apparently unconscious both of the gaze of such as stood still, or the greeting of those who passed on, his mind seeming altogether engrossed with the apparent labour of some arduous task in poetry or music. He walked fast or slow as best suited the progress of composition. At times he stopped to mark hastily down on his tablets something which seemed to occur to him as deserving of preservation; at other times he dashed out what he had written, and flung down the pencil as if in a sort of despair. On these occasions, the Sibylline leaf was carefully picked up by a beautiful page, his only attendant, who reverently observed the first suitable opportunity of restoring it again to his royal hand. The same youth bore a viol, on which, at a signal from his master, he occasionally struck a few musical notes, to which the old King listened, now with a soothed and satisfied air, now with a discontented and anxious brow. At times, his enthusiasm rose so high, that he even hopped and skipped with an activity which his years did not promise; at other times his motions were extremely slow, and occasionally he stood still, like one wrapped in the deepest and most anxious meditation. When he chanced to look on the group which seemed to watch his motions, and who ventured even to salute him with a murmur of applause, it was only to distinguish them with a friendly and good-humoured nod; a salutation with which, likewise, he failed not to reply to the greeting of the occasional passengers, when his earnest attention to his task, whatever it might be, permitted him to observe them.

At length the royal eye lighted upon Arthur, whose attitude of silent observation, and the distinction of his figure, pointed him out as a stranger. René beckoned to his page, who, receiving his master's commands in a whisper, descended from the royal chimney, to the broader platform beneath, which was open to general resort. The youth, addressing Arthur with much courtesy, informed him the King desired to speak with him. The young Englishman had no alternative but that of approaching, though pondering much in his own mind how he ought to comport himself towards such a singular specimen of royalty.

When he drew near, King René addressed him in a tone of courtesy not unmingled with dignity, and Arthur's awe in his immediate presence was greater than he himself could have anticipated from his previous conception of the royal character.

"You are, from your appearance, fair sir," said King René, "a stranger in this country. By what name must we call you, and to what business are we to ascribe the happiness of seeing you at our court?"

Arthur remained a moment silent, and the good old man, imputing it to awe and timidity, proceeded in an encouraging tone.

"Modesty in youth is ever commendable; you are doubtless an acolyte in the noble and joyous science of Minstrelsy and Music, drawn hither by the willing welcome which we afford to the professors of those arts, in which—praise be to Our Lady and the Saints!—we have ourself been deemed a proficient."

"I do not aspire to the honours of a Troubadour," answered Arthur.

"I believe you," answered the King, "for your speech smacks of the northern, or Norman-French, such as is spoken in England and other unrefined nations. But you are a minstrel, perhaps, from these ultramontane parts. Be assured we despise not their efforts; for we have listened, not without pleasure and instruction, to many of their bold and wild romaunts, which, though rude in device and language, and therefore far inferior to the regulated poetry of our Troubadours, have yet something in their powerful and rough measure, which occasionally rouses the heart like the sound of a trumpet."

"I have felt the truth of your Grace's observation, when I have heard the songs of my country," said Arthur; "but I have neither skill nor audacity to intimate what I admire—My latest residence has been in Italy."

"You are perhaps then a proficient in painting," said René; "an art which applies itself to the eye as poetry and music do to the ear, and is scarce less in esteem with us. If you are skilful in the art, you have come to a monarch who loves it, and the fair country in which it is practised."

"In simple truth, Sire, I am an Englishman, and my hand has been too much welk'd and hardened by practice of the bow, the lance, and the sword, to touch the harp or even the pencil."

"An Englishman!" said René, obviously relaxing in the warmth of his welcome; "and what brings you here? England and I have long had little friendship together."

"It is even on that account that I am here," said Arthur. "I come to pay my homage to your Grace's daughter, the Princess Margaret of Anjou, whom I and many true Englishmen regard still as our Queen, though traitors have usurped her title."

"Alas, good youth," said René, "I must grieve for you, while I respect your loyalty and faith. Had my daughter Margaret been of my mind, she had long since abandoned pretensions, which have drowned in seas of blood the noblest and bravest of her adherents."

The King seemed about to say more, but checked himself.

"Go to my palace," he said; "inquire for the Seneschal Hugh de Saint Cyr, he will give thee the means of seeing Margaret—that is, if it be her will to see thee. If not, good English youth, return to my palace, and thou shalt have hospitable entertainment; for a King who loves minstrelsy, music, and painting, is ever most sensible to the claims of honour, virtue, and loyalty; and I read in thy looks thou art possessed of these qualities, and willingly believe thou mayst, in more quiet times, aspire to share the honours of the joyous science. But if thou hast a heart to be touched by the sense of beauty and fair proportion, it will leap within thee at the first sight of my palace, the stately grace of which may be compared to the faultless form of some high-bred dame, or the artful, yet seemingly simple modulations of such a tune as we have been now composing."

The king seemed disposed to take his instrument, and indulge the youth with a rehearsal of the strain he had just arranged; but Arthur at that moment experienced the painful internal feeling of that peculiar species of shame, which well-constructed minds feel when they see others express a great assumption of importance, with a confidence that they are exciting admiration, when in fact they are only exposing themselves to ridicule. Arthur, in short, took leave, "in very shame," of the King of Naples, both the Sicilies, and Jerusalem, in a manner somewhat more abrupt than ceremony demanded. The King looked after him, with some wonder at this want of breeding, which, however, he imputed to his visitor's insular education, and then again began to twangle his viol.

"The old fool!" said Arthur; "his daughter is dethroned, his dominions crumbling to pieces, his family on the eve of becoming extinct, his grandson driven from one lurking-place to another, and expelled from his mother's inheritance,—and he can find amusement in these fopperies! I thought him, with his long white beard, like Nicholas Bonstetten; but the old Swiss is a Solomon compared with him."

As these and other reflections, highly disparaging to King René, passed through Arthur's mind, he reached the place of rendezvous, and found Thiebault beneath the steaming fountain, forced from one of those hot springs which had been the delight of the Romans from an early period. Thiebault, having assured his master that his retinue, horse and man, were so disposed as to be ready on an instant's call, readily undertook to guide him to King René's palace, which, from its singularity, and indeed its beauty of architecture, deserved the eulogium which the old monarch had bestowed upon it. The front consisted of three towers of Roman architecture, two of them being placed on the angles of the palace, and the third, which served the purpose of a mausoleum, forming a part of the group, though somewhat detached from the other buildings. This last was a structure of beautiful proportions. The lower part of the edifice was square, serving as a sort of pedestal to the upper part, which was circular, and surrounded by columns of massive granite. The other two towers at the angles of the palace were round, and also ornamented with pillars, and with a double row of windows. In front of, and connected with, these Roman remains, to which a date has been assigned as early as the fifth or sixth century, arose the ancient palace of the Counts of Provence, built a century or two later, but where a rich Gothic or Moorish front contrasted, and yet harmonised, with the more regular and massive architecture of the lords of the world. It is not more than thirty or forty years since this very curious remnant of antique art was destroyed, to make room for new public buildings, which have never yet been erected.

Arthur really experienced some sensation of the kind which the old King had prophesied, and stood looking with wonder at the ever-open gate of the palace, into which men of all kinds seemed to enter freely. After looking around for a few minutes, the young Englishman ascended the steps of a noble portico, and asked of a porter, as old and as lazy as a great man's domestic ought to be, for the seneschal named to him by the King. The corpulent janitor, with great politeness, put the stranger under the charge of a page, who ushered him to a chamber, in which he found another aged functionary of higher rank, with a comely face, a clear composed eye, and a brow which, having never been knit into gravity, intimated that the seneschal of Aix was a proficient in the philosophy of his royal master. He recognised Arthur the moment he addressed him.

"You speak northern French, fair sir; you have lighter hair and a fairer complexion than the natives of this country—you ask after Queen Margaret—By all these marks I read you English—Her Grace of England is at this moment paying a vow at the monastery of Mont Saint Victoire, and if your name be Arthur Philipson, I have commission to forward you to her presence immediately,—that is, as soon as you have tasted of the royal provision."

The young man would have remonstrated, but the seneschal left him no leisure.

"Meat and mass," he said, "never hindered work—it is perilous to youth to journey too far on an empty stomach—he himself would take a mouthful with the Queen's guest, and pledge him to boot in a flask of old Hermitage."

The board was covered with an alacrity which shewed that hospitality was familiarly exercised in King René's dominions. Pasties, dishes of game, the gallant boar's head, and other delicacies, were placed on the table, and the seneschal played the merry host, frequently apologising (unnecessarily) for shewing an indifferent example, as it was his duty to carve before King René, and the good King was never pleased unless he saw him feed lustily as well as carve featly.

" But for you, sir guest, eat freely, since you may not see food again till sunset; for the good Queen takes her misfortunes so to heart that sighs are her food, and her tears a bottle of drink, as the Psalmist hath it. But I bethink me you will need steeds for yourself and your equipage to reach Mont Saint Victoire, which is seven miles from Aix."

Arthur intimated that he had a guide and horses in attendance, and begged permission to take his adieu. The worthy seneschal, his fair round belly graced with a gold chain, accompanied him to the gate with a step, which a gentle fit of the gout had rendered uncertain, but which, he assured Arthur, would vanish before three days' use of the hot springs. Thiebault appeared before the gate, not with the tired steeds from which they had dismounted an hour since, but with fresh palfreys from the stable of the King.

"They are yours from the moment you have put foot in stirrup," said the seneschal; " the good King René never received back as his property a horse which he had lent to a guest; and that is perhaps one reason why his Highness and we of his household must walk often a-foot."

Here the seneschal exchanged greetings with his young visitor, who rode forth to seek Queen Margaret's place of temporary retirement at the celebrated monastery of Saint Victoire. He demanded of his guide in which direction it lay, who pointed, with an air of triumph, to a mountain three thousand feet and upwards in height, which arose at five or six miles' distance from the town, and which its bold and rocky summit rendered the most distinguished object of the landscape. Thiebault spoke of it with unusual glee and energy, so much so as to lead Arthur to conceive that his trusty squire had not neglected to avail himself of the lavish hospitality of *Le bon Roi Rene.* Thiebault, however, continued to expatiate on the fame of the mountain and monastery. They derived their name, he said, from a great victory which was gained by a Roman general, named Caio Mario, against two large armies of Saracens with ultramontane names, (the Teutones probably and Cimbri,) in gratitude to Heaven for which victory Caio Mario vowed to build a monastery on the mountain for the service of the Virgin Mary, in honour of whom he had been baptized. With all the importance of a local connoisseur, Thiebault proceeded to prove his general assertion by specific facts.

"Yonder," he said, "was the camp of the Saracens, from which, when the battle was apparently decided, their wives and women rushed, with horrible screams, dishevelled hair, and the gestures of furies, and for a time prevailed in stopping the flight of the men."

He pointed out to the river, for access to which, cut off by the superior generalship of the Romans, the barbarians, whom he called Saracens, hazarded the action, and whose streams they empurpled with their blood. In short, he mentioned many circumstances which shewed how accurately tradition will preserve the particulars of ancient events, even whilst forgetting, mistaking, and confounding dates and persons.

Perceiving that Arthur lent him a not unwilling ear,—for it may be supposed that the education of a youth bred up in the heat of civil wars, was not well qualified to criticise his account of the wars of a distant period,—the Provençal, when he had exhausted this topic, drew up close to his master's side, and asked, in a suppressed tone, whether he knew, or was desirous of being made acquainted with, the cause of Margaret's having left Aix, to establish herself in the monastery of Saint Victoire?

"For the accomplishment of a vow," answered Arthur; "all the world knows it."

"All Aix knows the contrary," said Thiebault; "and I can tell you the truth, so I were sure it would not offend your seignorie."

"The truth can offend no reasonable man, so it be expressed in the terms of which Queen Margaret must be spoken in the presence of an Englishman."

Thus replied Arthur, willing to receive what information he could gather, and desirous, at the same time, to check the petulance of his attendant.

"I have nothing," replied his follower, "to state in disparagement of the gracious Queen, whose only misfortune is, that like her royal father, she has more titles than towns. Besides, I know well that you Englishmen, though you speak wildly of your sovereigns yourselves, will not permit others to fail in respect to them."

"Say on, then," answered Arthur.

"Your seignorie must know, then," said Thiebault, "that the good King René has been much disturbed by the deep melancholy which afflicted Queen Margaret, and has bent himself with all his power to change it into a gayer humour. He made entertainments in public and in private; he assembled minstrels and troubadours, whose music and poetry might have drawn smiles from one on his deathbed. The whole country resounded with mirth and glee, and the gracious Queen could not stir abroad in the most private manner, but before she had gone a hundred paces, she lighted on an ambush, consisting of some pretty pageant, or festivous mummery, composed often by the good King himself, which interrupted her solitude, in purpose of relieving her heavy thoughts with some pleasant pastime. But the Queen's deep melancholy rejected all these modes of dispelling it, and at length she confined herself to her own apartments, and absolutely refused to see even her royal father, because he generally brought into her presence those whose productions he thought likely to soothe her sorrow. Indeed she seemed to hear the harpers with loathing, and, excepting one wandering Englishman, who sung a rude and melancholy ballad, which threw her into a flood of tears, and to whom she gave a chain of price, she never seemed to look at, or be conscious of the presence of any one. And at length, as I have had the honour to tell your seignorie, she refused to see even her royal father unless he came alone; and that he found no heart to do."

"I wonder not at it," said the young man; "by the White Swan, I am rather surprised his mummery drove her not to frenzy."

"Something like it indeed took place," said Thiebault; "and I will tell your seignorie how it chanced. You must know that good King René, unwilling to abandon his daughter to the foul fiend of melancholy, bethought him of making a grand effort. You must know further, that the King, powerful in all the craft of Troubadours and Jongleurs, is held in peculiar esteem for conducting mysteries, and other of those gamesome and delightful sports and processions, with which our holy Church permits her graver ceremonies to be relieved and diversified, to the cheering of the hearts of all true children of religion. It is admitted that no one has ever been able to approach his excellence in the arrangement of the Fête-Dieu; and the tune to which the devils cudgel King Herod, to the great edification of all Christian spectators, is of our good King's royal composition. He hath danced at Tarasconne in the ballet of Saint Martha and the Dragon, and was accounted in his own person, the only actor competent to present the Tarrasque. His Highness introduced also a new ritual into the consecration of the Boy Bishop, and composed an entire set of grotesque music for the Festival of Asses. In short, his Grace's strength lies in those pleasing and becoming festivities, which strew the path of edification with flowers, and send men dancing and singing on their way to Heaven.

"Now the good King René, feeling his own genius for such recreative compositions, resolved to exert it to the utmost, in the hope that he might thereby relieve the melancholy in which his daughter was plunged, and which infected all that approached her. It chanced, some short time since, that the Queen was absent for certain days, I know not where or on what business, but it gave the good King time to make his preparations. So when his daughter returned, he with much importunity prevailed on her to make part of a religious procession to Saint Sauveur, the principal church in Aix. The Queen, innocent of what was intended, decked herself with solemnity, to witness and partake of what she expected would prove a work of grave piety. But no sooner had she appeared on the esplanade in front of the palace, than more than an hundred masks, dressed up like Turks, Jews, Saracens, Moors, and I know not whom besides, crowded around to offer her their homage, in the character of the Queen of Sheba; and a grotesque piece of music called them to arrange themselves for a ludicrous ballet, in which they addressed the Queen in the most entertaining manner, and with the most extravagant gestures. The Queen, stunned with the noise, and affronted with the petulance of this unexpected onset, would have gone back into the palace; but the doors had been shut by the King's order so soon as she set forth; and her retreat in that direction was cut off.

Finding herself excluded from the palace, the Queen advanced to the front of the façade, and endeavoured by signs and words to appease the hubbub, but the maskers, who had their instructions, only answered with songs, music, and shouts."

"I would," said Arthur, "there had been a score of English yeomen in presence, with their quarter-staves, to teach the bawling villains respect for one that has worn the crown of England!"

"All the noise that was made before was silence and soft music," continued Thiebault, "till that when the good King himself appeared, grotesquely dressed in the character of King Solomon——"

"To whom, of all princes, he has the least resemblance," said Arthur——

"With such capers and gesticulations of welcome to the Queen of Sheba, as, I 'am assured by those who saw it, would have brought a dead man alive again, or killed a living man with laughing. Among other properties, he had in his hand a truncheon, somewhat formed like a fool's bauble——"

"A most fit sceptre for such a sovereign," said Arthur——

"Which was headed," continued Thiebault, "by a model of the Jewish Temple, finely gilded and curiously cut in pasteboard. He managed this with the utmost grace, and delighted every spectator by his gaiety and activity, excepting the Queen, who, the more he skipped and capered, seemed to be the more incensed, until, on his approaching her to conduct her to the procession, she seemed roused to a sort of frenzy, stuck the truncheon out of his hand, and breaking through the crowd, who felt as if a tigress had leapt amongst them from a showman's cart, rushed into the royal court-yard. Ere the order of the scenic representation, which her violence had interrupted, could be restored, the Queen again issued forth, mounted and attended by two or three English cavaliers of her Majesty's suite. She forced her way through the crowd, without regarding either their safety or her own, flew like a hail-storm along the streets, and never drew bridle till she was as far up this same Mont Saint Victoire as the road would permit. She was then received into the convent, and has since remained there; and a vow of penance is the pretext to cover over the quarrel betwixt her and her father."

"How long may it be," said Arthur, "since these things chanced?"

"It is but three days since Queen Margaret left Aix in the manner I have told you.—But we are come as far up the mountain as men usually ride. See, yonder is the monastery rising betwixt two huge rocks, which form the very top of Mont Saint Victoire. There is no more open ground than is afforded by the cleft, into which the convent of Saint Mary of Victory is, as it were, niched; and the access is guarded by the most dangerous precipices. To ascend the mountain, you must keep that narrow path which, winding and turning among the cliffs, leads at length to the summit of the hill, and the gate of the monastery."

"And what becomes of you and the horses?" said Arthur.

ANNE OF GEIERSTEIN. 257

"We will rest," said Thiebault, "in the hospital maintained by the good fathers at the bottom of the mountain, for the accommodation of those who attend on pilgrims;—for I promise you the shrine is visited by many who come from afar, and are attended both by man and horse.—Care not for me,—I

RUINS AT AIX : PROVENCE.

shall be first under cover; but there muster yonder in the west some threatening clouds, from which your seignorie may suffer inconvenience, unless you reach the convent in time. I will give you an hour to do the feat, and will say you are as active as a chamois hunter, if you reach it within the time."

VOL. II.—17

Arthur looked around him, and did indeed remark a mustering of clouds in the distant west, which threatened soon to change the character of the day, which had hitherto been brilliantly clear, and so serene that the falling of a leaf might have been heard. He therefore turned him to the steep and rocky path which ascended the mountain, sometimes by scaling almost precipitous rocks, and sometimes by reaching their tops by a more circuitous process. It winded through thickets of wild boxwood and other low aromatic shrubs, which afforded some pasture for the mountain goats, but were a bitter annoyance to the traveller who had to press through them. Such obstacles were so frequent, that the full hour allowed by Thiebault had elapsed before he stood on the summit of Mont Saint Victoire, and in front of the singular convent of the same name.

We have already said, that the crest of the mountain, consisting entirely of one bare and solid rock, was divided by a cleft or opening into two heads or peaks, between which the convent was built, occupying all the space between them. The front of the building was of the most ancient and sombre cast of the old Gothic, or rather, as it has been termed, the Saxon; and in that respect corresponded with the savage exterior of the naked cliffs, of which the structure seemed to make a part, and by which it was entirely surrounded, excepting a small open space of more level ground, where, at the expense of much toil, and by carrying earth up the hill, from different spots where they could collect it in small quantities, the good fathers had been able to arrange the accommodations of a garden.

A bell summoned a lay-brother, the porter of this singularly situated monastery, to whom Arthur announced himself as an English merchant, Philipson by name, who came to pay his duty to Queen Margaret. The porter, with much respect, shewed the stranger into the convent, and ushered him into a parlour, which, looking towards Aix, commanded an extensive and splendid prospect over the southern and western parts of Provence. This was the direction in which Arthur had approached the mountain from Aix; but the circuitous path by which he had ascended had completely carried him round the hill. The western side of the monastery, to which the parlour looked, commanded the noble view we have mentioned; and a species of balcony, which, connecting the two twin crags, at this place not above four or five yards asunder, ran along the front of the building, and appeared to be constructed for the purpose of enjoying it. But on stepping from one of the windows of the parlour upon this battlemented bartizan, Arthur became aware that the wall on which the parapet rested stretched along the edge of a precipice, which sunk sheer down five hundred feet at least from the foundations of the convent. Surprised and startled at finding himself on so giddy a verge, Arthur turned his eyes from the gulf beneath him to admire the distant landscape, partly illumined, with ominous lustre, by the now westerly sun. The setting beams shewed in dark red splendour a vast variety of hill and dale, champaign and cultivated ground, with towns, churches, and castles, some of which rose from among trees, while others seemed founded on rocky eminences; others again lurked by the side of streams or lakes, to which the heat and drought of the climate naturally attracted them.

The rest of the landscape presented similar objects when the weather was serene, but they were now rendered indistinct, or altogether obliterated, by the sullen shade of the approaching clouds, which gradually spread over great part of the horizon, and threatened altogether to eclipse the sun, though the lord of the horizon still struggled to maintain his influence, and, like a dying hero, seemed most glorious even in the moment of defeat. Wild sounds, like groans and howls, formed by the wind in the numerous caverns of the rocky mountain, added to the terrors of the scene, and seemed to foretell the fury of some distant storm, though the air in general was even unnaturally calm and breathless. In gazing on this extraordinary scene, Arthur did justice to the monks who had chosen this wild and grotesque situation, from which they could witness Nature in her wildest and grandest demonstrations, and compare the nothingness of humanity with her awful convulsions.

So much was Arthur awed by the scene before him, that he had almost forgotten, while gazing from the bartizan, the important business which had brought him to this place, when it was suddenly recalled by finding himself in the presence of Margaret of Anjou, who, not seeing him in the parlour of reception, had stept upon the balcony, that she might meet with him the sooner.

The Queen's dress was black, without any ornament except a gold coronal of an inch in breadth, restraining her long black tresses, of which advancing years, and misfortunes, had partly altered the hue. There was placed within the circlet a black plume with a red rose, the last of the season, which the good father who kept the garden had presented to her that morning, as the badge of her husband's house. Care, fatigue, and sorrow, seemed to dwell on her brow and her features. To another messenger, she would in all probability have administered a sharp rebuke, for not being alert in his duty to receive her as she entered; but Arthur's age and appearance corresponded with that of her loved and lost son. He was the son of a lady whom Margaret had loved with almost sisterly affection, and the presence of Arthur continued to excite in the dethroned Queen the same feelings of maternal tenderness which had been awakened on their first meeting in the Cathedral of Strasburg. She raised him as he kneeled at her feet, spoke to him with much kindness, and encouraged him to detail at full length his father's message, and such other news as his brief residence at Dijon had made him acquainted with.

She demanded which way Duke Charles had moved with his army.

"As I was given to understand by the master of his artillery," said Arthur, "towards the Lake of Neufchatel, on which side he proposes his first attack on the Swiss."

"The headstrong fool!" said Queen Margaret,—"he resembles the poor lunatic, who went to the summit of the mountain, that he might meet the rain half way.—Does thy father then," continued Margaret, "advise me to give up the last remains of the extensive territories, once the dominions of our royal House, and for some thousand crowns, and the paltry aid of a few hundred lances, to relinquish what is left of our patrimony to our proud and selfish kinsman of Burgundy, who extends his claim to our all, and affords so little help, or even promise of help, in return?"

"I should have ill discharged my father's commission," said Arthur, "if I had left your Highness to think that he recommends so great a sacrifice. He feels most deeply the Duke of Burgundy's grasping desire of dominion. Nevertheless, he thinks that Provence must, on King René's death, or sooner, fall either to the share of Duke Charles, or to Louis of France, whatever opposition your Highness may make to such a destination; and it may be that my father, as a knight and a soldier, hopes much from obtaining the means to make another attempt on Britain. But the decision must rest with your Highness."

"Young man," said the Queen, "the contemplation of a question so doubtful almost deprives me of reason!"

As she spoke, she sank down as one who needs rest, on a stone seat placed on the very verge of the balcony, regardless of the storm, which now began to rise with dreadful gusts of wind, the course of which being intermitted and altered by the crags round which they howled, it seemed as if in very deed Boreas, and Eurus, and Caurus, unchaining the winds from every quarter of heaven, were contending for mastery around the convent of our Lady of Victory. Amid the tumult, and amid billows of mist which concealed the bottom of the precipice, and masses of clouds which racked fearfully over their heads, the roar of the descending waters rather resembled the fall of cataracts than the rushing of torrents of rain. The seat on which Margaret had placed herself was in a considerable degree sheltered from the storm, but its eddies, varying in every direction, often tossed aloft her dishevelled hair; and we cannot describe the appearance of her noble and beautiful, yet ghastly and wasted features, agitated strongly by anxious hesitation, and conflicting thoughts, unless to those of our readers who have had the advantage of having seen our inimitable Siddons in such a character as this. Arthur, confounded by anxiety and terror, could only beseech her Majesty to retire before the fury of the approaching storm, into the interior of the convent.

"No," she replied with firmness; "roofs and walls have ears, and monks, though they have forsworn the world, are not the less curious to know what passes beyond their cells. It is in this place you must hear what I have to say; as a soldier you should scorn a blast of wind or a shower of rain; and to me, who have often held counsel amidst the sound of trumpets and clash of arms, prompt for instant fight, the war of elements is an unnoticed trifle. I tell thee, young Arthur Vere, as I would to your father—as I would to my son—if indeed Heaven had left such a blessing to a wretch forlorn——"

She paused, and then proceeded.

"I tell thee, as I would have told my beloved Edward, that Margaret, whose resolutions were once firm and immovable as these rocks among which we are placed, is now doubtful and variable as the clouds which are drifting around us. I told your father, in the joy of meeting once more a subject of such inappreciable loyalty, of the sacrifices I would make to assure the assistance of Charles of Burgundy, to so gallant an undertaking as that proposed to him by the faithful Oxford. But since I saw him, I have had cause of deep reflection. I met my aged father only to offend, and, I say it with shame, to insult the old man in presence of his people. Our tempers are as opposed as the sunshine, which a short space since gilded a serene and beautiful landscape, differs from the tempests which are now wasting it. I spurned with open scorn and contempt what he, in his mistaken affection, had devised for means of consolation, and, disgusted with the idle follies which he had devised for curing the melancholy of a dethroned Queen, a widowed spouse—and, alas! a childless mother,—I retired hither from the noisy and idle mirth, which was the bitterest aggravation of my sorrows. Such and so gentle is René's temper, that even my unfilial conduct will not diminish my influence over him; and if your father had announced that the Duke of Burgundy, like a knight and a sovereign, had cordially and nobly entered into the plan of the faithful Oxford, I could have found it in my heart to obtain the cession of territory his cold and ambitious policy requires, in order to ensure the assistance, which he now postpones to afford till he has gratified his own haughty humour by settling needless quarrels with his unoffending neighbours. Since I have been here, and calmness and solitude have given me time to reflect, I have thought on the offences I have given the old man, and on the wrongs I was about to do him. My father, let me do him justice, is also the father of his people. They have dwelt under their vines and fig-trees, in ignoble ease, perhaps, but free from oppression and exaction, and their happiness has been that of their good King. Must I change all this?—Must I aid in turning over these contented people to a fierce, headlong, arbitrary prince?—May I not break even the easy and thoughtless heart of my poor old father, should I succeed in urging him to do so?—These are questions which I shudder even to ask myself. On the other hand, to disappoint the toils, the venturous hopes of your father, to forego the only opportunity which may ever again offer itself, of revenge on the bloody traitors of York, and restoration of the House of Lancaster!—Arthur, the scene around us is not so convulsed by the fearful tempest and the driving clouds, as my mind is by doubt and uncertainty."

"Alas!" replied Arthur, "I am too young and inexperienced to be your Majesty's adviser in a case so arduous. I would my father had been in presence himself."

"I know what he would have said," replied the

Queen; "but knowing all, I despair of aid from human counsellors—I have sought others, but they also are deaf to my entreaties. Yes, Arthur, Margaret's misfortunes have rendered her superstitious. Know, that beneath these rocks, and under the foundation of this convent, there runs a cavern, entering by a secret and defended passage a little to the westward of the summit, and running through the mountain, having an opening to the south, from which, as from this bartizan, you can view the landscape so lately seen from this balcony, or the strife of winds and confusion of clouds which we now behold. In the middle of this cavernous thoroughfare is a natural pit, or perforation, of great, but unknown depth. A stone dropped into it is heard to dash from side to side, until the noise of its descent, thundering from cliff to cliff, dies away in distant and faint tinkling, less loud than that of a sheep's bell at a mile's distance. The common people, in their jargon, call this fearful gulf, Lou Garagoule; and the traditions of the monastery annex wild and fearful recollections to a place in itself sufficiently terrible. Oracles, it is said, spoke thence in pagan days, by subterranean voices, arising from the abyss; and from these the Roman general is said to have heard, in strange and uncouth rhymes, promises of the victory which gives name to this mountain. These oracles, it is averred, may be yet consulted after performance of strange rites, in which heathen ceremonies are mixed with Christian acts of devotion. The abbots of Mont Saint Victoire have denounced the consultation of Lou Garagoule, and the spirits who reside there, to be criminal. But as the sin may be expiated by presents to the church, by masses, and penances, the door is sometimes opened by the complaisant fathers to those whose daring curiosity leads them, at all risks, and by whatever means, to search into futurity. Arthur, I have made the experiment, and am even now returned from the gloomy cavern, in which, according to the traditional ritual, I have spent six hours by the margin of the gulf, a place so dismal, that after its horrors even this tempestuous scene is refreshing."

The Queen stopped, and Arthur, the more struck with the wild tale, that it reminded him of his place of imprisonment at La Ferette, asked anxiously, if her inquiries had obtained any answer.

"None whatever," replied the unhappy Princess. "The demons of Garagoule, if there be such, are deaf to the suit of an unfortunate wretch like me, to whom neither friends nor fiends will afford counsel or assistance. It is my father's circumstances which prevent my instant and strong resolution. Were my own claims on this piping and paltry nation of Troubadours alone interested, I could, for the chance of once more setting my foot in merry England, as easily and willingly resign them, and their paltry coronet, as I commit to the storm this idle emblem of the royal rank which I have lost."

As Margaret spoke, she tore from her hair the sable feather and rose which the tempest had detached from the circlet in which they were placed, and tossed them from the battlement with a gesture of wild energy. They were instantly whirled off in a bickering eddy of the agitated clouds, which swept the feather far distant into empty space, through which the eye could not pursue it. But while that of Arthur involuntarily strove to follow its course, a contrary gust of wind caught the red rose, and drove it back against his breast, so that it was easy for him to catch hold of and retain it.

"Joy, joy, and good fortune, royal mistress!" he said, returning to her the emblematic flower; "the tempest brings back the badge of Lancaster to its proper owner."

"I accept the omen," said Margaret; "but it concerns yourself, noble youth, and not me. The feather which is borne away to waste and desolation, is Margaret's emblem. My eyes will never see the restoration of the line of Lancaster. But you will live to behold it, and to aid to achieve it, and to dye our red rose deeper yet in the blood of tyrants and traitors. My thoughts are so strangely poised, that a feather or a flower may turn the scale. But my head is still giddy, and my heart sick.—To-morrow you shall see another Margaret, and till then adieu."

It was time to retire, for the tempest began to be mingled with fiercer showers of rain. When they re-entered the parlour, the Queen clapped her hands, and two female attendants entered.

"Let the Father Abbot know," she said, "that it is our desire that this young gentleman receive for this night such hospitality as befits an esteemed friend of ours.—Till to-morrow, young sir, farewell."

With a countenance which betrayed not the late emotion of her mind, and with a stately courtesy, that would have become her when she graced the halls of Windsor, she extended her hand, which the youth saluted respectfully. After her leaving the parlour, the Abbot entered, and in his attention to Arthur's entertainment and accommodation for the evening, shewed his anxiety to meet and obey Queen Margaret's wishes.

CHAPTER THE THIRTY-FIRST.

―――Want you a man
Experienced in the world and its affairs?
Here he is for your purpose.—He's a monk.
He hath forsworn the world and all its work
The rather that he knows it passing well,
Special the worst of it, for he's a monk.
                              OLD PLAY.

WHILE the dawn of the morning was yet grey, Arthur was awakened by a loud ringing at the gate of the monastery, and presently afterwards the porter entered the cell which had been allotted to him for his lodgings, to tell him, that if his name was Arthur Philipson, a brother of their order had brought him despatches from his father. The youth started up, hastily attired himself, and was introduced, in the parlour, to a Carmelite monk, being of the same order with the community of Saint Victoire.

"I have ridden many a mile, young man, to present you with this letter," said the monk, "having undertaken to your father that it should be delivered without delay. I came to Aix last night during the storm, and learning at the palace that you had ridden hither, I mounted as soon as the tempest abated, and here I am."

"I am beholden to you, father," said the youth, "and if I could repay your pains with a small donative to your convent――"

"By no means," answered the good father; "I took my personal trouble out of friendship to your father, and mine own errand led me this way. The expenses of my long journey have been amply provided for. But open your packet, I can answer your questions at leisure."

The young man accordingly stepped into an embrasure of the window, and read as follows:—

"SON ARTHUR,—Touching the state of the country, in so far as concerns the safety of travelling, know that the same is precarious. The Duke hath taken the towns of Brie and Granson, and put to death five hundred men, whom he made prisoners in garrison there. But the Confederates are approaching with a large force, and God will judge for the right. Howsoever the game may go, these are sharp wars, in which little quarter is spoken of on either side, and therefore there is no safety for men of our profession, till something decisive shall happen. In the meantime, you may assure the widowed lady that our correspondent continues well disposed to purchase the property which she has in hand; but will scarce be able to pay the price till his present pressing affairs shall be settled, which I hope will be in time to permit us to embark the funds in the profitable adventure I told our friend of. I have employed a friar, travelling to Provence, to carry this letter, which I trust will come safe. The bearer may be trusted.

"Your affectionate father,
"JOHN PHILIPSON."

Arthur easily comprehended the latter part of the epistle, and rejoiced he had received it at so critical a moment. He questioned the Carmelite on the amount of the Duke's army, which the monk stated to amount to sixty thousand men, while he said the Confederates, though making every exertion, had not yet been able to assemble the third part of that number. The young Ferrand de Vaudemont was with their army, and had received, it was thought, some secret assistance from France; but as he was little known in arms, and had few followers, the empty title of General which he bore, added little to the strength of the Confederates. Upon the whole, he reported, that every chance appeared to be in favour of Charles, and Arthur, who looked upon his success as presenting the only chance in favour of his father's enterprise, was not a little pleased to find it ensured, as far as depended on a great superiority of force. He had no leisure to make farther inquiries, for the Queen at that moment entered the apartment, and the Carmelite, learning her quality, withdrew from her presence in deep reverence.

The paleness of her complexion still bespoke the fatigues of the day preceding; but as she graciously bestowed on Arthur the greetings of the morning, her voice was firm, her eye clear, and her countenance steady. "I meet you," she said, "not as I left you, but determined in my purpose. I am satisfied, that if René does not voluntarily yield up his throne of Provence, by some step like that which we propose, he will be hurled from it by violence, in which, it may be, his life will not be spared. We will, therefore, to work with all speed—the worst is, that I cannot leave this convent till I have made the necessary penances for having visited the Garagoule, without performing which, I were no Christian woman. When you return to Aix, inquire at the palace for my secretary, with whom this line will give you credence. I have, even before this door of hope opened to me, endeavoured to form an estimate of King René's situation, and collected the documents for that purpose. Tell him to send me, duly sealed, and under fitting charge, the small cabinet hooped with silver. Hours of penance for past errors may be employed to prevent others; and, from the contents of that cabinet, I shall learn whether I am, in this weighty matter, sacrificing my father's interests to my own half-desperate hopes. But of this I have little or no doubt. I can cause the deeds of resignation and transference to be drawn up here under my own direction, and arrange the execution of them when I return to Aix, which shall be the first moment after my penance is concluded."

"And this letter, gracious madam," said Arthur, "will inform you what events are approaching, and of what importance it may be to take time by the forelock. Place me but in possession of these momentous deeds, and I will travel night and day till I reach the Duke's camp. I shall find him most likely in the moment of victory, and with his heart too much open to refuse a boon to the royal kinswoman who is surrendering to him all. We will—we must—in such an hour, obtain princely succours; and we shall soon see if the licentious Edward of York, the savage

Richard, the treacherous and perjured Clarence, are hereafter to be lords of merry England, or whether they must give place to a more rightful sovereign and better man. But O! royal madam, all depends on haste."

"True—yet a few days may—nay, must—cast the die between Charles and his opponents; and, ere making so great a surrender, it were as well to be assured that he whom we would propitiate, is in capacity to assist us.—All the events of a tragic and varied life have led me to see there is no such thing as an inconsiderable enemy. I will make haste, however, trusting in the interim we may have good news from the banks of the lake at Neufchatel."

"But who shall be employed to draw these most important deeds?" said the young man.

Margaret mused ere she replied,—"The Father Guardian is complaisant, and I think faithful; but I would not willingly repose confidence in one of the Provençal monks. Stay, let me think—your father says the Carmelite who brought the letter may be trusted—he shall do the turn. He is a stranger, and will be silent for a piece of money. Farewell, Arthur de Vere.—You will be treated with all hospitality by my father. If thou dost receive farther tidings, thou wilt let me know them; or, should I have instructions to send, thou wilt hear from me. — So, benedicite."

Arthur proceeded to wind down the mountain at a much quicker pace than he had ascended on the day before. The weather was now gloriously serene, and the beauties of vegetation, in a country where it never totally slumbers, were at once delicious and refreshing. His thoughts wandered from the crags of Mont Saint Victoire, to the cliff of the canton of Unterwalden, and fancy recalled the moments when his walks through such scenery were not solitary, but when there was a form by his side, whose simple beauty was engraved on his memory. Such thoughts were of a pre-occupying nature; and I grieve to say, that they entirely drowned the recollection of the mysterious caution given him by his father, intimating that Arthur might not be able to comprehend such letters as he should receive from him, till they were warmed before a fire.

The first thing which reminded him of this singular caution, was the seeing a chafing dish of charcoal in the kitchen of the hostelrie at the bottom of the mountain, where he found Thiebault and his horses. This was the first fire which he had seen since receiving his father's letter, and it reminded him not unnaturally of what the Earl had recommended. Great was his surprise to see, that after exposing the paper to the fire as if to dry it, a word emerged in an important passage of the letter, and the concluding words now read—"The bearer may *not* be trusted." Well-nigh choked with shame and vexation, Arthur could think of no other remedy than instantly to return to the convent, and acquaint the Queen with this discovery, which he hoped still to convey to her in time to prevent any risk being incurred by the Carmelite's treachery.

Incensed at himself, and eager to redeem his fault, he bent his manly breast against the steep hill,

TOWN OF AIX ; PROVENCE

which was probably never scaled in so short time as by the young heir of De Vere; for, within forty minutes from his commencing the ascent, he stood breathless and panting in the presence of Queen Margaret, who was alike surprised at his appearance and his exhausted condition.

"Trust not the Carmelite!"—he exclaimed—" You are betrayed, noble Queen, and it is by my negligence. Here is my dagger—bid me strike it into my heart!"

Margaret demanded and obtained a more special explanation, and when it was given, she said, "It is an unhappy chance; but your father's instructions ought to have been more distinct. I have told yonder Carmelite the purpose of the contracts, and engaged with him to draw them. He has but now left me to serve at the choir. There is no withdrawing the confidence I have unhappily placed; but I can easily prevail with the Father Guardian to prevent the monk from leaving the convent till we are indifferent to his secrecy. It is our best chance to secure it, and we will take care that what inconvenience he sustains by his detention shall be well recompensed. Meanwhile, rest thou, good Arthur, and undo the throat of thy mantle. Poor youth, thou art well-nigh exhausted with thy haste."

Arthur obeyed, and sat down on a seat in the parlour; for the speed which he had exerted rendered him almost incapable of standing.

"If I could but see," he said, "the false monk, I would find a way to charm him to secrecy!"

"Better leave him to me," said the Queen; "and

in a word, I forbid you to meddle with him. The coif can treat better with the cowl than the casque can do. Say no more of him. I joy to see you wear around your neck the holy relic I bestowed on you;—but what Moorish charmlet is that you wear beside it? Alas! I need not ask. Your heightened colour, almost as deep as when you entered a quarter of an hour hence, confesses a true-love token. Alas! poor boy, hast thou not only such a share of thy country's woes to bear, but also thine own load of affliction, not the less poignant now that future time will shew thee how fantastic it is! Margaret of Anjou could once have aided wherever thy affections were placed; but now she can only contribute to the misery of her friends, not to their happiness. But this lady of the chain, Arthur, is she fair—is she wise and virtuous—is she of noble birth—and does she love?"—She perused his countenance with the glance of an eagle, and continued, "To all, thou wouldst answer Yes, if shamefacedness permitted thee. Love her then in turn, my gallant boy, for love is the parent of brave actions. Go, my noble youth—high-born and loyal, valorous and virtuous, enamoured and youthful, to what mayest thou not rise? The chivalry of ancient Europe only lives in a bosom like thine. Go, and let the praises of a Queen fire thy bosom with the love of honour and achievement. In three days we meet at Aix."

Arthur, highly gratified with the Queen's condescension, once more left her presence.

Returning down the mountain with a speed very different from that which he had used in the ascent, he again found his Provençal squire, who had remained in much surprise at witnessing the confusion in which his master had left the inn, almost immediately after he had entered it without any apparent haste or agitation. Arthur explained his hasty return by alleging he had forgot his purse at the convent. "Nay, in that case," said Thiebault, "considering what you left and where you left it, I do not wonder at your speed; though, our Lady save me, as I never saw living creature, save a goat with a wolf at his heels, make his way over crag and briers with half such rapidity as you did."

They reached Aix after about an hour's riding, and Arthur lost no time in waiting upon the good King René, who gave him a kind reception, both in respect of the letter from the Duke of Burgundy, and in consideration of his being an Englishman, the avowed subject of the unfortunate Margaret. The placable monarch soon forgave his young guest the want of complaisance with which he had eschewed to listen to his compositions; and Arthur speedily found, that to apologise for his want of breeding in that particular, was likely to lead to a great deal more rehearsing than he could find patience to tolerate. He could only avoid the old King's extreme desire to recite his own poems, and perform his own music, by engaging him in speaking of his daughter Margaret. Arthur had been sometimes induced to doubt the influence which the Queen boasted herself to possess over her aged father; but on being acquainted with him personally, he became convinced that her powerful understanding and violent passions inspired the feeble-minded and passive King with a mixture of pride, affection, and fear, which united to give her the most ample authority over him.

Although she had parted with him but a day or two since, and in a manner so ungracious on her side, René was as much overjoyed at hearing of the probability of her speedy return, as the fondest father could have been at the prospect of being reunited to the most dutiful child, whom he had not seen for years. The old King was impatient as a boy for the day of her arrival, and, still strangely unenlightened on the difference of her taste from his own, he was with difficulty induced to lay aside a project of meeting her in the character of old Palemon,—

"The prince of shepherds, and their pride,"

at the head of an Arcadian procession of nymphs and swains, to inspire whose choral dances and songs, every pipe and tambourine in the country was to be placed in requisition. Even the old seneschal, however, intimated his disapprobation of this species of *joyeuse entrée*; so that René suffered himself at length to be persuaded that the Queen was too much occupied by the religious impressions to which she had been of late exposed, to receive any agreeable sensation from sights or sounds of levity. The King gave way to reasons which he could not sympathise with; and thus Margaret escaped the shock of welcome, which would perhaps have driven her in her impatience back to the mountain of Saint Victoire, and the sable cavern of Lou Garagoule.

During the time of her absence, the days of the court of Provence were employed in sports and rejoicings of every description; tilting at the barrier with blunted spears, riding at the ring, parties for hare-hunting and falconry, frequented by the youth of both sexes, in the company of whom the King delighted, while the evenings were consumed in dancing and music.

Arthur could not but be sensible, that not long since all this would have made him perfectly happy; but the last months of his existence had developed his understanding and passions. He was now initiated in the actual business of human life, and looked on its amusements with an air of something like contempt; so that among the young and gay noblesse, who composed this merry court, he acquired the title of the youthful philosopher, which was not bestowed upon him, it may be supposed, as inferring anything of peculiar compliment.

On the fourth day news were received, by an express messenger, that Queen Margaret would enter Aix before the hour of noon, to resume her residence in her father's palace. The good King René seemed, as it drew nigh, to fear the interview with his daughter as much as he had previously desired it, and contrived to make all around him partake of his fidgety anxiety. He tormented his steward and cooks to recollect what dishes they had ever observed her to taste of with approbation—he pressed the musicians to remember the tunes which she approved, and when one of them boldly replied he had never known her Majesty endure any strain with patience, the old monarch threatened to turn him out of his service for slandering the taste of his daughter. The banquet was ordered to be served at half-past eleven, as if accelerating it would have had the least effect upon hurrying the arrival of the expected guests; and the old King, with his napkin over his arm, traversed the hall from window to window, wearying every one with questions, whether they saw anything of the Queen of England. Exactly as the bells tolled noon, the Queen, with a very small retinue, chiefly English, and in mourning habits like herself, rode into the town of Aix. King René, at the head of his court, failed not to descend from the front of his stately palace, and move along the street to meet his daughter. Lofty, proud, and jealous of incurring ridicule, Margaret was not pleased with this public greeting in the market-place. But she was desirous at present to make amends for her late petulance, and therefore she descended from her palfrey; and although something shocked at seeing René equipped with a napkin, she humbled herself to bend the knee to him, asking at once his blessing and forgiveness.

"Thou hast—thou hast my blessing, my suffering dove," said the simple King to the proudest and most impatient princess that ever wept for a lost crown.—" And for thy pardon, how canst thou ask it, who never didst me an offence since God made me father to so gracious a child?—Rise, I say rise—nay, it is for me to ask thy pardon—True, I said in my ignorance, and thought within myself, that my heart had indited a goodly thing—but it vexed thee. It is therefore for me to crave pardon."—And down sunk good King René upon both knees; and the people, who are usually captivated with anything resembling the trick of the scene, applauded with much noise, and some smothered laughter, a situation in which the royal daughter and her parent seemed about to rehearse the scene of the Roman Charity.

Margaret, sensitively alive to shame, and fully aware that her present position was sufficiently ludicrous in its publicity at least, signed sharply to Arthur, whom she saw in the King's suite, to come to her; and using his arm to rise, she muttered to him aside, and in English,—"To what saint shall I vow myself, that I may preserve patience when I so much need it!"

"For pity's sake, royal madam, recall your firmness of mind and composure," whispered her esquire, who felt at the moment more embarrassed than honoured by his distinguished office, for he could feel that the Queen actually trembled with vexation and impatience.

They at length resumed their route to the palace, the father and daughter arm-in-arm, a posture most agreeable to Margaret, who could bring herself to endure her father's effusions of tenderness, and the general tone of his conversation, so that he was not overheard by others. In the same manner, she bore with laudable patience the teazing attentions which he addressed to her at table, noticed some of his particular courtiers, inquired after others, led the way to his favourite subjects of conversation on poetry, painting, and music, till the good King was as much delighted with the unwonted civilities of his daughter, as ever was lover with the favourable confessions of his mistress, when after years of warm courtship, the ice of her bosom is at length thawed. It cost the haughty Margaret an effort to bend herself to play this part—her pride rebuked her for stooping to flatter her father's foibles, in order to bring him over to the resignation of his dominions—yet having undertaken to do so, and so much having been already hazarded upon this sole remaining chance of success in an attack upon England, she saw, or was willing to see, no alternative.

Betwixt the banquet, and the ball by which it was to be followed, the Queen sought an opportunity of speaking to Arthur.

"Bad news, my sage counsellor," she said. "The Carmelite never returned to the convent after the service was over. Having learned that you had come back in great haste, he had, I suppose, concluded he might stand in suspicion, so he left the convent of Mont Saint Victoire."

"We must hasten the measures which your Majesty has resolved to adopt," answered Arthur.

"I will speak with my father to-morrow. Meanwhile, you must enjoy the pleasures of the evening, for to you they may be pleasures.—Young lady of Boisgelin, I give you this cavalier to be your partner for the evening."

The black-eyed and pretty Provençale courtesied with due decorum, and glanced at the handsome young Englishman with an eye of approbation; but whether afraid of his character as a philosopher, or his doubtful rank, added the saving clause,—"If my mother approves."

"Your mother, damsel, will scarce, I think, disapprove of any partner whom you receive from the hands of Margaret of Anjou. Happy privilege of youth," she added with a sigh, as the youthful couple went off to take their place in the *bransle*,* "which can snatch a flower even on the roughest road."

Arthur acquitted himself so well during the evening, that perhaps the young Countess was only sorry that so gay and handsome a gallant limited his compliments and attentions within the cold bounds of that courtesy enjoined by the rules of ceremony.

* Bransle, in English, brawl,—a species of dance.

CHAPTER THE THIRTY-SECOND.

> For I have given here my full consent,
> To undeck the pompous body of a king,
> Make glory base, and sovereignty a slave,
> Proud Majesty a subject, state a peasant.
>
> RICHARD II.

THE next day opened a grave scene. King René had not forgotten to arrange the pleasures of the day, when, to his horror and discomfiture, Margaret demanded an interview upon serious business. If there was a proposition in the world which René from his soul detested, it was any that related to the very name of business.

"What was it that his child wanted?" he said. "Was it money? He would give her whatever ready sums he had, though he owned his exchequer was somewhat bare; yet he had received his income for the season. It was ten thousand crowns. How much should he desire to be paid to her?—the half—three parts—or the whole? All was at her command."

"Alas, my dear father," said Margaret, "it is not my affairs, but your own, on which I desire to speak with you."

"If the affairs are mine," said René, "I am surely master to put them off to another day—to some rainy dull day, fit for no better purpose. See, my love, the hawking party are all on their steeds and ready—the horses are neighing and pawing—the gallants and maidens mounted, and ready with hawk on fist—the spaniels struggling in the leash. It were a sin, with wind and weather to friend, to lose so lovely a morning."

"Let them ride their way," said Queen Margaret, "and find their sport; for the matter I have to speak concerning involves honour and rank, life and means of living."

"Nay, but I have to hear and judge between Calezon and John of Acqua Mortis, the two most celebrated Troubadours."

"Postpone their cause till to morrow," said Margaret, "and dedicate an hour or two to more important affairs."

"If you are peremptory," replied King René, "you are aware, my child, I cannot say you nay."

And with reluctance he gave orders for the hawkers to go on and follow their sport, as he could not attend them that day.

The old King then suffered himself, like an unwilling greyhound withheld from the chase, to be led into a separate apartment. To ensure privacy, Margaret stationed her secretary, Mordaunt, with Arthur, in an antechamber, giving them orders to prevent all intrusion.

"Nay, for myself, Margaret," said the good-natured old man, "since it must be, I consent to be put *au secret;* but why keep old Mordaunt from taking a walk in this beautiful morning; and why prevent young Arthur from going forth with the rest? I promise you though they term him a philosopher, yet he shewed as light a pair of heels last night with the young Countess de Boisgelin, as any gallant in Provence."

"They are come from a country," said Margaret, "in which men are trained from infancy to prefer their duty to their pleasure."

The poor King, led into the council-closet, saw with internal shuddering, the fatal cabinet of ebony, bound with silver, which had never been opened but to overwhelm him with weariness, and dolefully calculated how many yawns he must strangle ere he sustained the consideration of its contents. They proved, however, when laid before him, of a kind that excited even his interest, though painfully.

His daughter presented him with a short and clear view of the debts which were secured on his dominions, and for which they were mortgaged in various pieces and parcels. She then shewed him, by another schedule, the large claims of which payment was instantly demanded, to discharge which no funds could be found or assigned. The King defended himself like others in his forlorn situation. To every claim of six, seven, or eight thousand ducats, he replied by the assertion, that he had ten thousand crowns in his chancery, and shewed some reluctance to be convinced, till repeatedly urged upon him, that the same sum could not be adequate to the discharge of thirty times the amount.

"Then," said the King, somewhat impatiently, "why not pay off those who are most pressing, and let the others wait till receipts come round?"

"It is a practice which has been too often resorted

to," replied the Queen, "and it is but a part of honesty to pay creditors who have advanced their all in your Grace's service."

"But are we not," said René, "King of both the Sicilies, Naples, Arragon, and Jerusalem? And why is the monarch of such fair kingdoms to be pushed to the wall, like a bankrupt yeoman, for a few bags of paltry crowns?"

"You are indeed monarch of these kingdoms," said Margaret; "but is it necessary to remind your Majesty that it is but as I am Queen of England, in which I have not an acre of land, and cannot command a penny of revenue? You have no dominions which are a source of revenue, save those which you see in this scroll, with an exact list of the income they afford. It is totally inadequate, you see, to maintain your state, and to pay the large engagements incurred to former creditors."

"It is cruel to press me to the wall thus," said the poor King. "What can I do? If I am poor, I cannot help it. I am sure I would pay the debts you talk of, if I knew the way."

"Royal father, I will shew it you.—Resign your useless and unavailing dignity, which, with the pretensions attending it, serves but to make your miseries ridiculous. Resign your rights as a sovereign, and the income which cannot be stretched out to the empty excesses of a beggarly court, will enable you to enjoy, in ease and opulence, all the pleasures you most delight in as a private baron."

"Margaret, you speak folly," answered René, somewhat sternly. "A king and his people are bound by ties which neither can sever without guilt. My subjects are my flock, I am their shepherd. They are assigned to my governance by Heaven, and I dare not renounce the charge of protecting them."

"Were you in condition to do so," answered the Queen, "Margaret would bid you fight to the death. But don your harness, long disused — mount your war-steed — cry, René for Provence! and see if a hundred men will gather round your standard. Your fortresses are in the hands of strangers; army you have none; your vassals may have good-will, but they lack all military skill and soldier-like discipline. You stand but the mere skeleton of monarchy, which France or Burgundy may prostrate on the earth, whichever first puts forth his arm to throw it down."

The tears trickled fast down the old King's cheeks, when this unflattering prospect was set before him, and he could not forbear owning his total want of power to defend himself, and his dominions, and admitting that he had often thought of the necessity of compounding for his resignation with one of his powerful neighbours.

"It was thy interest, Margaret, harsh and severe as you are, which prevented my entering, before now, into measures most painful to my feelings, but perhaps best calculated for my advantage. But I had hoped it would hold on for my day; and thou, my child, with the talents Heaven has given thee, wouldst, I thought, have found remedy for distresses, which I cannot escape, otherwise than by shunning the thought of them."

"If it is in earnest you speak of my interest," said

Margaret, "know, that your resigning Provence will satisfy the nearest, and almost the only wish that my bosom can form; but, so judge me Heaven, as it is on your account, gracious sire, as well as mine, that I advise your compliance."

"Say no more on't, child; give me the parchment of resignation, and I will sign it: I see thou hast it ready drawn; let us sign it, and then we will overtake the hawkers. We must suffer woe, but there is little need to sit down and weep for it."

"Do you not ask," said Margaret, surprised at his apathy, "to whom you cede your dominions?"

"What boots it," answered the King, "since they must be no more my own? It must be either to Charles of Burgundy, or my nephew Louis—both powerful and politic princes. God send my poor people may have no cause to wish their old man back again, whose only pleasure was to see them happy and mirthful."

"It is to Burgundy you resign Provence," said Margaret.

"I would have preferred him," answered René; "he is fierce, but not malignant. One word more—are my subjects' privileges and immunities fully secured?"

"Amply," replied the Queen; "and your own wants of all kinds honourably provided for. I would not leave the stipulations in your favour blank, though I might perhaps have trusted Charles of Burgundy, where money alone is concerned."

"I ask not for myself—with my viol and my pencil, René the Troubadour will be as happy as ever was René the King."

So saying, with practical philosophy he whistled the burden of his last composed ariette, and signed away the rest of his royal possessions without pulling off his glove, or even reading the instrument.

"What is this?" he said, looking at another and separate parchment of much briefer contents. "Must my kinsman Charles have both the Sicilies, Catalonia, Naples, and Jerusalem, as well as the poor remainder of Provence? Methinks, in decency, some greater extent of parchment should have been allowed to so ample a cession."

"That deed," said Margaret, "only disowns and relinquishes all countenance of Ferrand de Vaudemont's rash attempt on Lorraine, and renounces all quarrel on that account against Charles of Burgundy."

For once Margaret miscalculated the tractability of her father's temper. René positively started, coloured, and stammered with passion, as he interrupted her. — "*Only* disown — *only* relinquish — *only* renounce the cause of my grandchild, the son of my dear Yolande — his rightful claims on his mother's inheritance! — Margaret, I am ashamed for thee. Thy pride is an excuse for thy evil temper; but what is pride worth which can stoop to commit an act of dishonourable meanness? To desert, nay, disown my own flesh and blood, because the youth is a bold knight under shield, and disposed to battle for his right — I were worthy that harp and horn rung out shame on me, should I listen to thee."

Margaret was overcome in some measure by the old man's unexpected opposition. She endeavoured, however, to shew that there was no occasion, in point of honour, why René should engage in the cause of a wild adventurer, whose right, be it good be it bad, was only upheld by some petty and underhand supplies of money from France, and the countenance of a few of the restless banditti who inhabit the borders of all nations. But ere René could answer, voices raised to an unusual pitch were heard in the antechamber, the door of which was flung open by an armed knight, covered with dust, who exhibited all the marks of a long journey.

"Here I am," he said, "father of my mother—behold your grandson—Ferrand de Vaudemont; the son of your lost Yolande kneels at your feet, and implores a blessing on him and his enterprise."

"Thou hast it," replied René, "and may it prosper with thee, gallant youth, image of thy sainted mother—my blessings, my prayers, my hopes, go with you!"

"And you, fair aunt of England," said the young knight, addressing Margaret, "you who are yourself dispossessed by traitors, will you not own the cause of a kinsman who is struggling for his inheritance?"

"I wish all good to your person, fair nephew," answered the Queen of England, "although your features are strange to me. But to advise this old man to adopt your cause, when it is desperate in the eyes of all wise men, were impious madness."

"Is my cause then so desperate?" said Ferrand; "forgive me if I was not aware of it. And does my aunt Margaret say this, whose strength of mind supported Lancaster so long, after the spirits of her warriors had been quelled by defeat? What—forgive me, for my cause must be pleaded—what would you have said had my mother Yolande been capable to advise her father to disown your own Edward, had God permitted him to reach Provence in safety?"

"Edward," said Margaret, weeping as she spoke, "was incapable of desiring his friends to espouse a quarrel that was irremediable. His, too, was a cause for which mighty princes and peers laid lance in rest."

"Yet Heaven blessed it not," said Vaudemont.

"Thine," continued Margaret, "is but embraced by the robber nobles of Germany, the upstart burghers of the Rhine cities, the paltry and clownish Confederates of the Cantons."

"But Heaven *has blessed it*," replied Vaudemont. "Know, proud woman, that I come to interrupt your treacherous intrigues; no petty adventurer, subsisting and maintaining warfare by sleight rather than force, but a conqueror from a bloody field of battle, in which Heaven has tamed the pride of the tyrant of Burgundy."

"It is false!" said the Queen, starting; "I believe it not."

"It is true," said De Vaudemont, "as true as Heaven is above us.—It is four days since I left the field of Granson, heaped with Burgundy's mercenaries—his wealth, his jewels, his plate, his magnificent decorations, the prize of the poor Swiss, who scarce can tell their value. Know you this, Queen Margaret?" continued the young soldier, shewing the well-known jewel which decorated the Duke's order of the Golden Fleece; "think you not the lion was closely hunted when he left such trophies as these behind him?"

Margaret looked with dazzled eyes and bewildered thoughts, upon a token which confirmed the Duke's defeat, and the extinction of her last hopes. Her father, on the contrary, was struck with the heroism of the young warrior, a quality which, except as it existed in his daughter Margaret, had, he feared, taken leave of his family. Admiring in his heart the youth who exposed himself to danger for the meed of praise, almost as much as he did the poets by whom the warrior's fame is rendered immortal, he hugged his grandson to his bosom, bidding him "gird on his sword in strength," and assuring him, if money could advance his affairs, he, King René, could command ten thousand crowns, any part, or the whole of which, was at Ferrand's command; thus giving proof of what had been said of him, that his head was incapable of containing two ideas at the same time.

We return to Arthur, who, with the Queen of England's secretary, Mordaunt, had been not a little surprised by the entrance of the Count de Vaudemont, calling himself Duke of Lorraine, into the anteroom, in which they kept a kind of guard, followed by a tall strong Swiss, with a huge halberd over his shoulder. The prince naming himself, Arthur did not think it becoming to oppose his entrance to the presence of his grandfather and aunt, especially as it was obvious that his opposition must have created an affray. In the huge staring halberdier, who had sense enough to remain in the anteroom, Arthur was not a little surprised to recognise Sigismund Biederman, who, after staring wildly at him for a moment, like a dog which suddenly recognises a favourite, rushed up to the young Englishman with a wild cry of gladness, and in hurried accents, told him how happy he was to meet with him, and that he had matters of importance to tell him. It was at no time easy for Sigismund to arrange his ideas, and now they were altogether confused by the triumphant joy which he expressed for the recent victory of his countrymen over the Duke of Burgundy; and it was with wonder that Arthur heard his confused and rude, but faithful tale.

"Look you, King Arthur, the Duke had come up with his huge army as far as Granson, which is near the outlet of the great lake of Neufchatel. There were five or six hundred Confederates in the place, and they held it till provisions failed, and then you know they were forced to give it over. But though hunger is hard to bear, they had better have borne it a day or two longer, for the butcher Charles hung them all up by the neck, upon trees round the place, —and there was no swallowing for them, you know, after such usage as that. Meanwhile all was busy on our hills, and every man that had a sword or lance accoutred himself with it. We met at Neufchatel, and some Germans joined us with the noble Duke of Lorraine. Ah, King Arthur, there is a leader!—we all think him second but to Rudolph of Donnerhugel—you saw him even now—it was he that went into that room—and you saw him before, —it is he that was the Blue Knight of Bâle; but we

PORTRAIT OF QUEEN MARGARET,
FROM THE LATE COLLECTION AT STRAWBERRY HILL.

called him Laurenz then, for Rudolph said his presence among us must not be known to our father, and I did not know myself at that time who he really was. Well, when we came to Neufchatel we were a goodly company; we were fifteen thousand stout Confederates, and of others, Germans and Lorraine men, I will warrant you five thousand more. We heard that the Burgundian was sixty thousand in the field; but we heard at the same time, that Charles had hung up our brethren like dogs, and the man was not among us—among the Confederates, I mean —who would stay to count heads, when the question was to avenge them. I would you could have heard the roar of fifteen thousand Swiss demanding to be led against the butcher of their brethren! My father himself, who you know, is usually so eager for peace, now gave the first voice for battle; so, in the grey of the morning we descended the lake towards Granson, with tears in our eyes and weapons in our hands, determined to have death or vengeance. We came to a sort of strait, between Vauxmoreux and the lake; there were horse on the level ground between the mountain and the lake, and a large body of infantry on the side of the hill. The Duke of Lorraine and his followers engaged the horse, while we climbed the hill to dispossess the infantry. It was with us the affair of a moment. Every man of us was at home among the crags, and Charles's men were stuck among them as thou wert, Arthur, when thou didst first come to Geierstein. But there were no kind maidens to lend them their hands to help them down. No, no—There were pikes, clubs, and halberds, many a one, to dash and thrust them from places where they could hardly keep their feet had there been no one to disturb them. So the horsemen, pushed by the Lorrainers, and seeing us upon their flanks, fled as fast as their horses could carry them. Then we drew together again on a fair field, which is *buon campagna,* as the Italian says, where the hills retire from the lake. But lo you, we had scarce arrayed our ranks, when we heard such a din and clash of instruments, such a trample of their great horses, such a shouting and crying of men, as if all the soldiers, and all the minstrels in France and Germany, were striving which should make the loudest noise. Then there was a huge cloud of dust approaching us, and we began to see we must do or die, for this was Charles and his whole army come to support his vanguard. A blast from the mountain dispersed the dust, for they had halted to prepare for battle. O, good Arthur! you would have given ten years of life but to have seen the sight. There were thousands of horse, all in complete array, glancing against the sun, and hundreds of knights with crowns of gold and silver on their helmets, and thick masses of spears on foot, and cannon, as they call them. I did not know what things they were, which they drew on heavily with bullocks and placed before their army, but I knew more of them before the morning was over. Well, we were ordered to draw up in a hollow square, as we are taught at exercise, and before we pushed forwards, we were commanded, as is the godly rule and guise of our warfare, to kneel down and pray to God, Our Lady, and the blessed saints; and we afterwards learned that Charles, in his arrogance, thought we asked for mercy —Ha! ha! ha! a proper jest. If my father once knelt to him, it was for the sake of Christian blood and godly peace; but on the field of battle, Arnold Biederman would not have knelt to him and his whole chivalry, though he had stood alone with his sons on that field. Well, but Charles, supposing we asked grace, was determined to shew us that we had asked it at a graceless face, for he cried, 'Fire my cannon on the coward slaves; it is all the mercy they have to expect from me!'—Bang—bang—bang —off went the things I told you of, like thunder and lightning, and some mischief they did, but the less that we were kneeling; and the saints doubtless gave the huge balls a hoist over the heads of those who were asking grace from them, but from no mortal creatures. So we had the signal to rise and rush on, and I promise you there were no sluggards. Every man felt ten men's strength. My halberd is no child's toy—if you have forgotten it, there it is—and yet it trembled in my grasp as if it had been a willow wand to drive cows with. On we went, when suddenly the cannon were silent, and the earth shook with another and continued growl and battering, like thunder under ground. It was the men-at-arms rushing to charge us. But our leaders knew their trade, and had seen such a sight before—It was Halt, halt—kneel down in the front—stoop in the second rank—close shoulder to shoulder like brethren, lean all spears forward and receive them like an iron wall! On they rushed, and there was a rending of lances that would have served the Unterwalden old women with splinters of firewood for a twelvemonth. Down went armed horse — down went accoutred knight—down went banner and bannerman—down went peaked boot and crowned helmet, and of those who fell not a man escaped with life. So they drew off in confusion, and were getting in order to charge again, when the noble Duke Ferrand and his horsemen dashed at them in their own way, and we moved onward to support him. Thus on we pressed, and the foot hardly waited for us, seeing their cavalry so handled. Then if you had seen the dust and heard the blows! the noise of a hundred thousand thrashers, the flight of the chaff which they drive about, would be but a type of it. On my word, I almost thought it shame to dash about my halberd, the rout was so helplessly piteous. Hundreds were slain unresisting, and the whole army was in complete flight."

"My father—my father!" exclaimed Arthur; "in such a rout, what can have become of him?"

"He escaped safely," said the Swiss; "fled with Charles."

"It must have been a bloody field ere he fled," replied the Englishman.

"Nay," answered Sigismund, "he took no part in the fight, but merely remained by Charles; and prisoners said it was well for us, for that he is a man of great counsel and action in the wars. And as to flying, a man in such a matter must go back if he cannot press forward, and there is no shame in it, especially if you be not engaged in your own person."

As he spoke thus, their conversation was interrupted by Mordaunt, with "Hush, hush—the King and Queen come forth."

"What am I to do?" said Sigismund, in some alarm. "I care not for the Duke of Lorraine; but what am I to do when Kings and Queens enter?"

"Do nothing but rise, unbonnet yourself, and be silent."

Sigismund did as he was directed.

King René came forth arm in arm with his grandson; and Margaret followed, with deep disappointment and vexation on her brow. She signed to Arthur as she passed, and said to him—"Make thyself master of the truth of this most unexpected news, and bring the particulars to me. Mordaunt will introduce thee."

She then cast a look on the young Swiss, and replied courteously to his awkward salutation. The royal party then left the room, René bent on carrying his grandson to the sporting-party, which had been interrupted, and Margaret to seek the solitude of her private apartment, and await the confirmation of what she regarded as evil tidings.

They had no sooner passed, than Sigismund observed, —"And so that is a King and Queen!— Peste! the King looks somewhat like old Jacomo, the violer, that used to scrape on the fiddle to us when he came to Geierstein in his rounds. But the Queen is a stately creature. The chief cow of the herd, who carries the bouquets and garlands, and leads the rest to the chalet, has not a statelier pace. And how deftly you approached her and spoke to her! I could not have done it with so much grace

—but it is like that you have served apprentice to the court trade?"

"Leave that for the present, good Sigismund," answered Arthur, "and tell me more of this battle."

"By Saint Mary, but I must have some victuals and drink first," said Sigismund, "if your credit in this fine place reaches so far."

"Doubt it not, Sigismund," said Arthur; and, by the intervention of Mordaunt, he easily procured, in a more retired apartment, a collation and wine, to which the young Biederman did great honour, smacking his lips with much gusto after the delicious wines, to which, in spite of his father's ascetic precepts, his palate was beginning to be considerably formed and habituated. When he found himself alone with a flask of *cote roti* and a biscuit, and his friend Arthur, he was easily led to continue his tale of conquest.

"Well—where was I—Oh, where we broke their infantry — well — they never rallied, and fell into greater confusion at every step—and we might have slaughtered one half of them, had we not stopped to examine Charles's camp. Mercy on us, Arthur, what a sight was there! Every pavilion was full of rich clothes, splendid armour, and great dishes and flagons, which some men said were of silver; but I knew there was not so much silver in the world, and was sure they must be of pewter, rarely burnished. Here there were hosts of laced lacqueys, and grooms, and pages, and as many attendants as there were soldiers in the army; and thousands, for what I knew, of pretty maidens. By the same token, both menials and maidens placed themselves at the disposal of the victors; but I promise you that my father was right severe on any who would abuse the rights of war. But some of our young men did not mind him, till he taught them obedience with the staff of his halberd. Well, Arthur, there was fine plundering, for the Germans and French that were with us rifled everything, and some of our men followed the example—it is very catching—So I got into Charles's own pavilion, where Rudolph and some of his people were trying to keep out every one, that he might have the spoiling of it himself, I think; but neither he, nor any Bernese of them all, dared lay truncheon over my pate; so I entered, and saw them putting piles of pewter-trenchers, so clean as to look like silver, into chests and trunks. I pressed through them into the inner-place, and there was Charles's pallet-bed—I will do him justice, it was the only hard one in his camp—and there were fine sparkling stones and pebbles lying about among gauntlets, boots, vambraces, and such like gear—So I thought of your father and you, and looked for something, when what should I see but my old friend here," (here he drew Queen Margaret's necklace from his bosom,) " which I knew, because you remember I recovered it from the Scharfgerichter at Brisach.—'Oho! you pretty sparklers,' said I, 'you shall be Burgundian no longer, but go back to my honest English friends,' and therefore——"

"It is of immense value," said Arthur, "and belongs not to my father or to me, but to the Queen you saw but now."

"And she will become it rarely," answered Sigismund. "Were she but a score, or a score and a half years younger, she were a gallant wife for a Swiss landholder. I would warrant her to keep his household in high order."

"She will reward thee liberally for recovering her property," said Arthur, scarce suppressing a smile at the idea of the proud Margaret becoming the housewife of a Swiss shepherd.

"How—reward!" said the Swiss. "Bethink thee, I am Sigismund Biederman, the son of the Landamman of Unterwalden—I am not a base *lanz-knecht*, to be paid for courtesy with piastres. Let her grant me a kind word of thanks, or the matter of a kiss, and I am well contented."

"A kiss of her hand, perhaps," said Arthur, again smiling at his friend's simplicity.

"Umph, the hand! Well! it may do for a Queen of some fifty years and odd, but would be poor homage to a Queen of May."

Arthur here brought back the youth to the subject of his battle, and learned that the slaughter of the Duke's forces in the flight had been in no degree equal to the importance of the action.

"Many rode off on horseback," said Sigismund; "and our German *reiters* flew on the spoil when they should have followed the chase. And, besides, to speak truth, Charles's camp delayed our very selves in the pursuit; but had we gone half a mile further and seen our friends hanging on trees, not a Confederate would have stopped from the chase while he had limbs to carry him in pursuit."

"And what has become of the Duke?"

"Charles has retreated into Burgundy, like a boar who has felt the touch of the spear, and is more enraged than hurt; but is, they say, sad and sulky. Others report that he has collected all his scattered army, and immense forces besides, and has screwed his subjects to give him money, so that we may expect another brush. But all Switzerland will join us after such a victory."

"And my father is with him?" said Arthur.

"Truly he is, and has in a right godly manner tried to set afoot a treaty of peace with my own father. But it will scarce succeed. Charles is as mad as ever; and our people are right proud of our victory, and so they well may. Nevertheless, my father for ever preaches that such victories, and such heaps of wealth, will change our ancient manners, and that the ploughman will leave his labour to turn soldier. He says much about it; but why money, choice meat and wine, and fine clothing, should do so much harm, I cannot bring my poor brains to see— And many better heads than mine are as much puzzled—Here's to you, friend Arthur—This is choice liquor!"

"And what brings you and your General, Prince Ferrand, post to Nancy?" said the young Englishman.

"Faith, you are yourself the cause of our journey."

"I the cause?" said Arthur.—"Why, how could that be?"

"Why, it is said you and Queen Margaret are urging this old fiddling King René to yield up his territories to Charles, and to disown Ferrand in his claim upon Lorraine. And the Duke of Lorraine sent a man that you know well—that is, you do not know *him*, but you know some of his family, and he knows more of you than you wot—to put a spoke in your wheel, and prevent your getting for Charles the county of Provence, or preventing Ferrand being troubled or traversed in his natural rights over Lorraine."

"On my word, Sigismund, I cannot comprehend you," said Arthur.

"Well," replied the Swiss, "my lot is a hard one. All our house say that I can comprehend nothing, and I shall be next told that nobody can comprehend me.—Well, in plain language, I mean my uncle, Count Albert, as he calls himself, of Geierstein,—my father's brother."

"Anne of Geierstein's father?" echoed Arthur.

"Ay, truly; I thought we should find some mark to make you know him by."

"But I never saw him."

"Ay, but you have though—An able man he is, and knows more of every man's business than the man does himself. Oh! it was not for nothing that he married the daughter of a Salamander!"

"Pshaw, Sigismund, how can you believe that nonsense?" answered Arthur.

"Rudolph told me you were as much bewildered as I was, that night at Graff's-lust," answered the Swiss.

"If I were so, I was the greater ass for my pains," answered Arthur.

"Well, but this uncle of mine has got some of the

old conjuring books from the library at Arnheim, and they say he can pass from place to place with more than mortal speed; and that he is helped in his designs by mightier counsellors than mere men. Always, however, though so ably and highly endowed, his gifts, whether coming from a lawful or unlawful quarter, bring him no abiding advantage. He is eternally plunged into strife and danger."

"I know few particulars of his life," said Arthur, disguising as much as he could his anxiety to hear more of him; "but I have heard that he left Switzerland to join the Emperor."

"True," answered the young Swiss, "and married the young Baroness of Arnheim,—but afterwards he incurred my namesake's imperial displeasure, and not less that of the Duke of Austria. They say you cannot live in Rome and strive with the Pope; so my uncle thought it best to cross the Rhine, and betake himself to Charles's court, who willingly received noblemen from all countries, so that they had good sounding names, with the title of Count, Marquis, Baron, or suchlike, to march in front of them. So my uncle was most kindly received; but within this year or two all this friendship has been broken up. Uncle Albert obtained a great lead in some mysterious societies of which Charles disapproved, and set so hard at my poor uncle, that he was fain to take orders and shave his hair, rather than lose his head. But though he cut off his hair, his brain remains as busy as ever; and although the Duke suffered him to be at large, yet he found him so often in his way, that all men believed he waited but an excuse for seizing upon him and putting him to death. But my uncle persists that he fears not Charles; and that, Duke as he is, Charles has more occasion to be afraid of him.—And so you saw how boldly he played his part at La Ferette."

"By Saint George of Windsor!" exclaimed Arthur, "the Black Priest of Saint Paul's!"

"Oh, ho! you understand me now. Well, he took it upon him that Charles would not dare to punish him for his share in De Hagenbach's death; and no more did he, although uncle Albert sat and voted in the Estates of Burgundy, and stirred them up all he could to refuse giving Charles the money he asked of them. But when the Swiss war broke out, uncle Albert became assured his being a clergyman would be no longer his protection, and that the Duke intended to have him accused of corresponding with his brother and countrymen; and so he appeared suddenly in Ferrand's camp at Neufchatel, and sent a message to Charles that he renounced his allegiance, and bid him defiance."

"A singular story of an active and versatile man," said the young Englishman.

"Oh, you may seek the world for a man like uncle Albert. Then he knows every thing; and he told Duke Ferrand what you were about here, and offered to go and bring more certain information—ay, though he left the Swiss camp but five or six days before the battle, and the distance between Arles and Neufchatel be four hundred miles complete, yet he met him on his return, when Duke Ferrand, with me to shew him the way, was hastening hitherward, having set off from the very field of battle."

"Met him!" said Arthur—"Met whom?—Met the Black Priest of Saint Paul's?"

"Ay, I mean so," replied Sigismund; "but he was habited as a Carmelite monk."

"A Carmelite!" said Arthur, a sudden light flashing on him; "and I was so blind as to recommend his services to the Queen! I remember well that he kept his face much concealed in his cowl—and I, foolish beast, to fall so grossly into the snare!—And yet perhaps it is as well the transaction was interrupted, since I fear, if carried successfully through, all must have been disconcerted by this astounding defeat."

Their conversation had thus far proceeded, when Mordaunt, appearing, summoned Arthur to his royal mistress's apartment. In that gay palace, a gloomy room, whose windows looked upon some part of the ruins of the Roman edifice, but excluded every other object, save broken walls and tottering columns, was the retreat which Margaret had chosen for her own. She received Arthur with a kindness, more touching that it was the inmate of so proud and fiery a disposition,—of a heart assailed with many woes, and feeling them severely.

"Alas, poor Arthur!" she said, "thy life begins where thy father's threatens to end, in useless labour to save a sinking vessel. The rushing leak pours in its waters faster than human force can lighten or discharge. All—all goes wrong, when our unhappy cause becomes connected with it---Strength becomes weakness, wisdom folly, and valour cowardice. The Duke of Burgundy, hitherto victorious in all his bold undertakings, has but to entertain the momentary thought of yielding succour to Lancaster, and behold his sword is broken by a peasant's flail; and his disciplined army, held to be the finest in the world, flies like chaff before the wind; while their spoils are divided by renegade German hirelings, and barbarous Alpine shepherds!—What more hast thou learned of this strange tale?"

"Little, madam, but what you have heard. The worst additions are, that the battle was shamefully cowardlike, and completely lost, with every advantage to have won it—the best, that the Burgundian army has been rather dispersed than destroyed, and that the Duke himself has escaped, and is rallying his forces in Upper Burgundy."

"To sustain a new defeat, or engage in a protracted and doubtful contest, fatal to his reputation as defeat itself. Where is thy father?"

"With the Duke, madam, as I have been informed," replied Arthur.

"Hie to him, and say I charge him to look after his own safety, and care no farther for my interests. This last blow has sunk me—I am without an ally, without a friend, without treasure——"

"Not so, madam," replied Arthur. "One piece of good fortune has brought back to your Grace this inestimable relic of your fortunes."—And producing the precious necklace, he gave the history of its recovery.

"I rejoice at the chance which has restored these

diamonds," said the Queen, "that in point of gratitude, at least, I may not be utterly bankrupt. Carry them to your father,—tell him my schemes are over—and my heart, which so long clung to hope, is broken at last.—Tell him the trinkets are his own, and to his own use let him apply them. They will but poorly repay the noble earldom of Oxford, lost in the cause of her who sends them."

"Royal madam," said the youth, "be assured my father would sooner live by service as a *schwarzreiter*, than become a burden on your misfortunes."

"He never yet disobeyed command of mine," said Margaret; "and this is the last I will lay upon him. If he is too rich or too proud to benefit by his Queen's behest, he will find enough of poor Lancastrians who have fewer means or fewer scruples."

"There is yet a circumstance I have to communicate," said Arthur, and recounted the history of Albert of Geierstein, and the disguise of a Carmelite monk.

"Are you such a fool," answered the Queen, "as to suppose this man has any supernatural powers to aid him in his ambitious projects and his hasty journeys?"

"No, madam—but it is whispered that the Count Albert of Geierstein, or this Black Priest of Saint Paul's, is a chief amongst the Secret Societies of Germany, which even princes dread whilst they hate them; for the man that can command a hundred daggers, must be feared even by those who rule thousands of swords."

"Can this person," said the Queen, "being now a

churchman, retain authority amongst those who deal in life and death? It is contrary to the canons."

"It would seem so, royal madam; but every thing in these dark institutions differs from what is practised in the light of day. Prelates are often heads of a Vehmique bench, and the Archbishop of Cologne exercises the dreadful office of their chief, as Duke of Westphalia, the principal region in which these societies flourish.* Such privileges attach to the secret influence of the chiefs of this dark association, as may well seem supernatural to those who are unapprised of circumstances, of which men shun to speak in plain terms."

"Let him be wizard or assassin," said the Queen, "I thank him for having contributed to interrupt my plan of the old man's cession of Provence, which, as events stand, would have stripped René of his dominions, without furthering our plan of invading England.—Once more, be stirring with the dawn, and bend thy way back to thy father, and charge him to care for himself and think no more of me. Bretagne, where the heir of Lancaster resides, will be the safest place of refuge for its bravest followers. Along the Rhine, the Invisible Tribunal, it would

* The Archbishop of Cologne was recognised as head of all the Free Tribunals (*i. e.*, the Vehmique benches) in Westphalia, by a writ of privilege granted in 1335, by the Emperor Charles IV. Winceslaus confirmed this act by a privilege dated 1382, in which the Archbishop is termed Grand Master of the Vehme, or Grand Inquisitor. And this prelate and other priests were encouraged to exercise such office by Pope Boniface III., whose ecclesiastical discipline permitted them in such cases to assume the right of judging in matters of life and death.

seem, haunts both shores, and to be innocent of ill is no security; even here the proposed treaty with Burgundy may take air, and the Provençaux carry daggers as well as crooks and pipes. But I hear the horses fast returning from the hawking party, and the silly old man, forgetting all the eventful proceedings of the day, whistling as he ascends the steps. Well, we will soon part, and my removal will be, I think, a relief to him. Prepare for banquet and ball, for noise and nonsense—above all, to bid adieu to Aix with morning dawn."

Thus dismissed from the Queen's presence, Arthur's first care was to summon Thiebault to have all things in readiness for his departure; his next to prepare himself for the pleasures of the evening, not perhaps so heavily affected by the failure of his negotiation as to be incapable of consolation in such a scene; for the truth was, that his mind secretly revolted at the thoughts of the simple old King being despoiled of his dominions to further an invasion of England, in which, whatever interest he might have in his daughter's rights, there was little chance of success.

If such feelings were censurable, they had their punishment. Although few knew how completely the arrival of the Duke of Lorraine, and the intelligence he brought with him, had disconcerted the plans of Queen Margaret, it was well known there had been little love betwixt the Queen and his mother Yolande; and the young Prince found himself at the head of a numerous party in the court of his grandfather, who disliked his aunt's haughty manners, and were wearied by the unceasing melancholy of her looks and conversation, and her undisguised contempt of the frivolities which passed around her. Ferrand, besides, was young, handsome, a victor just arrived from a field of battle, fought gloriously, and gained against all chances to the contrary. That he was a general favourite, and excluded Arthur Philipson, as an adherent of the unpopular Queen, from the notice her influence had on a former evening procured him, was only a natural consequence of their relative condition. But what somewhat hurt Arthur's feelings was, to see his friend Sigismund the Simple, as his brethren called him, shining with the reflected glory of the Duke Ferrand of Lorraine, who introduced to all the ladies present, the gallant young Swiss, as Count Sigismund of Geierstein. His care had procured for his follower a dress rather more suitable for such a scene than the country attire of the Count, otherwise Sigismund Biederman.

For a certain time, whatever of novelty is introduced into society is pleasing, though it has nothing else to recommend it. The Swiss were little known personally out of their own country, but they were much talked of; it was a recommendation to be of that country. Sigismund's manners were blunt; a mixture of awkwardness and rudeness, which was termed frankness during the moment of his favour. He spoke bad French and worse Italian—it gave *naïveté* to all he said. His limbs were too bulky to be elegant; his dancing, for Count Sigismund failed not to dance, was the bounding and gamboling of a young elephant; yet they were preferred to the handsome proportions and courtly movements of the youthful Englishman, even by the black-eyed Countess, in whose good graces Arthur had made some progress on the preceding evening. Arthur, thus thrown into the shade, felt as Mr. Pepys afterwards did when he tore his camlet cloak, — the damage was not great, but it troubled him.

Nevertheless, the passing evening brought him some revenge. There are some works of art, the defects of which are not seen till they are injudiciously placed in too strong a light, and such was the case with Sigismund the Simple. The quick-witted, though fantastic Provençaux, soon found out the heaviness of his intellect, and the extent of his good-nature, and amused themselves at his expense, by ironical compliments and well-veiled raillery. It is probable they would have been less delicate on the subject, had not the Swiss brought into the dancing-room along with him his eternal halberd, the size, and weight, and thickness of which boded little good to any one whom the owner might detect in the act of making merry at his expense. But Sigismund did no further mischief that night, except that, in achieving a superb *entrechat*, he alighted with his whole weight on the miniature foot of his pretty partner, which he well-nigh crushed to pieces.

Arthur had hitherto avoided looking towards Queen Margaret during the course of the evening, lest he should disturb her thoughts from the channel in which they were rolling, by seeming to lay a claim on her protection. But there was something so whimsical in the awkward physiognomy of the mal-adroit

Swiss, that he could not help glancing an eye to the alcove where the Queen's chair of state was placed, to see if she observed him. The very first view was such as to rivet his attention. Margaret's head was reclined on the chair, her eyes scarcely open, her features drawn up and pinched, her hands closed with effort. The English lady of honour who stood behind her,—old, deaf, and dim-sighted,—had not discovered anything in her mistress's position more than the abstracted and indifferent attitude with which the Queen was wont to be present in body and absent in mind, during the festivities of the Provençal court. But when Arthur, greatly alarmed, came behind the seat to press her attention to her mistress, she exclaimed, after a minute's investigation, "Mother of Heaven, the Queen is dead!" And it was so. It seemed that the last fibre of life, in that fiery and ambitious mind, had, as she herself prophesied, given way at the same time with the last thread of political hope.

CHAPTER THE THIRTY-THIRD.

> Toll, toll the bell!
> Greatness is o'er,
> The heart has broke,
> To ache no more;
> An unsubstantial pageant all—
> Drop o'er the scene the funeral pall.
>
> OLD POEM.

THE commotion and shrieks of fear and amazement which were excited among the ladies of the court by an event so singular and shocking, had begun to abate, and the sighs, more serious though less intrusive, of the few English attendants of the deceased Queen began to be heard, together with the groans of old King René, whose emotions were as acute as they were shortlived. The leeches had held a busy but unavailing consultation, and the body that was once a Queen's, was delivered to the Priest of Saint Sauveur, that beautiful church in which the spoils of Pagan temples have contributed to fill up the magnificence of the Christian edifice. The stately pile was duly lighted up, and the funeral provided with such splendour as Aix could supply. The Queen's papers being examined, it was found, that Margaret, by disposing of jewels and living at small expense, had realized the means of making a decent provision for life, for her very few English atten-

DEATH OF QUEEN MARGARET.

dants. Her diamond necklace, described in her last will, as in the hands of an English merchant named John Philipson, or his son, or the price thereof, if by them sold or pledged, she left to the said John Philipson and his son Arthur Philipson, with a view to the prosecution of the design which they had been destined to advance, or if that should prove impossible, to their own use and profit. The charge of her funeral rites was wholly intrusted to Arthur, called Philipson, with a request that they should be conducted entirely after the forms observed in England. This trust was expressed in an addition to her will, signed the very day on which she died.

Arthur lost no time in despatching Thiebault express to his father, with a letter, explaining in such terms as he knew would be understood, the tenor of all that had happened since he came to Aix, and above all, the death of Queen Margaret.

Finally, he requested directions for his motions, since the necessary delay occupied by the obsequies of a person of such eminent rank must detain him at Aix till he should receive them.

The old King sustained the shock of his daughter's death so easily, that on the second day after the event, he was engaged in arranging a pompous procession for the funeral, and composing an elegy, to be sung to a tune also of his own composing, in honour of the deceased Queen, who was likened to the goddesses of heathen mythology, and to Judith, Deborah, and all the other holy women, not to mention the saints of the Christian dispensation. It cannot be concealed, that when the first burst of grief was over, King Rene could not help feeling that Margaret's death cut a political knot which he might have otherwise found it difficult to untie, and permitted him to take open part with his grandson, so far indeed as to afford him a considerable share of the contents of the Provençal treasury, which amounted to no larger sum than ten thousand crowns. Ferrand having received the blessing of his grandfather, in a form which his affairs rendered most important to him, returned to the resolutes whom he commanded; and with him, after a most loving farewell to Arthur, went the stout but simple-minded young Swiss, Sigismund Biederman.

The little court of Aix were left to their mourning. King René, for whom ceremonial and show, whether of a joyful or melancholy character, was always matter of importance, would willingly have bestowed in solemnizing the obsequies of his daughter Margaret what remained of his revenue, but was prevented from doing so, partly by remonstrances from his ministers, partly by the obstacles opposed by the young Englishman, who, acting upon the presumed will of the dead, interfered to prevent any such fantastic exhibitions being produced at the obsequies of the Queen, as had disgusted her during her life.

The funeral, therefore, after many days had been spent in public prayers, and acts of devotion, was solemnized with the mournful magnificence due to the birth of the deceased, and with which the Church of Rome so well knows how to affect at once the eye, ear, and feelings.

Amid the various nobles who assisted on the solemn occasion, there was one who arrived just as the tolling of the great bells of Saint Sauveur had announced that the procession was already on its way to the Cathedral. The stranger hastily exchanged his travelling dress for a suit of deep mourning, which was made after the fashion proper to England. So attired, he repaired to the Cathedral, where the noble mien of the cavalier imposed such respect on the attendants, that he was permitted to approach close to the side of the bier; and it was across the coffin of the Queen for whom he had acted and suffered so much, that the gallant Earl of Oxford exchanged a melancholly glance with his son. The assistants, especially the English servants of Margaret, gazed on them both with respect and wonder, and the elder cavalier, in particular, seemed to them no unapt representative of the faithful subjects of England, paying their last duty at the tomb of her who had so long swayed the sceptre, if not faultlessly, yet always with a bold and resolved hand.

The last sound of the solemn dirge had died away, and almost all the funeral attendants had retired, when the father and son still lingered in mournful silence beside the remains of their Sovereign. The clergy at length approached, and intimated they were about to conclude the last duties, by removing the body which had been lately occupied and animated by so haughty and restless a spirit, to the dust, darkness, and silence of the vault, where the long-descended Counts of Provence awaited dissolution. Six priests raised the bier on their shoulders, others bore huge waxen torches before and behind the body, as they carried it down a private staircase which yawned in the floor to admit their descent. The last notes of the requiem, in which the churchmen joined, had died away along the high and fretted arches of the Cathedral, the last flash of light which arose from the mouth of the vault had glimmered and disappeared, when the Earl of Oxford, taking his son by the arm, led him in silence forth into a small cloistered court behind the building, where they found themselves alone. They were silent for a few minutes, for both, and particularly the father, were deeply affected. At length the Earl spoke.

"And this, then, is her end," said he. "Here, royal lady, all that we have planned and pledged life upon falls to pieces with thy dissolution! The heart of resolution, the head of policy is gone; and what avails it that the limbs of the enterprise still have motion and life? Alas, Margaret of Anjou! may Heaven reward thy virtues, and absolve thee from the consequence of thine errors! Both belonged to thy station, and if thou didst hoist too high a sail in prosperity, never lived there princess who defied more proudly the storms of adversity, or bore up against them with such dauntless nobility of determination. With this event the drama has closed, and our parts, my son, are ended."

"We bear arms, then, against the infidels, my lord?" said Arthur, with a sigh that was, however, hardly audible.

"Not," answered the Earl, "until I learn that Henry of Richmond, the undoubted heir of the House of Lancaster, has no occasion for my services. In these jewels, of which you wrote me, so strangely lost and recovered, I may be able to supply him with resources more needful than either your services or mine. But I return no more to the camp of the Duke of Burgundy; for in him there is no help."

"Can it be possible that the power of so great a sovereign has been overthrown in one fatal battle?" said Arthur.

"By no means," replied his father. "The loss at Granson was very great; but to the strength of Burgundy it is but a scratch on the shoulders of a giant. It is the spirit of Charles himself, his wisdom at least, and his foresight, which have given way under the mortification of a defeat, by such as he accounted inconsiderable enemies, and expected to have trampled down with a few squadrons of his men-at-arms. Then his temper is become froward, peevish, and arbitrary, devoted to those who flatter, and, as there is too much reason to believe, betray him; and suspicious of those counsellors who give him wholesome advice. Even I have had my share of distrust. Thou knowest I refused to bear arms against our late hosts the Swiss; and he saw in that no reason for rejecting my attendance on his march. But since the defeat of Granson, I have observed a strong and sudden change, owing, perhaps, in some degree to the insinuations of Campo-Basso, and not a little to the injured pride of the Duke, who was unwilling that an indifferent person in my situation, and thinking as I do, should witness the disgrace of his arms. He spoke in my hearing of lukewarm friends, cold-blooded neu-trials,—of those who, not being with him, must be against him. I tell thee, Arthur de Vere, the Duke has said that which touched my honour so nearly, that nothing but the commands of Queen Margaret, and the interests of the House of Lancaster, could have made me remain in his camp. That is over—My royal mistress has no more occasion for my poor services—the Duke can spare no aid to our cause—and if he could, we can no longer dispose of the only bribe which might have induced him to afford us succours. The power of seconding his views on Provence is buried with Margaret of Anjou."

"What, then, is your purpose?" demanded his son.

"I propose," said Oxford, "to wait at the court of King René until I can hear from the Earl of Richmond, as we must still call him. I am aware that banished men are rarely welcome at the court of a foreign prince; but I have been the faithful follower of his daughter Margaret. I only propose to reside in disguise, and desire neither notice nor maintenance; so methinks King René will not refuse to permit me to breathe the air of his dominions, until I learn in what direction fortune or duty shall call me."

"Be assured he will not," answered Arthur. "René is incapable of a base or ignoble thought; and if he could despise trifles as he detests dishonour, he might be ranked high in the list of monarchs."

This resolution being adopted, the son presented his father at King René's court, whom he privately made acquainted that he was a man of quality, and a distinguished Lancastrian. The good King would in his heart have preferred a guest of lighter accomplishments and gayer temper, to Oxford, a statesman and a soldier of melancholy and grave habits. The Earl was conscious of this, and seldom troubled his benevolent and light-hearted host with his presence. He had, however, an opportunity of rendering the old King a favour of peculiar value. This was in conducting an important treaty betwixt René and Louis XI. of France, his nephew. Upon that crafty monarch, René finally settled his principality, for the necessity of extricating his affairs by such a measure was now apparent even to himself, every thought of favouring Charles of Burgundy in the arrangement having died with Queen Margaret. The policy and wisdom of the English Earl, who was intrusted with almost the sole charge of this secret and delicate measure, were of the utmost advantage to good King René, who was freed from personal and pecuniary vexations, and enabled to go piping and tabouring to his grave. Louis did not fail to propitiate the plenipotentiary, by throwing out distant hopes of aid to the efforts of the Lancastrian party in England. A faint and insecure negotiation was entered into upon the subject; and these affairs, which rendered two journeys to Paris necessary on the part of Oxford and his son, in the spring and summer of the year 1476, occupied them until that year was half spent.

In the meanwhile, the wars of the Duke of Burgundy with the Swiss Cantons and Count Ferrand of Lorraine, continued to rage. Before midsummer, 1476, Charles had assembled a new army of at least sixty thousand men, supported by one hundred and fifty pieces of cannon, for the purpose of invading Switzerland, where the warlike mountaineers easily levied a host of thirty thousand Switzers, now accounted almost invincible, and called upon their confederates, the Free Cities on the Rhine, to support them with a powerful body of cavalry. The first efforts of Charles were successful. He overran the Pays de Vaud, and recovered most of the places which he had lost after the defeat at Granson. But instead of attempting to secure a well-defended frontier, or what would have been still more politic, to achieve a peace upon equitable terms with his redoubtable neighbours, this most obstinate of princes resumed the purpose of penetrating into the recesses of the Alpine mountains, and chastising the mountaineers even within their own strongholds, though experience might have taught him the danger, nay desperation, of the attempt. Thus the news received by Oxford and his son, when they returned to Aix in midsummer, was, that Duke Charles had advanced to Morat, (or Murten,) situated upon a lake of the same name, at the very entrance of Switzerland. Here report said, that Adrian de Bubenberg, a veteran knight of Berne, commanded, and maintained the most obstinate defence, in expectation of the relief which his countrymen were hastily assembling.

"Alas, my old brother-in-arms!" said the Earl to his son, on hearing these tidings, "this town besieged, these assaults repelled, this vicinity of an enemy's country, this profound lake, these inaccessible cliffs, threaten a second part of the tragedy of Granson, more calamitous perhaps than even the former."

On the last week of July, the capital of Provence was agitated by one of those unauthorized, yet generally received rumours, which transmit great events with incredible swiftness, as an apple flung from hand to hand by a number of people will pass a given space infinitely faster than if borne by the most rapid series of expresses. The report announced a second defeat of the Burgundians, in terms so exaggerated, as induced the Earl of Oxford to consider the greater part, if not the whole, as a fabrication.

CHAPTER THE THIRTY-FOURTH.

And is the hostile troop arrived,
And have they won the day?
It must have been a bloody field
Ere Darwent fled away!
　　　　　THE ETTRICK SHEPHERD.

SLEEP did not close the eyes of the Earl of Oxford or his son; for although the success or defeat of the Duke of Burgundy could not now be of importance to their own private or political affairs, yet the father did not cease to interest himself in the fate of his former companion-in-arms; and the son, with the fire of youth, always eager after novelty,* expected to find something to advance or thwart his own progress in every remarkable event which agitated the world.

Arthur had risen from his bed, and was in the act of attiring himself, when the tread of a horse arrested his attention. He had no sooner looked out of the window, than exclaiming, "News, my father, news from the army!" he rushed into the street, where a cavalier, who appeared to have ridden very hard, was inquiring for the two Philipsons, father and son. He had no difficulty in recognising Colvin, the master of the Burgundian ordnance. His ghastly look bespoke distress of mind; his disordered array and

* Cupidus novarum rerum.

broken armour, which seemed rusted with rain, or stained with blood, gave the intelligence of some affray in which he had probably been worsted; and so exhausted was his gallant steed, that it was with difficulty the animal could stand upright. The condition of the rider was not much better. When he alighted from his horse to greet Arthur, he reeled so much that he would have fallen without instant support. His horny eye had lost the power of speculation; his limbs possessed imperfectly that of motion, and it was with a half suffocated voice that he muttered, "Only fatigue—want of rest and of food."

Arthur assisted him into the house, and refreshments were procured; but he refused all except a bowl of wine, after tasting which he set it down, and looking at the Earl of Oxford with an eye of the deepest affliction, he ejaculated, "The Duke of Burgundy!"

"Slain?" replied the Earl; "I trust not!"

"It might have been better if he were," said the Englishman; "but dishonour has come before death."

"Defeated, then?" said Oxford.

"So completely and fearfully defeated," answered the soldier, "that all that I have seen of loss before was slight in comparison."

"But how, or where?" said the Earl of Oxford; "you were superior in numbers, as we were informed."

"Two to one at least," answered Colvin; "and when I speak of our encounter at this moment, I could rend my flesh with my teeth for being here to tell such a tale of shame. We had sat down for about a week before that paltry town of Murten, or Morat, or whatever it is called. The Governor, one of those stubborn mountain-bears of Berne, bade us defiance. He would not even condescend to shut his gates, but when we summoned the town, returned for answer, we might enter if we pleased,—we should be suitably received. I would have tried to bring him to reason by a salvo or two of artillery, but the Duke was too much irritated to listen to good counsel. Stimulated by that black traitor, Campo-Basso, he deemed it better to run forward with his whole force upon a place, which, though I could soon have battered it about their German ears, was yet too strong to be carried by swords, lances, and hagbuts. We were beaten off with great loss, and much discouragement to the soldiers. We then commenced more regularly, and my batteries would have brought these mad Switzers to their senses. Walls and ramparts went down before the lusty cannoniers of Burgundy; we were well secured also by intrenchments against those whom we heard of as approaching to raise the siege. But on the evening of the twentieth of this month, we learned that they were close at hand, and Charles, consulting only his own bold spirit, advanced to meet them, relinquishing the advantage of our batteries and strong position. By his orders, though against my own judgment, I accompanied him with twenty good pieces, and the flower of my people. We broke up on the next morning, and had not advanced far before we saw the lances and thick array of halberds and two-handed swords which crested the mountain. Heaven, too, added its terrors—A thunder-storm, with all the fury of those tempestuous climates, descended on both armies, but did most annoyance to ours, as our troops, especially the Italians, were more sensible to the torrents of rain which poured down, and the rivulets, which swelled into torrents, inundated and disordered our position. The Duke for once saw it necessary to alter his purpose of instant battle. He rode up to me, and directed me to defend with the cannon the retreat which he was about to commence, adding, that he himself would in person sustain me with the men-at arms. The order was given to retreat. But the movement gave new spirit to an enemy already sufficiently audacious. The ranks of the Swiss instantly prostrated themselves in prayer—a practice on the field of battle which I have ridiculed—but I will do so no more. When, after five minutes, they sprung again on their feet, and began to advance rapidly, sounding their horns and crying their war-cries with all their usual ferocity—behold, my lord, the clouds of Heaven opened, shedding on the Confederates the blessed light of the returning sun, while our ranks were still in the gloom of the tempest. My men were discouraged. The host behind them was retreating; the sudden light thrown on the advancing Switzers shewed along the mountains a profusion of banners, a glancing of arms, giving to the enemy the appearance of double the numbers that had hitherto been visible to us. I exhorted my followers to stand fast, but in doing so I thought a thought, and spoke a word, which was a grievous sin. 'Stand fast, my brave cannoniers,' I said, 'we will presently let them hear louder thunders, and shew them more fatal lightnings, than their prayers have put down!'—My men shouted—But it was an impious thought—a blasphemous speech—and evil came after it. We levelled our guns on the advancing masses as fairly as cannon were ever pointed— I can vouch it, for I laid the Grand Duchess of Burgundy myself—Ah, poor Duchess! what rude hands manage thee now!—The volley was fired, and ere the smoke spread from the muzzles, I could see many a man, and many a banner, go down. It was natural to think such a discharge would have checked the attack, and whilst the smoke hid the enemy from us, I made every effort again to load our cannon, and anxiously endeavoured to look through the mist to discover the state of our opponents. But ere our smoke was cleared away, or the cannon again loaded, they came headlong down on us, horse and foot, old men and boys, men-at-arms and varlets, charging up to the muzzle of the guns, and over them, with total disregard to their lives. My brave fellows were cut down, pierced through, and overrun, while they were again loading their pieces, nor do I believe that a single cannon was fired a second time."

"And the Duke?" said the Earl of Oxford, "did he not support you?"

"Most loyally and bravely," answered Colvin, "with his own body guard of Walloons and Burgundians. But a thousand Italian mercenaries went off, and never shewed face again. The pass, too, was cumbered with the artillery, and in itself narrow, bordering on mountains and cliffs, a deep lake close beside. In short it was a place totally unfit for horsemen to act in. In spite of the Duke's utmost exertions, and those of the gallant Flemings who fought around him, all were borne back in complete disorder. I was on foot, fighting as I could, without hopes of my life, or indeed thoughts of saving it, when I saw the guns taken and my faithful cannoniers slain. But I saw Duke Charles hard pressed, and took my horse from my page that held him.— Thou, too, art lost, my poor orphan boy!—I could only aid Monseigneur de la Croye and others to extricate the Duke. Our retreat became a total rout, and when we reached our rear-guard, which we had left strongly encamped, the banners of the Switzers were waving on our batteries, for a large division had made a circuit, through mountain-passes known only to themselves, and attacked our camp, vigorously seconded by that accursed Adrian de Bubenberg, who sallied from the beleaguered town, so that our intrenchments were stormed on both sides at once.— I have more to say, but having ridden day and night to bring you these evil tidings, my tongue clings to the roof of my mouth, and I feel that I can speak no more. The rest is all flight and massacre, disgraceful to every soldier that shared in it. For my part, I confess my contumelious self-confidence and insolence to man, as well as blasphemy to Heaven. If I live, it is but to hide my disgraced head in a cowl, and expiate the numerous sins of a licentious life."

With difficulty the broken-minded soldier was prevailed upon to take some nourishment and repose, together with an opiate, which was prescribed by the physician of King René, who recommended it as necessary to preserve even the reason of his patient, exhausted by the events of the battle, and subsequent fatigue.

The Earl of Oxford, dismissing other assistance, watched alternately with his son at Colvin's bed-side. Notwithstanding the draught that had been administered, his repose was far from sound. Sudden starts, the perspiration which sprung from his brow, the distortions of his countenance, and the manner in which he clenched his fists and flung about his limbs, shewed that in his dreams he was again encountering the terrors of a desperate and forlorn combat. This lasted for several hours; but about noon fatigue and medicine prevailed over nervous excitation, and the defeated commander fell into a deep and untroubled repose till evening. About sunset he awakened, and, after learning with whom and where he was, he partook of refreshments, and without any apparent consciousness of having told them before, he detailed once more all the particulars of the battle of Murten.

"It were little wide of truth," he said, "to calculate that one half of the Duke's army fell by the sword, or were driven into the lake. Those who escaped are great part of them scattered, never again to unite. Such a desperate and irretrievable rout was never witnessed. We fled like deer, sheep, or any other timid animals which only remain in company because they are afraid to separate, but never think of order or of defence."

"And the Duke?" said the Earl of Oxford.

COSTUME OF PRINCESS IN THE COURT OF KING RENÉ.

"We hurried him with us," said the soldier, "rather from instinct than loyalty, as men flying from a conflagration snatch up what they have of value without knowing what they are doing. Knight and knave, officer and soldier, fled in the same panic, and each blast of the horn of Uri in our rear added new wings to our flight."

"And the Duke?" repeated Oxford.

"At first he resisted our efforts, and strove to turn back on the foe; but when the flight became general, he galloped along with us, without a word spoken or a command issued. At first we thought his silence and passiveness, so unusual in a temper so fiery, were fortunate for securing his personal safety. But when we rode the whole day, without being able to obtain a word of reply to all our questions,—when he sternly refused refreshments of every kind, though he had tasted no food all that disastrous day,—when every variation of his moody and uncertain temper was sunk into silent and sullen despair, we took counsel what was to be done, and it was by the general voice that I was despatched to entreat that you, for whose counsels alone Charles has been known to have had some occasional deference, would come instantly to his place of retreat, and exert all your influence to awaken him from this lethargy, which may otherwise terminate his existence."

"And what remedy can I interpose?" said Oxford. "You know how he neglected my advice, when following it might have served my interest as well as his own. You are aware that my life was not safe among the miscreants that surrounded the Duke, and exercised influence over him."

"Most true," answered Colvin; "but I also know he is your ancient companion-in-arms, and it would ill become me to teach the noble Earl of Oxford what the laws of chivalry require. For your lordship's safety, every honest man in the army will give willing security."

"It is for that I care least," said Oxford, indifferently; "and if indeed my presence can be of service to the Duke,—if I could believe that he desired it——"

"He does—he does, my lord!" said the faithful soldier, with tears in his eyes. "We heard him name your name, as if the words escaped him in a painful dream."

"I will go to him, such being the case," said Oxford.—"I will go instantly. Where did he purpose to establish his head-quarters?"

"He had fixed nothing for himself on that or other matters; but Monsieur de Contay named La Rivière, near Salins, in Upper Burgundy, as the place of his retreat."

"Thither, then, will we, my son, with all haste of preparation. Thou, Colvin, hadst better remain here, and see some holy man, to be assoilzied for thy hasty speech on the battle-field of Morat. There was offence in it without doubt, but it will be ill-atoned for by quitting a generous master when he hath most need of your good service; and it is but an act of cowardice to retreat into the cloister, till we have no longer active duties to perform in this world."

"It is true," said Colvin, " that should I leave the Duke now, perhaps not a man would stay behind that could stell a cannon properly. The sight of your lordship cannot but operate favourably on my noble master, since it has waked the old soldier in myself. If your lordship can delay your journey till to-morrow, I will have my spiritual affairs settled, and my bodily health sufficiently restored, to be your guide to La Rivière; and, for the cloister, I will think of it when I have regained the good name which I have lost at Murten. But I will have masses said, and these right powerful, for the souls of my poor cannoniers."

The proposal of Colvin was adopted, and Oxford, with his son, attended by Thiebault, spent the day in preparation, excepting the time necessary to take formal leave of King René, who seemed to part with them with regret. In company with the ordnance officer of the discomfited Duke, they traversed those parts of Provence, Dauphiné, and Franche Compté, which lie between Aix and the place to which the Duke of Burgundy had retreated; but the distance and inconvenience of so long a route consumed more than a fortnight on the road, and the month of July 1476 was commenced, when the travellers arrived in Upper Burgundy, and at the Castle of La Rivière, about twenty miles to the south of the town of Salins. The castle, which was but of small size, was surrounded by very many tents, which were pitched in a crowded, disordered, and unsoldierlike manner, very unlike the discipline usually observed in the camp of Charles the Bold. That the Duke was present there, however, was attested by his broad banner, which, rich with all its quarterings, streamed from the battlements of the castle. The guard turned out to receive the strangers, but in a manner so disorderly, that the Earl looked to Colvin for explanation. The master of the ordnance shrugged up his shoulders, and was silent.

Colvin having sent in notice of his arrival, and that of the English Earl, Monsieur de Contay caused them presently to be admitted, and expressed much joy at their arrival.

"A few of us," he said, "true servants of the Duke, are holding council here, at which your assistance, my noble Lord of Oxford, will be of the utmost importance. Messieurs de la Croye, De Craon, Rubempré, and others, nobles of Burgundy, are now assembled to superintend the defence of the country at this exigence."

They all expressed delight to see the Earl of Oxford, and had only abstained from thrusting their attentions on him the last time he was in the Duke's camp, as they understood it was his wish to observe incognito.

"His Grace," said De Craon, "has asked after you twice, and on both times by your assumed name of Philipson."

"I wonder not at that, my Lord of Craon," replied the English nobleman; "the origin of the name took its rise in former days, when I was here during my first exile. It was then said that we poor Lancastrian nobles must assume other names than our own, and the good Duke Philip said, as I was brother-in-arms to his son Charles, I must be called after himself, by the name of Philipson. In memory of the good sovereign, I took that name when the day of need actually arrived, and I see that the Duke thinks of our early intimacy by his distinguishing me so.— How fares his Grace?"

The Burgundians looked at each other, and there was a pause.

"Even like a man stunned, brave Oxford," at length De Contay replied. "Sieur d'Argentin, you can best inform the noble Earl of the condition of our sovereign."

"He is like a man distracted," said the future historian of that busy period. "After the battle of Granson, he was never, to my thinking, of the same sound judgment as before. But then, he was capricious, unreasonable, peremptory, and inconsistent, and resented every counsel that was offered, as if it had been meant in insult; was jealous of the least trespass in point of ceremonial, as if his subjects were holding him in contempt. Now there is a total change, as if this second blow had stunned him, and suppressed the violent passions which the first called into action. He is silent as a Carthusian, solitary as a hermit, expresses interest in nothing, least of all in the guidance of his army. He was, you know, anxious about his dress; so much so, that there was some affectation even in the rudenesses which he practised in that matter. But, woe's me, you will see a change now; he will not suffer his hair or nails to be trimmed or arranged. He is totally heedless of respect or disrespect towards him, takes little or no nourishment, uses strong wines, which, however, do not seem to affect his understanding; he will hear nothing of war or state affairs, as little of hunting or of sport. Suppose an anchorite, brought from a cell to govern a kingdom, you see in him, except in point of devotion, a picture of the fiery, active Charles of Burgundy."

"You speak of a mind deeply wounded, Sieur d'Argentin," replied the Englishman. "Think you it fit I should present myself before the Duke?"

"I will inquire," said Contay; and leaving the apartment, returned presently, and made a sign to the Earl to follow him.

In a cabinet, or closet, the unfortunate Charles reclined in a large arm-chair, his legs carelessly stretched on a footstool, but so changed that the Earl of Oxford could have believed what he saw to be the ghost of the once fiery Duke. Indeed, the shaggy length of hair which, streaming from his head, mingled with his beard; the hollowness of the caverns, at the bottom of which rolled his wild eyes; the falling in of the breast, and the advance of the shoulders, gave the ghastly appearance of one who has suffered the final agony which takes from mortality the signs of life and energy. His very costume (a cloak flung loosely over him) increased his resemblance to a shrouded phantom. De Contay named the Earl of Oxford; but the Duke gazed on him with a lustreless eye, and gave him no answer.

"Speak to him, brave Oxford," said the Burgundian in a whisper; " he is even worse than usual, but perhaps he may know your voice."

Never, when the Duke of Burgundy was in the most palmy state of his fortunes, did the noble Englishman kneel to kiss his hand with such sincere reverence. He respected in him, not only the afflicted friend, but the humbled sovereign, upon whose tower of trust the lightning had so recently broken. It was probably the falling of a tear upon his hand which seemed to awake the Duke's attention, for he looked towards the Earl, and said, "Oxford—Philipson—my old—my only friend, hast thou found me out in this retreat of shame and misery?"

"I am not your only friend, my lord," said Oxford. "Heaven has given you many affectionate friends among your natural and loyal subjects. But though a stranger, and saving the allegiance I owe to my lawful sovereign, I will yield to none of them in the respect and deference which I have paid to your Grace in prosperity, and now come to render to you in adversity."

"Adversity, indeed!" said the Duke; "irremediable, intolerable adversity! I was lately Charles of Burgundy, called the Bold—now am I twice beaten by a scum of German peasants; my standard taken, my men-at-arms put to flight, my camp twice plundered, and each time of value more than equal to the price of all Switzerland fairly lost; myself hunted like a caitiff goat or chamois.—The utmost spite of hell could never accumulate more shame on the head of a sovereign!"

"On the contrary, my lord," said Oxford, "it is a trial of Heaven, which calls for patience and strength of mind. The bravest and best knight may lose the saddle; he is but a laggard who lies rolling on the sand of the lists after the accident has chanced."

"Ha, laggard, sayst thou?" said the Duke, some part of his ancient spirit awakened by the broad taunt; "Leave my presence, sir, and return to it no more, till you are summoned thither——"

"Which I trust will be no later than your Grace quits your dishabille, and disposes yourself to see your vassals and friends with such ceremony as befits you and them," said the Earl composedly.

"How mean you by that, Sir Earl? You are unmannerly."

"If I be, my lord, I am taught my ill-breeding by circumstances. I can mourn over fallen dignity; but I cannot honour him who dishonours himself by bending, like a regardless boy, beneath the scourge of evil fortune."

"And who am I that you should term me such?" said Charles, starting up in all his natural pride and ferocity; "or who are you but a miserable exile, that you should break in upon my privacy with such disrespectful upbraiding?"

"For me," replied Oxford, "I am, as you say, an unrespected exile; nor am I ashamed of my condition, since unshaken loyalty to my king and his successors has brought me to it. But in you, can I recognise the Duke of Burgundy in a sullen hermit, whose guards are a disorderly soldiery, dreadful only to their friends; whose councils are in confusion for want of their sovereign, and who himself lurks, like a lamed wolf in its den, in an obscure castle, waiting but a blast of the Switzer's horn to fling open its gates, which there are none to defend; who wears not a knightly sword to protect his person, and cannot even die like a stag at bay, but must be worried like a hunted fox?"

"Death and hell, slanderous traitor!" thundered the Duke, glancing a look at his side, and perceiving himself without a weapon,—"It is well for thee I have no sword, or thou shouldst never boast of thine insolence going unpunished.—Contay, step forth like a good knight, and confute the calumniator. Say, are not my soldiers arrayed, disciplined, and in order?"

"My lord," said Contay, trembling (brave as he was in battle) at the frantic rage which Charles exhibited, "there are a numerous soldiery yet under your command, but they are in evil order, and in worse discipline, I think, than they were wont."

"I see it—I see it," said the Duke; "idle and evil counsellors are ye all. — Hearken, Sir of Contay, what have you and the rest of you been doing, holding as you do large lands and high fiefs of us, that I cannot stretch my limbs on a sick-bed, when my heart is half-broken, but my troops must fall into such scandalous disorder as exposes me to the scorn and reproach of each beggarly foreigner?"

"My lord," replied Contay more firmly, "we have done what we could. But your Grace has accustomed your mercenary generals and leaders of Free Companies, to take their orders only from your own mouth, or hand. They clamour also for pay, and the treasurer refuses to issue it without your Grace's order, as he alleges it might cost him his head;

and they will not be guided and restrained, either by us or those who compose your council."

The Duke laughed sternly, but was evidently somewhat pleased with the reply.

"Ha, ha!" he said, "it is only Burgundy who can ride his own wild horses, and rule his own wild soldiery. Hark thee, Contay — To-morrow I ride forth to review the troops—for what disorder has passed allowance shall be made. Pay also shall be issued—but woe to those who shall have offended too deeply! Let my grooms of the chamber know to provide me fitting dress and arms. I have got a lesson," (glancing a dark look at Oxford,) "and I will not again be insulted without the means of wreaking my vengeance. Begone, both of you. And, Contay, send the treasurer hither with his accounts, and woe to his soul if I find aught to complain of! Begone, I say, and send him hither."

They left the apartment with suitable obeisance. As they retired, the Duke said abruptly, "Lord of Oxford, a word with you. Where did you study medicine? In your own famed university, I suppose. Thy physic hath wrought a wonder. Yet, Doctor Philipson, it might have cost thee thy life."

"I have ever thought my life cheap," said Oxford, "when the object was to help my friend."

"Thou art indeed a friend," said Charles, "and a fearless one. But go—I have been sore troubled, and thou hast tasked my temper closely. To-morrow we will speak further; meantime, I forgive thee, and I honour thee."

The Earl of Oxford retired to the Council-hall, where the Burgundian nobility, aware of what had passed, crowded around him with thanks, compliments, and congratulations. A general bustle now ensued; orders were hurried off in every direction. Those officers who had duties to perform which had been neglected, hastened to conceal or to atone for their negligence. There was a general tumult in the camp, but it was a tumult of joy; for soldiers are always most pleased when they are best in order for performing their military service; and license or inactivity, however acceptable at times, are not, when continued, so agreeable to their nature, as strict discipline and a prospect of employment.

The treasurer, who was, luckily for him, a man of sense and method, having been two hours in private with the Duke, returned with looks of wonder, and professed, that never, in Charles's most prosperous days, had he shewed himself more acute in the department of finance, of which he had but that morning seemed totally incapable; and the merit was universally attributed to the visit of Lord Oxford, whose timely reprimand had, like the shot of a cannon dispersing foul mists, awakened the Duke from his black and bilious melancholy.

On the following day, Charles reviewed his troops with his usual attention, directed new levies, made various dispositions of his forces, and corrected the faults of their discipline by severe orders which were enforced by some deserved punishments, (of which the Italian mercenaries of Campo-Basso had a large share,) and rendered palatable by the payment of arrears, which was calculated to attach them to the standard under which they served.

The Duke also, after consulting with his council, agreed to convoke meetings of the States in his different territories, redress certain popular grievances, and grant some boons which he had hitherto denied; and thus began to open a new account of popularity with his subjects, in place of that which his rashness had exhausted.

ZURICH PEASANTS.

ROMAN FOUNTAIN AT AIX.

CHAPTER THE THIRTY-FIFTH.

> ———Here's a weapon now,
> Shall shake a conquering general in his tent,
> A monarch on his throne, or reach a prelate,
> However holy be his offices,
> E'en while he serves the altar.
>
> OLD PLAY.

FROM this time all was activity in the Duke of Burgundy's court and army. Money was collected, soldiers were levied, and certain news of the Confederates' motions only were wanting to bring on the campaign. But although Charles was, to all outward appearance, as active as ever, yet those who were more immediately about his person were of opinion that he did not display the soundness of mind, or the energy of judgment, which had been admired in him before these calamities. He was still liable to fits of moody melancholy, similar to those which descended upon Saul, and was vehemently furious when aroused out of them. Indeed, the Earl of Oxford himself seemed to have lost the power which he had exercised over him at first. Nay, though in general Charles was both grateful and affectionate towards him, he evidently felt humbled by the recollection of his having witnessed his impotent and disastrous condition, and was so much afraid of Lord Oxford being supposed to lead his counsels, that he often repelled his advice, merely, as it seemed, to shew his own independence of mind.

In these froward humours, the Duke was much encouraged by Campo-Basso. That wily traitor now saw his master's affairs tottering to their fall, and he resolved to lend his lever to the work, so as to entitle him to a share of the spoil. He regarded Oxford as one of the most able friends and counsellors who adhered to the Duke; he thought he saw in his looks that he fathomed his own treacherous purpose, and therefore he hated and feared him. Besides, in order perhaps to colour over, even to his own eyes, the abominable perfidy he meditated, he affected to be exceedingly enraged against the Duke for the late punishment of marauders belonging to his Italian bands. He believed that chastisement to have been inflicted by the advice of Oxford; and he suspected that the measure was pressed with the hope of discovering that the Italians had not pillaged for their own emolument only, but for that of their commander. Believing that Oxford was thus hostile to him, Campo-Basso would have speedily found means to take him out of his path, had not the Earl himself found it prudent to observe some precautions; and the lords of Flanders and Burgundy, who loved him for the very reasons for which the Italian abhorred him, watched over his safety with a vigilance, of which he himself was ignorant, but which certainly was the means of preserving his life.

It was not to be supposed that Ferrand of Lorraine should have left his victory so long unimproved; but the Swiss Confederates, who were the strength of his forces, insisted that the first operations should take place in Savoy and the Pays de Vaud, where the Burgundians had many garrisons, which, though they received no relief, yet were not easily or speedily reduced. Besides, the Switzers being, like most of the national soldiers of the time, a kind of militia, most of them returned home, to get in their harvest, and to deposit their spoil in safety. Ferrand, therefore, though bent on pursuing his success with all the ardour of youthful chivalry, was prevented from making any movement in advance until the month of December, 1476. In the meantime, the Duke of Burgundy's forces, to be least burdensome to the country, were cantoned in distant places of his dominions, where every exertion was made to perfect the discipline of the new levies. The Duke, if left to himself, would have precipitated the struggle by again assembling his forces, and pushing forward into the Helvetian territories; but though he inwardly foamed at the recollection of Granson and Murten, the memory of these disasters was too recent to permit such a plan of the campaign. Meantime, weeks glided past, and the month of December was far advanced, when, one morning, as the Duke was sitting in council, Campo-Basso suddenly entered, with a degree of extravagant rapture in his countenance, singularly different from the cold, regulated, and subtle smile which was usually his utmost advance towards laughter. "*Guantes*," * he said, "*Guantes*, for luck's sake, if it please your Grace."

"And what of good fortune comes nigh us?"

EFFIGY OF KING RENÉ.

* *Guantes*, used by the Spanish as the French say étrennes, or the English handsell or luckpenny—phrases used by inferiors to their patrons as the bringers of good news.

said the Duke,—"Methought she had forgot the way to our gates."

"She has returned to them, please your Highness, with her cornucopia full of choicest gifts, ready to pour her fruit, her flowers, her treasures, on the head of the sovereign of Europe most worthy to receive them."

"The meaning of all this?" said Duke Charles; "riddles are for children."

"The harebrained young madman Ferrand, who calls himself of Lorraine, has broken down from the mountains, at the head of a desultory army of scapegraces like himself; and what think you,—ha! ha! ha!—they are overrunning Lorraine, and have taken Nancy—ha! ha! ha!"

"By my good faith, Sir Count," said Contay, astonished at the gay humour with which the Italian treated a matter so serious, "I have seldom heard a fool laugh more gaily at a more scurvy jest, than you, a wise man, laugh at the loss of the principal town of the province we are fighting for."

"I laugh," said Campo-Basso, "among the spears, as my war-horse does—ha! ha!—among the trumpets. I laugh also over the destruction of the enemy, and the dividing of the spoil, as eagles scream their joy over the division of their prey; I laugh——"

"You laugh," said the Lord of Contay, waxing impatient, "when you have all the mirth to yourself, as you laughed after our losses at Granson and Murten."

"Peace, sir!" said the Duke. "The Count of Campo-Basso has viewed the case as I do. This young knight-errant ventures from the protection of his mountains; and Heaven deal with me as I keep my oath, when I swear that the next fair field on which we meet shall see one of us dead! It is now the last week of the old year, and before Twelfth-Day we will see whether he or I shall find the bean in the cake.—To arms, my lords; let our camp instantly break up, and our troops move forward towards Lorraine. Send off the Italian and Albanian light cavalry, and the Stradiots, to scour the country in the van—Oxford, thou wilt bear arms in this journey, wilt thou not?"

"Surely," said the Earl. "I am eating your Highness's bread; and when enemies invade, it stands with my honour to fight for your Grace as if I was your born subject. With your Grace's permission, I will despatch a pursuivant, who shall carry letters to my late kind host, the Landamman of Unterwalden, acquainting him with my purpose."

The Duke having given a ready assent, the pursuivant was dismissed accordingly, and returned in a few hours, so near had the armies approached to each other. He bore a letter from the Landamman, in a tone of courtesy and even kindness, regretting that any cause should have occurred for bearing arms against his late guest, for whom he expressed high personal regard. The same pursuivant also brought greetings from the family of the Biedermans to their friend Arthur, and a separate letter, addressed to the same person, of which the contents ran thus:—

"Rudolph Donnerhugel is desirous to give the

young merchant, Arthur Philipson, the opportunity of finishing the bargain which remained unsettled between them in the castle-court of Geierstein. He is the more desirous of this, as he is aware that the said Arthur has done him wrong, in seducing the affections of a certain maiden of rank, to whom he, Philipson, is not, and cannot be, anything beyond an ordinary acquaintance. Rudolph Donnerhugel will send Arthur Philipson word, when a fair and equal meeting can take place on neutral ground. In the meantime, he will be as often as possible in the first rank of the skirmishers."

Young Arthur's heart leapt high as he read the defiance, the piqued tone of which shewed the state of the writer's feelings, and argued sufficiently Rudolph's disappointment on the subject of Anne of Geierstein, and his suspicion that she had bestowed her affections on the youthful stranger. Arthur found means of despatching a reply to the challenge of the Swiss, assuring him of the pleasure with which he would attend his commands, either in front of the line or elsewhere, as Rudolph might desire.

Meantime the armies were closely approaching to each other, and the light troops sometimes met. The Stradiots from the Venetian territory, a sort of cavalry resembling that of the Turks, performed much of that service on the part of the Burgundian army, for which, indeed, if their fidelity could have been relied on, they were admirably well qualified. The Earl of Oxford observed, that these men, who were under the command of Campo-Basso, always brought in intelligence that the enemy were in indifferent order, and in full retreat. Besides, information was communicated through their means, that sundry individuals, against whom the Duke of Burgundy entertained peculiar personal dislike, and whom he specially desired to get into his hands, had taken refuge in Nancy. This greatly increased the Duke's ardour for retaking that place, which became perfectly ungovernable when he learned that Ferrand and his Swiss allies had drawn off to a neighbouring position called Saint Nicholas, on the news of his arrival. The greater part of the Burgundian counsellors, together with the Earl of Oxford, protested against his besieging a place of some strength, while an active enemy lay in the neighbourhood to relieve it. They remonstrated on the smallness of his army, on the severity of the weather, on the difficulty of obtaining provisions, and exhorted the Duke, that having made such a movement as had forced the enemy to retreat, he ought to suspend decisive operations till spring. Charles at first tried to dispute and repel these arguments; but when his counsellors reminded him that he was placing himself and his army in the same situation as at Granson and Murten, he became furious at the recollection, foamed at the mouth, and only answered by oaths and imprecations, that he would be master of Nancy before Twelfth-Day.

Accordingly, the army of Burgundy sat down before Nancy, in a strong position, protected by the hollow of a water-course, and covered with thirty pieces of cannon, which Colvin had under his charge.

Having indulged his obstinate temper in thus arranging the campaign, the Duke seemed to give a little more heed to the advice of his counsellors touching the safety of his person, and permitted the Earl of Oxford, with his son, and two or three officers of his household, men of approved trust, to sleep within his pavilion, in addition to the usual guard.

It wanted three days of Christmas when the Duke sat down before Nancy, and on that very evening a tumult happened which seemed to justify the alarm for his personal safety. It was midnight, and all in the ducal pavilion were at rest, when a cry of treason arose. The Earl of Oxford, drawing his sword, and snatching up a light which burned beside him, rushed into the Duke's apartment, and found him standing on the floor totally undressed, but with his sword in his hand, and striking around him so furiously, that the Earl himself had difficulty in avoiding his blows. The rest of his officers rushed in, their weapons drawn, and their cloaks wrapped around their left arms. When the Duke was somewhat composed, and found himself surrounded by his friends, he informed them, with rage and agitation, that the officers of the Secret Tribunal had, in spite of the vigilant precautions taken, found means to gain entrance into his chamber, and charged him, under the highest penalty, to appear before the Holy Vehme upon Christmas night.

The bystanders heard this story with astonishment, and some of them were uncertain whether they ought to consider it as a reality, or a dream of the Duke's irritable fancy. But the citation was found on the Duke's toilet, written, as was the form, upon parchment, signeted with three crosses, and stuck to the table with a knife. A slip of wood had been also cut from the table. Oxford read the summons with attention. It named as usual a place, where the Duke was cited to come unarmed and unattended, and from which it was said he would be guided to the seat of judgment.

Charles, after looking at the scroll for some time, gave vent to his thoughts.

"I know from what quiver this arrow comes," he said. "It is shot by that degenerate noble, apostate priest, and accomplice of sorcerers, Albert of Geierstein. We have heard that he is among the motley group of murderers and outlaws, whom the old fiddler of Provence's grandson has raked together. But, by Saint George of Burgundy! neither monk's cowl, soldier's casque, nor conjuror's cap, shall save him after such an insult as this. I will degrade him from knighthood, hang him from the highest steeple in Nancy, and his daughter shall choose between the meanest herd-boy in my army, and the convent of *filles repentées!*"

"Whatever are your purposes, my lord," said Contay, "it were surely best be silent, when, from this late apparition, we may conjecture that more than we wot of may be within hearing."

The Duke seemed struck with this hint, and was silent, or at least only muttered oaths and threats betwixt his teeth, while the strictest search was made for the intruder on his repose. But it was in vain.

Charles continued his researches, incensed at a

flight of audacity higher than ever had been ventured upon by these Secret Societies, who, whatever might be the dread inspired by them, had not as yet attempted to cope with sovereigns. A trusty party of Burgundians were sent on Christmas night to watch the spot (a meeting of four cross roads), named in the summons, and make prisoners of any whom they could lay hands upon; but no suspicious persons appeared at or near the place. The Duke not the less continued to impute the affront he had received to Albert of Geierstein. There was a price set upon his head; and Campo-Basso, always willing to please his master's mood, undertook that some of his Italians, sufficiently experienced in such feats, should bring the obnoxious baron before him, alive or dead. Colvin, Contay, and others, laughed in secret at the Italian's promises.

"Subtle as he is," said Colvin, "he will lure the wild vulture from the heavens before he gets Albert of Geierstein into his power."

Arthur, to whom the words of the Duke had given subject for no small anxiety, on account of Anne of Geierstein, and of her father for her sake, breathed more lightly on hearing his menaces held so cheaply.

It was the second day after this alarm that Oxford felt a desire to reconnoitre the camp of Ferrand of Lorraine, having some doubts whether the strength and position of it were accurately reported. He obtained the Duke's consent for this purpose, who at the same time made him and his son a present of two noble steeds of great power and speed, which he himself highly valued.

So soon as the Duke's pleasure was communicated to the Italian Count, he expressed the utmost joy that he was to have the assistance of Oxford's age and experience upon an exploratory party, and selected a chosen band of a hundred Stradiots, whom he said he had sent sometimes to skirmish up to the very beards of the Switzers. The Earl shewed himself much satisfied with the active and intelligent manner in which these men performed their duty, and drove before them and dispersed some parties of Ferrand's cavalry. At the entrance of a little ascending valley, Campo-Basso communicated to the English noblemen, that if they could advance to the farther extremity, they would have a full view of the enemy's position. Two or three Stradiots then spurred on to examine this defile, and, returning back, communicated with their leader in their own language, who, pronouncing the passage safe, invited the Earl of Oxford to accompany him. They proceeded through the valley without seeing an enemy, but on issuing upon a plain at the point intimated by Campo-Basso, Arthur, who was in the van of the Stradiots, and separated from his father, did indeed see the camp of Duke Ferrand within half a mile's distance; but a body of cavalry had that instant issued from it, and were riding hastily towards the gorge of the valley, from which he had just emerged. He was about to wheel his horse and ride off, but, conscious of the great speed of the animal, he thought he might venture to stay for a moment's more accurate survey of the camp. The Stradiots who attended him did not wait his orders to retire, but went off, as was indeed their duty, when attacked by a superior force.

Meantime, Arthur observed that the knight, who seemed leader of the advancing squadron, mounted on a powerful horse that shook the earth beneath him, bore on his shield the bear of Berne, and had otherwise the appearance of the massive frame of Rudolph Donnerhugel. He was satisfied of this when he beheld the cavalier halt his party and advance towards him alone, putting his lance in rest, and moving slowly, as if to give him time for preparation. To accept such a challenge, in such a moment, was dangerous, but to refuse it was disgraceful; and while Arthur's blood boiled at the idea of chastising an insolent rival, he was not a little pleased at heart that their meeting on horseback gave him an advantage over the Swiss, through his perfect acquaintance with the practice of the tournay, in which Rudolph might be supposed more ignorant.

They met, as was the phrase of the time, "manful under shield." The lance of the Swiss glanced from the helmet of the Englishman, against which it was addressed, while the spear of Arthur, directed right against the centre of his adversary's body, was so justly aimed, and so truly seconded by the full fury of the career, as to pierce, not only the shield which hung round the ill-fated warrior's neck, but a breastplate, and a shirt of mail which he wore beneath it. Passing clear through the body, the steel point of the weapon was only stopped by the back-piece of the unfortunate cavalier, who fell headlong from his horse, as if struck by lightning, rolled twice or thrice over on the ground, tore the earth with his hands, and then lay prostrate a dead corpse.

There was a cry of rage and grief among those men-at-arms whose ranks Rudolph had that instant left, and many couched their lances to avenge him; but Ferrand of Lorraine, who was present in person, ordered them to make prisoner, but not to harm the successful champion. This was accomplished, for Arthur had not time to turn his bridle for flight, and resistance would have been madness.

When brought before Ferrand, he raised his visor, and said, "Is it well, my lord, to make captive an adventurous Knight, for doing his devoir against a personal challenger?"

"Do not complain, Sir Arthur of Oxford," said Ferrand, "before you experience injury — You are free, Sir Knight. Your father and you were faithful to my royal aunt Margaret, and although she was my enemy, I do justice to your fidelity in her behalf; and from respect to her memory, disinherited as she was like myself, and to please my grandfather, who I think had some regard for you, I give you your freedom. But I must also care for your safety during your return to the camp of Burgundy. On this side of the hill we are loyal and true-hearted men; on the other, they are traitors and murderers. — You, Sir Count, will, I think, gladly see our captive placed in safety."

The Knight to whom Ferrand addressed himself, a tall stately man, put himself in motion to attend on Arthur, while the former was expressing to the young Duke of Lorraine the sense he entertained of his chivalrous conduct. "Farewell, Sir Arthur de Vere," said Ferrand. "You have slain a noble champion, and to me a most useful and faithful friend. But it was done nobly and openly, with equal arms, and in the front of the line; and evil befall him who entertains feud first!" Arthur bowed to his saddlebow. Ferrand returned the salutation, and they parted.

Arthur and his new companion had ridden but a little way up the ascent, when the stranger spoke thus:—

"We have been fellow-travellers before, young man, yet you remember me not."

Arthur turned his eyes on the cavalier, and observing that the crest which adorned his helmet was fashioned like a vulture, strange suspicions began to cross his mind, which were confirmed, when the Knight, opening his helmet, shewed him the dark and severe features of the Priest of Saint Paul's.

"Count Albert of Geierstein!" said Arthur.

"The same," replied the Count, "though thou hast seen him in other garb and headgear. But tyranny drives all men to arms, and I have resumed, by the licence and command of my superiors, those which I had laid aside. A war against cruelty and oppression is holy as that waged in Palestine, in which priests bear armour."

"My Lord Count," said Arthur, eagerly, "I cannot too soon entreat you to withdraw to Sir Ferrand of Lorraine's squadron. Here you are in peril, where no strength or courage can avail you. The Duke has placed a price on your head; and the country betwixt this and Nancy swarms with Stradiots and Italian light horsemen."

"I laugh at them," answered the Count. "I have not lived so long in a stormy world, amid intrigues of war and policy, to fall by the mean hand of such as they—besides, thou art with me, and I have seen but now that thou canst bear thee nobly."

"In your defence, my lord," said Arthur, who thought of his companion as the father of Anne of Geierstein, "I should try to do my best."

"What, youth!" replied Count Albert with a stern sneer, that was peculiar to his countenance; "wouldst thou aid the enemy of the lord under whose banner thou servest, against his waged soldiers?"

Arthur was somewhat abashed at the turn given to his ready offer of assistance, for which he had expected at least thanks; but he instantly collected himself, and replied, "My Lord Count Albert, you have been pleased to put yourself in peril to protect me from partisans of your party—I am equally bound to defend you from those of our side."

"It is happily answered," said the Count;—"yet I think there is a little blind partisan, of whom troubadours and minstrels talk, to whose instigation I might, in case of need, owe the great zeal of my protector."

He did not allow Arthur, who was a good deal embarrassed, time to reply, but proceeded: "Hear me, young man—Thy lance has this day done an evil deed to Switzerland, to Berne, and Duke Ferrand, in slaying their bravest champion. But to me, the death of Rudolph Donnerhugel is a welcome event. Know that he was, as his services grew more indispensable, become importunate in requiring Duke Ferrand's interest with me for my daughter's hand. And the Duke himself, the son of a princess, blushed not to ask me to bestow the last of my house—for my brother's family are degenerate mongrels—upon a presumptuous young man, whose uncle was a domestic in the house of my wife's father, though they boasted some relationship, I believe, through an illegitimate channel, which yonder Rudolph was wont to make the most of, as it favoured his suit."

"Surely," said Arthur, "a match with one so unequal in birth, and far more in every other respect, was too monstrous to be mentioned?"

"While I lived," replied Count Albert, "never should such union have been formed, if the death both of bride and bridegroom by my dagger could have saved the honour of my house from violation. But when I—I whose days, whose very hours are numbered—shall be no more, what could prevent an undaunted suitor, fortified by Duke Ferrand's favour, by the general applause of his country, and perhaps by the unfortunate prepossession of my brother Arnold, from carrying his point against the resistance and scruples of a solitary maiden?"

"Rudolph is dead," replied Arthur, "and may Heaven assoilzie him from guilt! But were he alive, and urging his suit on Anne of Geierstein, he would find there was a combat to be fought——"

"Which has been already decided," answered

Count Albert. "Now, mark me, Arthur de Vere! My daughter has told me of the passages betwixt you and her. Your sentiments and conduct are worthy of the noble house you descend from, which I well know ranks with the most illustrious in Europe. You are indeed disinherited, but so is Anne of Geierstein, save such pittance as her uncle may impart to her of her paternal inheritance. If you share it together till better days, (always supposing your noble father gives his consent, for my child shall enter no house against the will of its head,) my daughter knows that she has my willing consent and my blessing. My brother shall also know my pleasure. He will approve my purpose; for though dead to thoughts of honour and chivalry, he is alive to social feelings, loves his niece, and has friendship for thee and for thy father. What say'st thou, young man, to take a beggarly Countess, to aid thee in the journey of life? I believe—nay, I prophesy, (for I stand so much on the edge of the grave, that methinks I command a view beyond it,) that a lustre will one day, after I have long ended my doubtful and stormy life, beam on the coronets of De Vere and Geierstein."

De Vere threw himself from his horse, clasped the hand of Count Albert, and was about to exhaust himself in thanks; but the Count insisted on his silence.

"We are about to part," he said. "The time is short—the place is dangerous. You are to me, personally speaking, less than nothing. Had any one of the many schemes of ambition which I have pursued led me to success, the son of a banished Earl had not been the son-in-law I had chosen. Rise and remount your horse—thanks are unpleasing when they are not merited."

Arthur arose, and, mounting his horse, threw his raptures into a more acceptable form, endeavouring to describe how his love for Anne, and efforts for her happiness, should express his gratitude to her father, and observing that the Count listened with some pleasure to the picture he drew of their future life, he could not help exclaiming,—" And you, my lord— you who have been the author of all this happiness, will you not be the witness and partaker of it? Believe me, we will strive to soften the effect of the hard blows which fortune has dealt to you, and should a ray of better luck shine upon us, it will be the more welcome that you can share it."

"Forbear such folly," said the Count Albert of Geierstein. "I know my last scene is approaching. —Hear and tremble. The Duke of Burgundy is sentenced to die, and the Secret and Invisible Judges, who doom in secret, and avenge in secret, like the Deity, have given the cord and the dagger to my hand!"

"Oh, cast from you these vile symbols!" exclaimed Arthur, with enthusiasm; "let them find butchers and common stabbers to do such an office, and not dishonour the noble Lord of Geierstein!"

"Peace, foolish boy!" answered the Count. "The oath by which I am sworn is higher than that clouded sky, more deeply fixed than those distant mountains. Nor think my act is that of an assassin, though for such I might plead the Duke's own example. I send not hirelings, like these base Stradiots, to hunt his life, without imperilling mine own. I give not his daughter—innocent of his offences—the choice betwixt a disgraceful marriage and a discreditable retreat from the world. No, Arthur de Vere, I seek Charles with the resolved mind of one, who, to take the life of an adversary, exposes himself to certain death."

"I pray you speak no farther of it," said Arthur, very anxiously. "Consider I serve for the present the Prince whom you threaten——"

"And art bound," interrupted the Count, "to unfold to him what I tell you. I desire you should do so; and though he hath already neglected a summons of the Tribunal, I am glad to have this opportunity of sending him personal defiance. Say to Charles of Burgundy, that he has wronged Albert of Geierstein. He who is injured in his honour loses all value for his life, and whoever does so has full command over that of another man. Bid him keep himself well from me, since if he see a second sun of the approaching year rise over the distant Alps, Albert of Geierstein is forsworn.—And now begone, for I see a party approach under a Burgundian banner. They will ensure your safety, but, should I remain longer, would endanger mine."

So saying, the Count of Geierstein turned his horse and rode off.

CHAPTER THE THIRTY-SIXTH.

*Faint the din of battle bray'd
Distant down the heavy wind,
War and terror fled before,
Wounds and death were left behind.*
MICKLE.

ARTHUR, left alone, and desirous perhaps to cover the retreat of Count Albert, rode towards the approaching body of Burgundian cavalry, who were arrayed under the Lord Contay's banner.

"Welcome, welcome," said that nobleman, advancing hastily to the young knight. "The Duke of Burgundy is a mile hence, with a body of horse to support the reconnoitring party. It is not half-an-hour since your father galloped up, and stated that you had been led into an ambuscade by the treachery of the Stradiots, and made prisoner. He has impeached Campo-Basso of treason, and challenged him to the combat. They have both been sent to the camp, under charge of the Grand Marshal, to prevent their fighting on the spot, though I think our Italian shewed little desire to come to blows. The Duke holds their gages, and they are to fight upon Twelfth-Day."

"I doubt that day will never dawn for some who look for it," said Arthur; "but if it do, I will myself claim the combat, by my father's permission."

He then turned with Contay, and met a still larger body of cavalry under the Duke's broad banner. He was instantly brought before Charles. The Duke heard, with some apparent anxiety, Arthur's support of his father's accusations against the Italian, in whose favour he was so deeply prejudiced. When assured that the Stradiots had been across the hill, and communicated with their leader just before he encouraged Arthur to advance, as it proved, into the midst of an ambush, the Duke shook his head, lowered his shaggy brows, and muttered to himself, —"Ill will to Oxford, perhaps — these Italians are vindictive."—Then raising his head, he commanded Arthur to proceed.

He heard with a species of ecstasy the death of Rudolph Donnerhugel, and, taking a ponderous gold chain from his own neck, flung it over Arthur's.

"Why, thou hast forestalled all our honours, young Arthur—this was the biggest bear of them all —the rest are but suckling whelps to him! I think I have found a youthful David to match their huge thick-headed Goliath. But the idiot to think his peasant hand could manage a lance! Well, my brave boy—what more? How camest thou off? By some wily device or agile stratagem, I warrant."

"Pardon me, my lord," answered Arthur. "I was protected by their chief, Ferrand, who considered my encounter with Rudolph Donnerhugel as a personal duel; and desirous to use fair war, as he said, dismissed me honourably, with my horse and arms."

"Umph!" said Charles, his bad humour returning; "your Prince Adventurer must play the generous—Umph—well, it belongs to his part, but shall not be a line for me to square my conduct by. Proceed with your story, Sir Arthur de Vere."

As Arthur proceeded to tell how and under what circumstances Count Albert of Geierstein named himself to him, the Duke fixed on him an eager look, and trembled with impatience as he fiercely interrupted him with the question — "And you — you struck him with your poniard under the fifth rib, did you not?"

"I did not, my Lord Duke—we were pledged in mutual assurance to each other."

"Yet you knew him to be my mortal enemy?" said the Duke. "Go, young man, thy lukewarm indifference has cancelled thy merit. The escape of Albert of Geierstein hath counterbalanced the death of Rudolph Donnerhugel."

"Be it so, my lord," said Arthur, boldly. "I neither claim your praises, nor deprecate your censure. I had to move me in either case motives personal to myself, — Donnerhugel was my enemy, and to Count Albert I owe some kindness."

The Burgundian nobles who stood around, were terrified for the effect of this bold speech. But it was never possible to guess with accuracy how such things would affect Charles. He looked around him with a laugh—"Hear you this English cockerel, my lords—what a note will he one day sound, that already crows so bravely in a prince's presence!"

A few horsemen now came in from different quarters, recounting that the Duke Ferrand and his company had retired into their encampment, and the country was clear of the enemy.

"Let us then draw back also," said Charles, "since there is no chance of breaking spears to-day. And thou, Arthur de Vere, attend me closely."

Arrived at the Duke's pavilion, Arthur underwent an examination, in which he said nothing of Anne of Geierstein, or her father's designs concerning him, with which he considered Charles as having nothing to do; but he frankly conveyed to him the personal threats which the Count had openly used. The Duke listened with more temper, and when he heard the expression, "That a man who is desperate of his own life might command that of any other person," he said, "But there is a life beyond this, in which he who is treacherously murdered, and his base and desperate assassin, shall each meet their deserts." He then took from his bosom a gold cross, and kissed it, with much appearance of devotion. "In this," said he, "I will place my trust. If I fail in this world, may I find grace in the next.—Ho, Sir Marshal!" he exclaimed—"Let your prisoners attend us."

The Marshal of Burgundy entered with the Earl of Oxford, and stated that his other prisoner, Campo-Basso, had desired so earnestly that he might be suffered to go and post his sentinels on that part of the camp intrusted to the protection of his troops, that he, the Marshal, had thought fit to comply with his request.

"It is well," said Burgundy, without further remark.—"Then to you, my Lord Oxford, I would present your son, had you not already locked him in your arms. He has won great *los* and honour, and done me brave service. This is a period of the year when good men forgive their enemies;—I know not why,—my mind was little apt to be charged with such matters,—but I feel an unconquerable desire to stop the approaching combat betwixt you and Campo-Basso. For my sake, consent to be friends, and to receive back your gage of battle, and let me conclude this year — perhaps the last I may see — with a deed of peace."

"My lord," said Oxford, "it is a small thing you ask of me, since your request only enforces a Christian duty. I was enraged at the loss of my son. I am grateful to Heaven and your Grace for restoring him. To be friends with Campo-Basso is to me impossible. Faith and treason, truth and falsehood, might as soon shake hands and embrace. But the Italian shall be to me no more than he has been before this rupture; and that is literally nothing. I put my honour in your Grace's hands;—if he receives back his gage, I am willing to receive mine. John de Vere needs not be apprehensive that the world will suppose that he fears Campo-Basso."

The Duke returned sincere thanks, and detained the officers to spend the evening in his tent. His manners seemed to Arthur to be more placid than he had ever seen them before, while to the Earl of Oxford they recalled the earlier days in which their intimacy commenced, ere absolute power and unbounded success had spoiled Charles's rough, but not ungenerous disposition. The Duke ordered a distribution of provisions and wine to the soldiers, and expressed an anxiety about their lodgings, the cure of the wounded, and the health of the army, to which he received only unpleasing answers. To some of his counsellors, apart, he said, "Were it not for our vow, we would relinquish this purpose till spring, when our poor soldiers might take the field with less of suffering."

Nothing else remarkable appeared in the Duke's manner, save that he inquired repeatedly after Campo-Basso, and at length received accounts that he was indisposed, and that his physician had recommended rest; he had therefore retired to repose himself, in order that he might be stirring on his duty at peep of day, the safety of the camp depending much on his vigilance.

The Duke made no observation on the apology, which he considered as indicating some lurking disinclination, on the Italian's part, to meet Oxford. The guests at the ducal pavilion were dismissed an hour before midnight.

When Oxford and his son were in their own tent, the Earl fell into a deep reverie, which lasted nearly ten minutes. At length, starting suddenly up, he said, "My son, give orders to Thiebault and thy yeoman to have our horses before the tent by break of day, or rather before it; and it would not be amiss if you ask our neighbour Colvin to ride along with us. I will visit the outposts by daybreak."

"It is a sudden resolution, my lord," said Arthur.

"And yet it may be taken too late," said his father. "Had it been moonlight, I would have made the rounds to-night."

"It is as dark as a wolf's throat," said Arthur. "But wherefore, my lord, can this night in particular excite your apprehensions?"

"Son Arthur, perhaps you will hold your father credulous. But my nurse, Martha Nixon, was a northern woman, and full of superstitions. In particular, she was wont to say, that any sudden and causeless change of a man's nature, as from licence to sobriety, from temperance to indulgence, from avarice to extravagance, from prodigality to love of money, or the like, indicates an immediate change of his fortunes—that some great alteration of circumstances, either for good or evil, (and for evil most likely, since we live in an evil world,) is impending over him whose disposition is so much altered. This old woman's fancy has recurred so strongly to my mind, that I am determined to see with mine own eyes, ere to-morrow's dawn, that all our guards and patrols around the camp are on the alert."

Arthur made the necessary communications to Colvin and to Thiebault, and then retired to rest.

It was ere daybreak of the first of January, 1474, a period long memorable for the events which marked it, that the Earl of Oxford, Colvin, and the young Englishman, followed only by Thiebault and two other servants, commenced their rounds of the Duke of Burgundy's encampment. For the greater part of their progress, they found sentinels and guards all on the alert and at their posts. It was a bitter morning. The ground was partly covered with snow,—that snow had been partly melted by a thaw, which had prevailed for two days, and partly congealed into ice by a bitter frost, which had commenced the preceding evening, and still continued. A more dreary scene could scarcely be witnessed.

But what were the surprise and alarm of the Earl of Oxford and his companions, when they came to that part of the camp which had been occupied the day before by Campo-Basso and his Italians, who, reckoning men-at-arms and Stradiots, amounted to nigh two thousand men—not a challenge was given —not a horse neighed—no steeds were seen at picquet—no guard on the camp. They examined several of the tents and huts—they were empty.

"Let us back to alarm the camp," said the Earl of Oxford; "here is treachery."

"Nay, my lord," said Colvin, "let us not carry back imperfect tidings. I have a battery an hundred yards in advance, covering the access to this hollow way; let us see if my German cannoniers are at their post, and I think I can swear that we shall find them so. The battery commands a narrow pass, by which alone the camp can be approached; and if my men are at their duty, I will pawn my life that we make the pass good till you bring up succours from the main body."

"Forward, then, in God's name!" said the Earl of Oxford.

They galloped, at every risk, over broken ground, slippery with ice in some places, encumbered with snow in others. They came to the cannon, judiciously placed to sweep the pass, which rose towards the artillery on the outward side, and then descended gently from the battery into the lower ground. The waning winter moon, mingling with the dawning light, shewed them that the guns were in their places, but no sentinel was visible.

"The villains cannot have deserted!" said the astonished Colvin—"But see, there is light in their cantonment.—Oh, that unhallowed distribution of wine! Their usual sin of drunkenness has beset them. I will soon drive them from their revelry."

He sprung from his horse, and rushed into the tent from whence the light issued. The cannoniers, or most of them, were still there, but stretched on the ground, their cups and flagons scattered around them; and so drenched were they in wassail, that Colvin could only, by commands and threats, awaken two or three, who, staggering, and obeying him rather from instinct than sense, reeled forward to man the battery. A heavy rushing sound, like that of men marching fast, was now heard coming up the pass.

"It is the roar of a distant avalanche," said Arthur.

"It is an avalanche of Switzers, not of snow," said Colvin.—"Oh, these drunken slaves!—The cannon are deeply loaded, and well pointed—this volley must check them if they were fiends, and the report will alarm the camp sooner than we can do.—But, oh, these drunken villains!"

"Care not for their aid," said the Earl; "my son and I will each take a linstock, and be gunners for once."

They dismounted, and bade Thiebault and the grooms look to the horses, while the Earl of Oxford and his son took each a linstock from one of

the helpless gunners, three of whom were just sober
enough to stand by their guns.

"Bravo!" cried the bold Master of Ordnance,
"never was a battery so noble. Now, my mates—
your pardon, my lords, for there is no time for ceremony—and you, ye drunken knaves, take heed not
to fire till I give the word, and, were the ribs of these
tramplers as flinty as their Alps, they shall know
how old Colvin loads his guns."

They stood breathless, each by his cannon. The
dreaded sound approached nearer and more near, till
the imperfect light shewed a dark and shadowy but
dense column of men, armed with long spears, pole-
axes, and other weapons, amidst which banners dimly floated. Colvin suffered them to approach to the
distance of about forty yards, and then gave the word,
Fire! But his own piece alone exploded; a slight
flame flashed from the touch-hole of the others, which
had been spiked by the Italian deserters, and left in
reality disabled, though apparently fit for service.
Had they been all in the same condition with that
fired by Colvin, they would probably have verified
his prophecy; for even that single discharge produced an awful effect, and made a long lane of dead
and wounded through the Swiss column, in which
the first and leading banner was struck down.

"Stand to it yet," said Colvin, "and aid me if
possible to reload the piece."

For this, however, no time was allowed. A stately
form, conspicuous in the front of the staggered column, raised up the fallen banner, and a voice as of
a giant exclaimed, "What, countrymen! have you

seen Murten and Granson, and are you daunted by a single gun? — Berne — Uri — Schwitz — banners forward! Unterwalden, here is your standard!—Cry your war-cries, wind your horns; Unterwalden, follow your Landamman!"

They rushed on like a raging ocean, with a roar as deafening, and a course as impetuous. Colvin, still labouring to reload his gun, was struck down in the act. Oxford and his son were overthrown by the multitude, the closeness of which prevented any blows being aimed at them. Arthur partly saved himself by getting under the gun he was posted at; his father, less fortunate, was much trampled upon, and must have been crushed to death but for his armour of proof. The human inundation, consisting of at least four thousand men, rushed down into the camp, continuing their dreadful shouts, soon mingled with shrill shrieks, groans, and cries of alarm.

A broad red glare rising behind the assailants, and putting to shame the pallid lights of the winter morning, first recalled Arthur to a sense of his condition. The camp was on fire in his rear, and resounded with all the various shouts of conquest and terror that are heard in a town which is stormed. Starting to his feet, he looked around him for his father. He lay near him senseless, as were the gunners, whose condition prevented their attempting an eacape. Having opened his father's casque, he was rejoiced to see him give symptoms of reanimation.

"The horses, the horses!" said Arthur. "Thiebault, where art thou?"

"At hand, my lord," said that trusty attendant,

who had saved himself and his charge by a prudent retreat into a small thicket, which the assailants had avoided that they might not disorder their ranks.

"Where is the gallant Colvin?" said the Earl; "get him a horse, I will not leave him in jeopardy."

"His wars are ended, my lord," said Thiebault; "he will never mount steed more."

A look and a sigh as he saw Colvin, with the ramrod in his hand, before the muzzle of the piece, his head cleft by a Swiss battle-axe, was all the moment permitted.

"Whither must we take our course?" said Arthur to his father.

"To join the Duke," said the Earl of Oxford. "It is not on a day like this that I will leave him."

"So please you," said Thiebault, "I saw the Duke, followed by some half-score of his guards, riding at full speed across this hollow water-course, and making for the open country to the northward. I think I can guide you on the track."

"If that be so," replied Oxford, "we will mount and follow him. The camp has been assailed on several places at once, and all must be over since he has fled."

With difficulty they assisted the Earl of Oxford to his horse, and rode as fast as his returning strength permitted, in the direction which the Provençal pointed out. Their other attendants were dispersed or slain.

They looked back more than once on the camp, now one great scene of conflagration, by whose red and glaring light they could discover on the ground the traces of Charles's retreat. About three miles from the scene of their defeat, the sound of which they still heard, mingled with the bells of Nancy, which were ringing in triumph, they reached a half-frozen swamp, round which lay several dead bodies. The most conspicuous was that of Charles of Burgundy, once the possessor of such unlimited power— such unbounded wealth. He was partly stripped and plundered, as were those who lay round him. His body was pierced with several wounds, inflicted by various weapons. His sword was still in his hand, and the singular ferocity which was wont to animate his features in battle, still dwelt on his stiffened countenance. Close behind him, as if they had fallen in the act of mutual fight, lay the corpse of Count Albert of Geierstein; and that of Ital Schreckenwald, the faithful though unscrupulous follower of the latter, lay not far distant. Both were in the dress of the men-at-arms composing the Duke's guard, a disguise probably assumed to execute the fatal commission of the Secret Tribunal. It is supposed that a party of the traitor Campo-Basso's men had been engaged in the skirmish in which the Duke fell, for six or seven of them, and about the same number of the Duke's guards, were found near the spot.

The Earl of Oxford threw himself from his horse, and examined the body of his deceased brother-in-arms, with all the sorrow inspired by early remembrance of his kindness. But as he gave way to the feelings inspired by so melancholy an example of the fall of human greatness, Thiebault, who was looking

DISCOVERY OF THE BODY OF CHARLES THE BOLD.

out on the path they had just pursued, exclaimed, "To horse, my lord! here is no time to mourn the dead, and little to save the living—the Swiss are upon us."

"Fly thyself, good fellow," said the Earl; "and do thou, Arthur, fly also, and save thy youth for happier days. I cannot and will not fly farther. I will render me to the pursuers; if they take me to grace, it is well; if not, there is ONE above that will receive me to His."

"I will not fly," said Arthur, "and leave you defenceless; I will stay and share your fate."

"And I will remain also," said Thiebault; "the Switzers make fair war when their blood has not been heated by much opposition, and they have had little enough to-day."

The party of Swiss which came up proved to be Sigismund, with his brother Ernest, and some of the youths of Unterwalden. Sigismund kindly and joyfully received them to mercy; and thus, for the third time, rendered Arthur an important service, in return for the kindness he had expressed towards him.

"I will take you to my father," said Sigismund, "who will be right glad to see you; only that he is ill at ease just now for the death of brother Rudiger, who fell with the banner in his hand, by the only cannon that was fired this morning; the rest could not bark; Campo-Basso had muzzled Colvin's mastiffs, or we should many more of us have been served like poor Rudiger. But Colvin himself is killed."

"Campo-Basso then was in your correspondence?" said Arthur.

"Not in ours—we scorn such companions — but some dealing there was between the Italian and Duke Ferrand; and having disabled the cannon, and filled the German gunners soundly drunk, he came off to our camp with fifteen hundred horse, and offered to act with us. 'But no, no!' said my father,—'traitors come not into our Swiss host;' and so, though we walked in at the door which he left open, we would not have his company. So he marched with Duke Ferrand to attack the other extremity of the camp, where he found them entrance by announcing them as the return of a reconnoitring party."

EFFIGY OF CHARLES THE BOLD.

ANNE OF GEIERSTEIN. 385

"Nay, then," said Arthur, "a more accomplished traitor never drew breath, nor one who drew his net with such success."

"You say well," answered the young Swiss. "The Duke will never, they say, be able to collect another army?"

"Never, young man," said the Earl of Oxford, "for he lies dead before you."*

Sigismund started; for he had an inherent respect,

---

* The following very striking passage is that in which Philip de Commines sums up the last scene of Charles the Bold, whose various fortunes he had long watched with a dark anticipation that a character so reckless, and capable of such excess, must sooner or later lead to a tragical result:—

"As soon as the Count de Campo-Basso arrived in the Duke of Lorrain's army, word was sent him to leave the camp immediately, for they would not entertain, nor have any communication with such traytors. Upon which message he retir'd with his party to a Castle and Pass not far off, where he fortified himself with carts and other things as well as he could, in hopes, that if the Duke of Burgundy was routed, he might have an opportunity of coming in for a share of the plunder, as he did afterwards. Nor was this practice with the Duke of Lorrain the most execrable action that Campo-Basso was guilty of; but before he left the army he conspired with several other officers (finding it was impracticable to attempt anything against the Duke of Burgundy's person) to leave him just as they came to charge, for at that time he suppos'd it would put the Duke into the greatest terror and consternation, and if he fled, he was sure he could not escape alive, for he had order'd thirteen or fourteen sure men, some to run as soon as the Germans came up to charge 'em, and others to watch the Duke of Burgundy, and kill him in the rout, which was well enough contrived: I myself have seen two or three of those who were employed to kill the Duke. Having thus settled his conspiracy at home, he went over to the Duke of Lor-

and somewhat of fear, for the lofty name of Charles the Bold, and could hardly believe that the mangled corpse which now lay before him, was once the personage he had been taught to dread. But his surprise was mingled with sorrow, when he saw the body of his uncle, Count Albert of Geierstein.

rain upon the approach of the German army ; but finding they would not entertain him, he retired to Conde.

"The German army march'd forward, and with 'em a considerable body of French horse, whom the King had given leave to be present at that action. Several parties lay in ambush not far off, that if the Duke of Burgundy was routed, they might surprise some person of quality, or take some considerable booty. By this every one may see into what a deplorable condition this poor Duke had brought himself, by his contempt of good counsel. Both armies being joyn'd, the Duke of Burgundy's forces having been twice beaten before, and by consequence weak and dispirited, and ill provided besides, were quickly broken and entirely defeated: Many sav'd themselves and got off ; the rest were either taken or kill'd ; and among 'em the Duke of Burgundy himself was kill'd on the spot. One Monsieur Claude of Bausmont, Captain of the Castle of Dier in Lorrain, kill'd the Duke of Burgundy. Finding his army routed, he mounted a swift horse, and endeavouring to swim a little river in order to make his escape, his horse fell with him, and overset him : The Duke cry'd out for quarter to this gentleman who was pursuing him, but he being deaf, and not hearing him, immediately kill'd and stripp'd him, not knowing who he was, and left him naked in the ditch, where his body was found the next day after the battle ; which the Duke of Lorrain (to his eternal honour) buried with great pomp and magnificence in Saint George's Church, in the old town of Nancy, himself and all his nobility, in deep mourning, attending the corpse to the grave. The following epitaph was some time afterwards ingrav'd on his tomb :—

' *Carolus hoc busto Burgundæ gloria gentis*
Conditur, Europæ qui fuit ante timor.'

"Oh, my uncle!" he said—"my dear uncle Albert! has all your greatness and your wisdom brought you to a death, at the side of a ditch, like any crazed beggar?—Come, this sad news must be presently told to my father, who will be concerned to hear of his brother's death, which will add gall to

I saw a seal ring of his, since his death, at Milan, with his arms cut curiously upon a sardonix that I have seen him often wear in a ribbon at his breast, which was sold at Milan for two ducats, and had been stolen from him by a rascal that waited on him in his chamber. I have often seen the Duke dress'd and undress'd in great state and formality, and attended by very great persons; but at his death all this pomp and magnificence ceas'd, and his family was involved in the same ruin with himself, and very likely as a punishment for his having deliver'd up the Constable not long before, out of a base and avaricious principle; but God forgive him. I have known him a powerful and honourable Prince, in as great esteem, and as much courted by his neighbours, (when his affairs were in a prosperous condition,) as any Prince in Europe, and perhaps more; and I cannot conceive what should provoke God Almighty's displeasure so highly against him, unless it was his self-love and arrogance, in appropriating all the success of his enterprises, and all the renown he ever acquir'd, to his own wisdom and conduct, without attributing anything to God. Yet to speak truth, he was master of several good qualities: No Prince ever had a greater ambition to entertain young noblemen than he, nor was more careful of their education: His presents and bounty were never profuse and extravagant, because he gave to many, and had a mind everybody should taste of it. No Prince was ever more easie of access to his servants and subjects. Whilst I was in his service he was never cruel, but a little before his death he took up that humour, which was an infallible sign of the shortness of his life. He was very splendid and curious in his dress, and in everything else, and indeed a little too much. He paid great honours to all ambassadors and foreigners, and enter-

bitterness, coming on the back of poor Rudiger's. It is some comfort, however, that father and uncle never could abide each other."

With some difficulty they once more assisted the Earl of Oxford to horseback, and were proceeding to

tain'd them nobly: His ambitious desire of fame was insatiable, and it was that which induced him to be eternally in wars, more than any other motive. He ambitiously desired to imitate the old Kings and Heroes of antiquity, whose actions still shine in History, and are so much talked of in the world, and his courage was equal to any Prince's of his time.

"But all his designs and imaginations were vain and extravagant, and turn'd afterwards to his own dishonour and confusion, for 'tis the conquerors and not the conquer'd that purchase to themselves renown. I cannot easily determine towards whom God Almighty show'd his anger most, whether towards him who died suddenly without pain or sickness in the field of battle, or towards his subjects who never enjoy'd peace after his death, but were continually involv'd in wars, against which they were not able to maintain themselves, upon account of the civil dissensions and cruel animosities that arose among 'em; and that which was the most insupportable, was, that the very people, to whom they were now obliged for their defence and preservation, were the Germans, who were strangers, and not long since their profess'd enemies. In short, after the Duke's death, there was not a neighbouring state that wish'd them to prosper, nor even Germany that defended 'em. And by the management of their affairs, their understanding seem'd to be as much infatuated as their master's, for they rejected all good counsel, and pursued such methods as directly tended to their destruction; and they are still in such a condition, that though they have at present some little ease and relaxation from their sorrows, yet it is with great danger of a relapse, and 'tis well if it turns not in the end to their utter ruin.

"I am partly of their opinion who maintain, that God gives Princes, as he in his wisdom thinks fit, to punish or chastise

set forward when the English lord said,—"You will place a guard here, to save these bodies from farther dishonour, that they may be interred with due solemnity."

"By our Lady of Einsiedlen! I thank you for the

the subjects; and he disposes the affection of subjects to their Princes, as he has determin'd to raise or depress 'em. Just so it has pleas'd him to deal with the House of Burgundy; for after a long series of riches and prosperity, and six-and-twenty years' peace under three Illustrious Princes, predecessors to this Charles, (all of 'em excellent persons, and of great prudence and discretion,) it pleased God to send this Duke Charles, who involv'd them in bloody wars, as well winter as summer, to their great affliction and expense, in which most of their richest and stoutest men were either killed or utterly undone. Their misfortunes continu'd successively to the very hour of his death; and after such a manner, that at the last, the whole strength of their country was destroy'd, and all kill'd or taken prisoners who had any zeal or affection for the House of Burgundy, and had power to defend the state and dignity of that family; so that in a manner their losses were equal to, if not overbalanc'd their former prosperity; for as I have seen those Princes heretofore puissant, rich, and honourable, so it fared the same with their subjects; for I think, I have seen and known the greatest part of Europe; yet I never knew any province, or country, tho' perhaps of a larger extent, so abounding in money, so extravagantly fine in furniture for their horses, so sumptuous in their buildings, so profuse in their expenses, so luxurious in their feasts and entertainments, and so prodigal in all respects, as the subjects of these Princes, in my time: but it has pleased God at one blow to subvert and ruin this illustrious family. Such changes and revolutions in states and kingdoms God in his providence has wrought before we were born, and will do again when we are in our graves; for this is a certain maxim, that the prosperity or adversity of Princes are wholly at his disposal."—COMMINES, Book V. Chap 9.

hint," said Sigismund. "Yes, we should do all that the church can for uncle Albert. It is to be hoped he has not gambled away his soul beforehand, playing with Satan at odds and evens. I would we had a priest to stay by his poor body; but it matters not, since no one ever heard of a demon appearing just before breakfast."

They proceeded to the Landamman's quarters through sights and scenes which Arthur, and even his father, so well accustomed to war in all its shapes, could not look upon without shuddering. But the simple Sigismund, as he walked by Arthur's side, contrived to hit upon a theme so interesting as to divert his sense of the horrors around them.

"Have you farther business in Burgundy, now this Duke of yours is at an end?"

"My father knows best," said Arthur; "but I apprehend we have none. The Duchess of Burgundy, who must now succeed to some sort of authority in her late husband's dominion, is sister to this Edward of York, and a mortal enemy to the House of Lancaster, and to those who have stood by it faithfully. It were neither prudent nor safe to tarry where she has influence."

"In that case," said Sigismund, "my plan will fadge bravely. You shall go back to Geierstein, and take up your dwelling with us. Your father will be a brother to mine, and a better one than uncle Albert, whom he seldom saw or spoke with; while with your father he will converse from morning till night, and leave us all the work of the farm. And you, Arthur, you shall go with us, and be a brother to us all, in place of poor Rudiger, who was, to be sure, my real brother, which you cannot be: nevertheless, I did not like him so well, in respect he was not so good-natured. And then Anne—cousin Anne—is left all to my father's charge, and is now at Geierstein—and you know, King Arthur, we used to call her Queen Guenover."

"You spoke great folly then," said Arthur.

"But it is great truth—For, look you, I loved to tell Anne tales of our hunting, and so forth, but she would not listen a word till I threw in something of King Arthur, and then I warrant she would sit still as a heath-hen when the hawk is in the heavens. And now Donnerhugel is slain, you know you may marry my cousin when you and she will, for nobody hath interest to prevent it."

Arthur blushed with pleasure under his helmet, and almost forgave that new-year's morning all its complicated distresses.

"You forget," he replied to Sigismund, with as much indifference as he could assume, "that I may be viewed in your country with prejudice on account of Rudolph's death."

"Not a whit, not a whit; we bear no malice for what is done in fair fight under shield. It is no more than if you had beat him in wrestling or at quoits — only it is a game cannot be played over again."

They now entered the town of Nancy; the windows were hung with tapestry, and the streets crowded with tumultuous and rejoicing multitudes, whom the success of the battle had relieved from great alarm for the formidable vengeance of Charles of Burgundy.

The prisoners were received with the utmost kindness by the Landamman, who assured them of his protection and friendship. He appeared to support the death of his son Rudiger with stern resignation.

"He had rather," he said, "his son fell in battle, than that he should live to despise the old simplicity of his country, and think the object of combat was the gaining of spoil. The gold of the dead Burgundy," he added, "would injure the morals of Switzerland more irretrievably than ever his sword did their bodies."

He heard of his brother's death without surprise, but apparently with emotion.

"It was the conclusion," he said, "of a long tissue of ambitious enterprises, which often offered fair prospects, but uniformly ended in disappointment."

The Landamman farther intimated, that his brother had apprized him that he was engaged in an affair of so much danger, that he was almost certain to perish in it, and had bequeathed his daughter to her uncle's care, with instructions respecting her.

Here they parted for the present, but shortly after, the Landamman inquired earnestly of the Earl of Oxford, what his motions were like to be, and whether he could assist them.

"I think of choosing Bretagne for my place of refuge," answered the Earl, "where my wife has dwelt since the battle of Tewkesbury expelled us from England."

"Do not so," said the kind Landamman, "but

come to Geierstein with the Countess, where, if she can, like you, endure our mountain manners and mountain fare, you are welcome as to the house of a brother, to a soil where neither conspiracy nor treason ever flourished. Bethink you, the Duke of Bretagne is a weak prince, entirely governed by a wicked favourite, Peter Landais. He is as capable—I mean the minister — of selling brave men's blood, as a butcher of selling bullock's flesh; and you know, there are those, both in France and Burgundy, that thirst after yours."

The Earl of Oxford expressed his thanks for the proposal, and his determination to profit by it, if approved of by Henry of Lancaster, Earl of Richmond, whom he now regarded as his sovereign.

To close the tale, about three months after the battle of Nancy, the banished Earl of Oxford resumed his name of Philipson, bringing with his lady some remnants of their former wealth, which enabled them to procure a commodious residence near to Geierstein; and the Landamman's interest in the state procured for them the right of denizenship. The high blood, and the moderate fortunes, of Anne of Geierstein and Arthur de Vere, joined to their mutual inclination, made their marriage in every respect rational; and Annette with her bachelor took up their residence with the young people, not as servants, but mechanical aids in the duties of the farm; for Arthur continued to prefer the chase to the labours of husbandry, which was of little consequence, as his separate income amounted, in that poor country, to opulence. Time glided on, till it amounted to five years since the exiled family had been inhabitants of Switzerland. In the year 1482, the Landamman Biederman died the death of the righteous, lamented universally, as a model of the true and valiant, simple-minded and sagacious chiefs, who ruled the ancient Switzers in peace, and headed them in battle. In the same year, the Earl of Oxford lost his noble Countess.

But the star of Lancaster, at that period, began again to culminate, and called the banished lord and his son from their retirement, to mix once more in politics. The treasured necklace of Margaret was then put to its destined use, and the produce applied to levy those bands which shortly after fought the celebrated battle of Bosworth, in which the arms of Oxford and his son contributed so much to the success of Henry VII. This changed the destinies of De Vere and his lady. Their Swiss farm was conferred on Annette and her husband; and the manners and beauty of Anne of Geierstein attracted as much admiration at the English Court as formerly in the Swiss Chalet.

END OF ANNE OF GEIERSTEIN.

By W. HAMILTON GIBSON

EYE SPY. Illustrated by the Author. 8vo, Cloth, $2 50.

MY STUDIO NEIGHBORS. Illustrated by the Author. 8vo, Cloth, $2 50.

SHARP EYES: A Rambler's Calendar of Fifty-two Weeks among Insects, Birds, and Flowers. Illustrated by the Author. 8vo, Cloth, Ornamental, $2 50.

STROLLS BY STARLIGHT AND SUNSHINE. Illustrated by the Author. 8vo, Cloth, Ornamental, Gilt Edges, $3 50.

HAPPY HUNTING-GROUNDS. Illustrated by the Author. 4to, Cloth, Ornamental, Gilt Edges, $7 50.

HIGHWAYS AND BYWAYS. Illustrated by the Author. 4to, Cloth, Ornamental, $2 50.

PASTORAL DAYS. Illustrated by the Author. 4to, Cloth, Ornamental, Gilt Edges, $7 50.

CAMP LIFE IN THE WOODS, and the Tricks of Trapping and Trap-Making. Illustrated by the Author. 16mo, Cloth, $1 00.

OUR EDIBLE TOADSTOOLS AND MUSHROOMS. Illustrated by the Author. 8vo, Cloth, Ornamental, Gilt Edges, $7 50.

His graceful, poetical prose is nearly of equal value with his fine and delicate drawings. His style is full of glowing freshness.—*N. Y. Times.*

No one knows more of flowers, shrubs, trees, and birds than Mr. Gibson, or of the special haunts and homes of all of them; and even readers to whom botany is a sealed book may follow him into the fields and woods and marshes with a full certainty of being charmed and enlightened in unexpected ways.—*N. Y. Tribune.*

HARPER & BROTHERS, Publishers
NEW YORK AND LONDON

☞ *Any of the above works will be sent by mail, postage prepaid, to any part of the United States, Canada, or Mexico, on receipt of the price.*

By THOMAS HARDY

DESPERATE REMEDIES.	JUDE THE OBSCURE.
TWO ON A TOWER.	THE HAND OF ETHELBERTA.
THE WOODLANDERS.	A PAIR OF BLUE EYES.
FAR FROM THE MADDING CROWD.	THE MAYOR OF CASTERBRIDGE.
WESSEX TALES.	THE TRUMPET-MAJOR.
A LAODICEAN.	UNDER THE GREENWOOD TREE.
TESS OF THE D'URBERVILLES.	RETURN OF THE NATIVE.

THE WELL-BELOVED.

Uniform Edition. Illustrated. Crown 8vo, Cloth, $1 50 per volume.

WESSEX POEMS, and Other Verses. Illustrated by the Author. Crown 8vo, Cloth, $1 75.

LIFE'S LITTLE IRONIES. Tales. Post 8vo, Cloth, Ornamental, $1 25.

A GROUP OF NOBLE DAMES. Illustrated. 12mo, Cloth, Ornamental, $1 25.

FELLOW-TOWNSMEN. 32mo, Cloth, 35 cents.

Hardy has an exquisite vein of humor. . . . He has a reserve force, so to speak, of imagination, of invention, which keeps the interest undiminished always, though the personages in the drama may be few and their adventures unremarkable. But most of all he has shown the pity and the beauty of human life, most of all he has enlarged the boundaries of sympathy and charity.—*New York Tribune.*

HARPER & BROTHERS, PUBLISHERS

NEW YORK AND LONDON

☞ *Any of the above works will be sent by mail, postage prepaid, to any part of the United States, Canada, or Mexico, on receipt of the price.*

By WILL CARLETON

FARM BALLADS. Illustrated. Post 8vo, Cloth, Ornamental, $1 25.

FARM LEGENDS. Illustrated. Post 8vo, Cloth, Ornamental, $1 25.

FARM FESTIVALS. Illustrated. Post 8vo, Cloth, Ornamental, $1 25.

CITY BALLADS. Illustrated. Post 8vo, Cloth, Ornamental, $1 25.

CITY LEGENDS. Illustrated. Post 8vo, Cloth, Ornamental, $1 25.

CITY FESTIVALS. Illustrated. Post 8vo, Cloth, Ornamental, $1 25.

Old Edition. Illustrated. Square 8vo, Cloth, $2 00 per vol.; Gilt Edges, $2 50 per vol.; Full Seal, $4 00 per vol.

These ballads are tender, simple, and strike a responsive chord in the reader's heart. . . . Emphatically a home book.—*Christian at Work,* N. Y.

RHYMES OF OUR PLANET. Illustrated. Post 8vo, Cloth, $1 25.

THE OLD INFANT, AND SIMILAR STORIES. Illustrated. Post 8vo, Cloth, $1 25.

In his way, as truly a creator of character as Robert Browning, and we recognize in him not only the genius which creates, but the art which exhibits his creations with a skill that commands our attention.—*N. Y. Times.*

HARPER & BROTHERS, Publishers
NEW YORK AND LONDON

☞ *Any of the above works will be sent by mail, postage prepaid, to any part of the United States, Canada, or Mexico, on receipt of the price.*

By WILL N. HARBEN

WESTERFELT. Post 8vo, Ornamented Cloth, $1 50. ("American Contemporary Novels.")

A good, ingenious story, which grows more and more interesting as the author proceeds.—RICHARD HENRY STODDARD.

A work of potent imagination, with the play of human passions in an original rearrangement of the world-old drama.—W. D. HOWELLS, in "The Easy Chair."

A highly dramatic presentation of the warring forces of human passions, conscience, and distorted religious beliefs. The story from first page to last is vibrant with sustained power.—*The Outlook*, New York.

A decided success.—*Courier-Journal*, Louisville.

The story is intense, dramatic, and exciting.—*Sun*, Baltimore.

So perfectly natural are the scenes and incidents that between the lines we can almost catch the rhythmical music of the streams and breathe the sweet odor of the fields in bloom.—*Constitution*, Atlanta.

An unusually vivid picture of a little-known locality. The descriptions of the lawless mountaineers have all the reality of those of Mr. John Fox, Jr.—*Book Buyer*, New York.

The world knows very little about the folk found in North Georgia, and this book seems almost photographic in its realism.—*The Eagle*, Brooklyn.

HARPER & BROTHERS, PUBLISHERS
NEW YORK AND LONDON

☞ *The above book will be sent by mail, postage prepaid, to any part of the United States, Canada, or Mexico, on receipt of the price.*

By LILIAN BELL

SIR JOHN AND THE AMERICAN GIRL. Post 8vo, $1 15 *net*.

THE EXPATRIATES. A Novel. Post 8vo, Cloth, $1 50.

AS SEEN BY ME. With Frontispiece.

THE INSTINCT OF STEP-FATHERHOOD. Stories.

FROM A GIRL'S POINT OF VIEW.

The author is so good-humored, quaint, and clever that she has not left a dull page in her book.—*Saturday Evening Gazette*, Boston.

A LITTLE SISTER TO THE WILDERNESS. A Novel. New Edition.

Written from the heart and with rare sympathy. . . . The writer has a natural and fluent style, and her dialect has the double excellence of being novel and scanty. The scenes are picturesque and diversified.—*Churchman*, N. Y.

THE UNDER SIDE OF THINGS. A Novel. With a Portrait of the Author.

This is a tenderly beautiful story. . . . This book is Miss Bell's best effort, and most in the line of what we hope to see her proceed in, dainty and keen and bright, and always full of the fine warmth and tenderness of splendid womanhood.—*Interior*, Chicago.

THE LOVE AFFAIRS OF AN OLD MAID.

So much sense, sentiment, and humor are not often united in a single volume.—*Observer*, N. Y.

16mo, Ornamented Cloth, Uncut Edges and Gilt Tops, $1 25 per volume.
Postage Extra on Net Books.

HARPER & BROTHERS, PUBLISHERS
NEW YORK AND LONDON

☞ *Any of the above works will be sent by mail, postage prepaid, to any part of the United States, Canada, or Mexico, on receipt of the price.*

By HENRY SETON MERRIMAN

RODEN'S CORNER. A Novel. With Illustrations by T. DE THULSTRUP. Post 8vo, Ornamented Cloth, $1 75.

A story that is far too interesting to lay down until the last page is turned.—*St. James's Gazette*, London.

He handles it with vigor, and maintains in this new field the reputation gained by his former novels.—*Outlook*, N. Y.

THE SOWERS. A Novel. Post 8vo, Ornamented Cloth, $1 25.

"The Sowers," for subtlety of plot, for brilliancy of dialogue, and for epigrammatic analysis of character, is one of the cleverest books of the season.—*Churchman*, N. Y.

There have been few such good novels for years.—*Illustrated London News*.

WITH EDGED TOOLS. A Novel. Post 8vo, Ornamented Cloth, $1 25.

Mr. Merriman is so original, and has such a nice knack of putting things together, that he keeps up the interest on every page.—*N. Y. Times*.

FROM ONE GENERATION TO ANOTHER. A Novel. Post 8vo, Ornamented Cloth, $1 25.

A book of unusual force. It contains a remarkably acute study of a selfish and silly woman—one almost perfect in construction.—*N. Y. Tribune*.

THE PHANTOM FUTURE. A Novel. Post 8vo, Cloth, $1 25.

To those who relish a minute and searching analysis of character, and who appreciate refinement and purity of style, we may recommend "The Phantom Future." . . . A charming story.—*N. Y. Sun*.

HARPER & BROTHERS, PUBLISHERS
NEW YORK AND LONDON

☞ *Any of the above works will be sent by mail, postage prepaid, to any part of the United States, Canada, or Mexico, on receipt of the price.*